W9-BHU-103

THE **COMPLETE IDIOT'S GUIDE** TO

Private Investigating

Third Edition
by Steven Kerry Brown

ALPHA

A member of Penguin Group (USA) Inc.

I dedicate this book to my parents. My father D.K. Brown was a special agent in charge with the FBI for more than 30 years and then Undersheriff in Duval County, Florida, until his death. From him I inherited the investigative gene in my DNA. From my mother Brookie Bellamy Brown I inherited the ability to recognize the good side of a person, even in people who have committed the most heinous of acts.

ALPHA BOOKS

Published by Penguin Group (USA) Inc.

Penguin Group (USA) Inc., 375 Hudson Street, New York, New York 10014, USA • Penguin Group (Canada), 90 Eglinton Avenue East, Suite 700, Toronto, Ontario M4P 2Y3, Canada (a division of Pearson Penguin Canada Inc.) • Penguin Books Ltd., 80 Strand, London WC2R 0RL, England • Penguin Ireland, 25 St. Stephen's Green, Dublin 2, Ireland (a division of Penguin Books Ltd.) • Penguin Group (Australia), 250 Camberwell Road, Camberwell, Victoria 3124, Australia (a division of Pearson Australia Group Pty. Ltd.) • Penguin Books India Pvt. Ltd., 11 Community Centre, Panchsheel Park, New Delhi— 110 017, India • Penguin Group (NZ), 67 Apollo Drive, Rosedale, North Shore, Auckland 1311, New Zealand (a division of Pearson New Zealand Ltd.) • Penguin Books (South Africa) (Pty.) Ltd., 24 Sturdee Avenue, Rosebank, Johannesburg 2196, South Africa • Penguin Books Ltd., Registered Offices: 80 Strand, London WC2R 0RL, England

Copyright © 2013 by Penguin Group (USA) Inc.

All rights reserved. No part of this book may be reproduced, scanned, or distributed in any printed or electronic form without permission. Please do not participate in or encourage piracy of copyrighted materials in violation of the author's rights. Purchase only authorized editions. No patent liability is assumed with respect to the use of the information contained herein. Although every precaution has been taken in the preparation of this book, the publisher and author assume no responsibility for errors or omissions. Neither is any liability assumed for damages resulting from the use of information contained herein. For information, address Alpha Books, 800 East 96th Street, Indianapolis, IN 46240.

THE COMPLETE IDIOT'S GUIDE TO and Design are registered trademarks of Penguin Group (USA) Inc.

International Standard Book Number: 978-1-61564-250-2
Library of Congress Catalog Card Number: 2012949171

19 18   15 14 13 12 11 10 9 8

Interpretation of the printing code: The rightmost number of the first series of numbers is the year of the book's printing; the rightmost number of the second series of numbers is the number of the book's printing. For example, a printing code of 13-1 shows that the first printing occurred in 2013.

Printed in the United States of America

Note: This publication contains the opinions and ideas of its author. It is intended to provide helpful and informative material on the subject matter covered. It is sold with the understanding that the author and publisher are not engaged in rendering professional services in the book. If the reader requires personal assistance or advice, a competent professional should be consulted.

The author and publisher specifically disclaim any responsibility for any liability, loss, or risk, personal or otherwise, which is incurred as a consequence, directly or indirectly, of the use and application of any of the contents of this book.

Most Alpha books are available at special quantity discounts for bulk purchases for sales promotions, premiums, fund-raising, or educational use. Special books, or book excerpts, can also be created to fit specific needs. For details, write: Special Markets, Alpha Books, 375 Hudson Street, New York, NY 10014.

Publisher: *Mike Sanders*

Executive Managing Editor: *Billy Fields*

Executive Acquisitions Editor: *Lori Cates Hand*

Development Editor: *Jennifer Moore*

Senior Production Editor: *Kayla Dugger*

Copy Editor: *Krista Hansing Editorial Services, Inc.*

Cover Designer: *Rebecca Batchelor*

Book Designers: *William Thomas, Rebecca Batchelor*

Indexer: *Celia McCoy*

Layout: *Brian Massey*

Proofreader: *Virginia Vought*

Contents

Appendixes

Introduction

Welcome to the third edition of *The Complete Idiot's Guide to Private Investigating*. In this edition, you'll find a ton of new material and some of your old favorites. Even though I wrote this book, I still pull it off the shelf every couple of weeks to double-check something. For the professional, it's a valuable guide on how to do your work. For the student in a PI course, this book may well be your text. It's used in public and private schools across the nation. If you're a do-it-yourselfer, you cannot find a better resource for the price than this book.

A while back, I spent a day with a criminal defense attorney working a criminal rape case in which his client was the defendant. This attorney asked me if I'd read Erle Stanley Gardner's *Perry Mason* books.

I'd never read any but had certainly seen a lot of Perry Mason on television. This attorney said the criminal law in the Mason books and on TV was basically accurate, except that even the best trial lawyer will never get the guilty person to confess on the stand. So did I know why Perry Mason won all his cases? What was his secret to success?

"Paul Drake," he said, "Perry Mason's private investigator." A really good attorney understands how an excellent investigator can help him win cases. If an attorney doesn't understand that principle, then he's not a good trial attorney, for sure.

So what do private investigators really do to help attorneys win cases? To explain that, let me tell you about my college friend whose father was president of a company that made cans for vegetables and other food items. The company felt that business was stagnating and wanted to expand. It hired a consultant to originate ideas on increasing business. The board of directors met with the consultant after he'd done his research. When they were all seated, he said to the board, "Okay, what kind of business do you think this company is in?"

"That's simple—we're in the can business," the board told him.

"No, you aren't," the consultant said. "Your company is not in the can business; it's in the packaging business."

With that concept in mind, the company went on to greatly expand into all areas of packaging.

Likewise, the private investigator is not in the surveillance business, or the electronic countermeasure business, or the background investigative business. Well, if it's not any of those businesses, what kind of business is it?

The private investigative agency is in the information business. The PI's client needs to know something. The PI gets the information. The unusual techniques that a PI uses are the fun part of the business and are what separates it from other information businesses, but nonetheless, information is what a PI sells.

In this book, I teach you how to get the information using tricks of the trade. Whether you're a professional PI or you're doing it for yourself, the techniques are the same, and they're all here.

You have two choices: do it yourself or hire it out. I've tried to put all the basics in this book, to help you do it yourself or find the right PI for the job.

If you're already a professional PI, you'll find some useful advice in each chapter to help you build your business, be more professional, get more clients, and make more money.

Every chapter is woven through with real stories from the case files of my PI practice. The names and locations have been changed to protect my clients' identities, but the pertinent facts are there and the situations are real. The solutions are real, too. Real people, real facts, real life.

Among the many updates I include in this new edition is extended coverage of family law and criminal defense cases. I also bring you up to speed on the latest technology available to PIs, including GPS tracking devices and new online databases.

Now look through the table of contents to find your specific problem, and I'll show you how to get the information you need.

How This Book Is Organized

This book is presented in five parts:

Part 1, Private Investigation, Business or Fun?, talks about how to find a professional PI, the legal requirements of obtaining your own PI license, the skills and equipment you need, and how to get hired by a PI agency.

Part 2, Getting the Scoop, offers both basic and advanced techniques for skip tracing. These chapters teach you where to find information, how to dig up the dirt at the courthouse, where to access the public record databases, and how to log on to the secret "pay sites" that professional PIs use. I also give you a few tips on extracting information from the phone company.

Part 3, On-the-Job Training, is a crash course in investigative techniques. You're taught how to do interrogations and how to run stationary and moving surveillances. Plus, you get my favorite part, PI tricks and treats for both basic and advanced investigators.

Part 4, In the Field, offers step-by-step instructional information on a variety of different types of cases. You're taught in detail how to sift through the evidence of marital infidelity, how to catch the runaway teenager, and how to set up surveillance in your home. You're also taught the basics of how to check phones for illegal wiretaps.

Part 5, Advanced Techniques, teaches you how to perform in-depth background investigations and includes tips on setting up your own background-screening company. There's also a chapter for the professional PI on how to triple your hourly billing rate performing diligent adoption and estate searches. This part also shows how a professional should gather all the evidence, report it, and present it in court.

Extras

Some of the great features of *The Complete Idiot's Guides* are the sidebars placed throughout the chapters with additional information. In these sidebars, I've tried to explain some extra facets of investigation. I also include tips and warnings about using investigative techniques mentioned in the chapter.

HIDDEN HINT

Look here for new methods to see a subject that you might not have thought of otherwise.

LEGAL TRAP

Here I issue warnings and point out legal traps that can snare you.

DEFINITION

PIs speak their own language. Clue in on the definitions of the terms, slang, and jargon of the industry that you might not know.

THE SCOOP

Check out these sidebars for interesting facts, sidelights, and procedures relating to private investigation.

Acknowledgments

I'd like to thank Melanie Brown for making me walk a straight line. Also Frank Green and James N. Frey, who taught me everything I know about the craft of writing. Without Jessica Faust, my literary agent at BookEnds, this and previous editions of this book wouldn't have been written.

For their contributions, special thanks go to Robert Scott at Skipsmashers, to Mitch Davis at TSCM/Special Operations Group, and to Jimmie Mesis, publisher of *PI Magazine* and owner of PI Gear.

Thanks also to the folks at Alpha who worked on this edition: Lori Hand, Jennifer Moore, Kayla Dugger, and Krista Hansing.

Trademarks

All terms mentioned in this book that are known to be or are suspected of being trademarks or service marks have been appropriately capitalized. Alpha Books and Penguin Group (USA) Inc. cannot attest to the accuracy of this information. Use of a term in this book should not be regarded as affecting the validity of any trademark or service mark.

Private Investigation, Business or Fun?

Looking to change your career and become a PI? Or maybe you don't want to become a PI, but you just need some information. Did somebody steal the bicycles out of your garage, and you want them back? Looking for an old boyfriend or girlfriend? Want to check out a potential tenant, a new employee, or a new lover?

In this part, you learn the ins and outs of doing PI work. You discover how to find the information yourself, just like the pro PIs do. And if you want to become a professional PI, this part walks you through the process, shows you the vision, and helps you pursue that dream.

The Making of a PI

In This Chapter

- Meeting Mr. Pinkerton, America's first PI
- Getting your foot in the door
- Considering niches in the investigative field
- Honing your creative thinking skills
- Getting acquainted with the less-than-flashy side of detective work

As a PI, your most important client is the truth. You must be impartial in this pursuit. The irony is that your clients don't always want the truth. Does a husband really want to hear that his wife has been cheating on him with his best friend for the last three years? Or does an insurance company want to find out that the person it's accusing of insurance fraud is, in fact, telling the truth? The answer to these and many other questions posed by clients is a resounding *no*. Yet it's your job to dig up the facts, present them to your client, and let the chips fall as they may.

Ultimately, you're doing an important service for your clients even when you tell them things they don't want to hear. Your clients need to know the bad as well as the good. Nothing is worse for an attorney than to be blindsided in court by some derogatory or hurtful piece of information that he didn't know about—and should have. He needs to have all the facts beforehand, and that's the private investigator's side of the business.

In this chapter, I offer up a little 411 on the origins of private investigating and describe the most common types of work PIs do.

Tracking Down America's First PI

Allan Pinkerton is the father of private investigation in the United States. Born in Glasgow, Scotland, in 1819, he began his career in law enforcement as a deputy sheriff for Kane County, Illinois, in 1846. Four years later, he opened his detective agency in Chicago.

THE SCOOP

Some claim that Pinkerton's private detective agency, with its "all-seeing eye," is the origin of the term *private eye* that we use today.

Pinkerton played a significant role in the history of nineteenth-century America. Documented facts are hard to come by, but many historians contend that Pinkerton became aware of a plot to assassinate Abraham Lincoln while Lincoln was en route to his inauguration in Washington, D.C. Pinkerton overtook Lincoln's entourage and persuaded him to change his itinerary, thereby thwarting the attempted assassination.

In 1866, the railroads hired Pinkerton to put an end to the great train robbery gangs, including the Jesse James gang (also called the James–Younger gang). Early on, Pinkerton's agency didn't fare so well with the James–Younger gang. At least two Pinkerton operatives were killed in their attempts to arrest the Younger brothers. John Younger was also killed in one of those gunfights, a fierce shootout in St. Clair County, Missouri, in March 1874.

But thanks primarily to Pinkerton's aggressive pursuit, the railroad robbery gangs were out of business by the early 1900s. Many people believe that the Pinkertons sent a number of innocent men to jail in the train robbery gang cleanup; the term *railroading* came into use to describe law enforcement pressuring innocent people to admit guilt.

In 1999 Pinkerton's agency was acquired by Securitas (which also acquired the next largest security agency, Burns, in 2000). Securitas is a conglomerate listed on the Swiss stock exchange.

Breaking into the Business

Although getting your foot in the door can take some effort, when you're in the investigative business, you'll find that it's a lot more fun than a real job. People typically gain entry into the PI field through one of two doors:

- Gaining on-the-job experience as an intern for an established private investigative agency

- Working in an investigative position with law enforcement or the military

Even Mr. Pinkerton, the father of the PI business in the United States, did a stint as a deputy sheriff before starting his agency. But you don't need previous law enforcement experience to work as a PI. In many cases, you don't even need a license to do some investigative work. For several niches in the PI field, previous law enforcement training has no bearing on the work at all. Besides, in some states that require previous "investigative" experience before issuing a PI license, 25 years as a street cop doesn't meet the "investigative" requirement.

In the following sections, I provide an overview of the various niches in the field, clue you in on the type of work involved, and indicate whether you need a PI license to do the work.

Retrieving Public Records

You can make an entire career out of retrieving courthouse documents. (See Chapter 5 for details about accessing records at county and federal courthouses). Document retrievers earn very good incomes by circulating through local courthouses, pulling documents requested by clients, and searching civil and criminal histories.

You can make several thousand dollars a month doing this work, and it involves little overhead. In rural areas you can earn twice the amount you'd make in urban areas. In most states, you don't need a private investigator's license to pull records.

With advances in technology, the field of document retrieval is undergoing significant changes. Many county courthouses now provide access to their records online, often for free. However, in some counties, you still have to show up at the courthouse and get the files in person; in such cases, you can charge $75 and up for a trip to the courthouse to retrieve a record for a client.

Doing In-House Investigations

If you're interested in conducting background investigations only for yourself, maybe on your new boyfriend, you don't need a license. Similarly, most states allow in-house investigators to do background investigations and internal theft investigations without a license. If you're good at investigations and have picked up a little experience along the way, consider becoming an in-house investigator. Most investigators who are employed by law firms (as full employees, not subcontractors) can work without a license. Doing in-house work is good way to obtain the statutory experience needed for your own license. Check out Chapter 2 to find out which states require a PI license to do investigative work.

Serving Subpoenas for a Living

In most states, you don't need a PI license to serve *subpoenas*, although you often need PI skills to track down the people being served. Usually the local sheriff's office or the courts regulate the authorized servers (often referred to as *process servers*) and can help you get the information you need to enter this niche.

> **DEFINITION**
>
> A **subpoena** is a command from the judge of a court or an officer of the court, like an attorney, requiring that the person or representative of an institution named in the subpoena appear in court at a certain time.

Can you make a good living serving subpoenas? Absolutely. The keys to making money by serving subpoenas are high volume and high efficiency. In many ways, the financial aspect of a subpoena service business is similar to that of a PI agency. If you want a six-figure income, you need to have your own subpoena service company or your own PI agency. Normally, servers are paid based on the number of subpoenas they serve.

To be successful in this niche, strive to be more efficient than the local sheriff's office. The office often charges around $40 for the service, and frequently, its servers are slow. You might charge $50 or $60 for the service but provide a much quicker turnaround time and better reporting to the client after the process has been served. Nobody benefits if the subpoena is served after the trial is over.

> **HIDDEN HINT**
>
> Prompt and efficient client service is the key to building a business in the investigative field or any of its related service areas. Many process servers email or text their clients as soon as they complete a service. Others have websites where clients can enter a secure area via password and find out what subpoenas have been served and when, as well as which are still outstanding.

Skip Tracing, Finding Deadbeat Parents, and Locating Missing Individuals

Some investigators focus exclusively on skip tracing, locating missing individuals, and hunting down deadbeat parents. In most states, you need a license for these types of jobs.

PIs refer to people who don't want to be found as *skips*, meaning people who are intentionally hiding (perhaps from creditors) or who have some other reason to keep their whereabouts a secret. *Skip tracing* is the process of tracking down those individuals through whatever means possible. When searching for skips, PIs often search public and private databases; contact the skip's friends, family, neighbors, and employees; and even use social networking sites such as Facebook to glean information about them. In Chapter 4, I provide a thorough overview of skip tracing.

I know of one agency that works only deadbeat parent cases—in other words, tracking down parents who owe back child support. The client signs a contract agreeing to pay the agency a percentage of the child support or alimony payments after it finds the parent. The agency is quite successful in locating the deadbeat parents and collecting the money they owe to the custodial parents.

Other agencies specialize in finding the birth parents of adopted children. This is a difficult area and has as many rewarding moments as it does disappointments. Here's just one example from my case files:

Mary Beth, a 30-year-old woman who lived in Maryland, contacted us and asked us to find her birth mother. The mother who'd adopted her told her she was born in Florida. When her adoptive mother died, Mary Beth began sorting out her papers and came across some notes her mother had made that included the name of her birth mother. Of course, 30 years later her birth mother had probably been married at least once and probably had a different name. Mary Beth had no idea if she was still alive or living in another state.

By searching state marriage records and other databases, we ascertained that her birth mother actually now resided in a very posh, gated community in the Jacksonville, Florida, area. We discreetly made contact with the birth mother, who denied ever having a daughter and certainly ever giving her up for adoption.

We contacted her again, and this time she told us that she didn't want anything to do with her daughter, that the child had been from a different part of her life, and asked us to please leave her alone. Sad, but true.

> **THE SCOOP**
>
> Don't reunite adopted children with their birth parents unless both parties agree. You need to respect either party's desire for privacy, as much as you may not want to.

Hiring the Hired Gun

Another niche area of the PI business is working in personal protection. For this line of work, you may need a PI license (check with your state's regulations), and you should also invest in some training using professional firearms and defensive tactics. A professional bodyguard demands a lot more than standing 6 feet, 4 inches tall and carrying a big gun—although that's a good start.

> **LEGAL TRAP**
>
> In our lawsuit-happy society, if a confrontation goes awry, then you, as body-guard, will probably end up being sued by both your client and the other parties involved. Make sure you have the proper training and insurance before you do any sort of protective services work.

The distinction between providing personal protective services and security guard services is hazy. Most states require different licenses for each service: a PI license for straight personal protection and a guard company license for the other. Most security guard services also provide some investigative services and frequently carry both licenses.

Another lucrative aspect of PI work that falls between personal protection and the security business is concert security and nightclub security.

Thinking Sideways: The Key to Success

No matter what area of investigative work appeals to you, you need to be creative and willing to think sideways. Successful PIs are able to look at a problem from different angles to find creative solutions for them.

An attorney who represented the Jacksonville Shipyards came to my firm with a problem. The Shipyards had an employee, Richard, who wasn't working due to an alleged knee injury he'd received while overhauling a ship in the yard. Some Shipyards employees, co-workers of Richard, had told the Shipyards manager that Richard was malingering. According to his co-workers, he was able to repair automobiles in his backyard, do household maintenance, and replace part of his roof. If he could do that, he certainly could find useful work at the shipyard.

The other employees were irked that Richard seemed perfectly healthy and was collecting a full paycheck without doing anything, while they had to work for their paychecks.

The Shipyards hired a PI firm to put Richard under surveillance. Richard had an 8-foot privacy fence surrounding the side- and backyards of his home. The firm set surveillance vans in Richard's neighborhood but never could catch him performing strenuous tasks. They heard metal banging on metal in the backyard, but they couldn't see through the privacy fence. They even hired a helicopter to fly over, but Richard stayed in the house that day.

More frustrated than ever, the Shipyards instructed its attorney to find another PI firm that might have better luck. This attorney recommended my firm because we'd helped him out in a previous case. (In that case, we had his claimant under surveillance, caught him working, and nailed him as much as anybody has ever been nailed before. His client had worked very hard laying a concrete driveway and we videotaped him for six hours straight as he worked without a break. As soon as the attorney saw our surveillance tapes, he dropped the client. For that reason, the attorney knew we could produce excellent results.)

The Shipyards wanted Richard either back to work or fired. They needed proof that he could work, and they didn't care what it cost to get that proof. I assigned the case to one of my senior investigators. After a couple days, the investigator told me it was impossible. Richard never came out of the house; if he was doing anything strenuous, he had to be doing it in the backyard. He, too, had heard noises coming from the back of the house, but he couldn't testify about what was taking place back there or who was doing it.

When presented with a problem like we had with Richard, a good investigator steps back and takes a look at the big picture. You need creativity and innovation. You have to think outside the box. Think sideways. Think laterally or upside down, if you have to. Attack the problem from a new angle. Let your mind roam, and make that intuitive leap.

I went to Richard's neighborhood and drove around the area. Behind Richard's house was a two-story apartment complex. I approached the manager and indicated my desire to rent one of the apartments. She showed me one of the vacant second-floor units. From its back window, it had a clear view over Richard's privacy fence, and I could see the entire rear yard and one side of his house.

The problem? They had a one-year minimum lease. I didn't think the Shipyards would pay the rent on an empty apartment for an entire year. They might have. They wanted this situation resolved. But there had to be a better solution. I confided in the apartment manager the basics of my situation, but I didn't tell her the name of the subject that I wanted to put under surveillance. I assured her there would be no wear and tear on the apartment; I would use the apartment only a few hours a day.

We struck a deal in which I would pay the apartment manager $25 cash for each day my investigators entered the apartment. She agreed not to rent the apartment until she had no other vacancies, and then she'd give us first right of refusal on the unit.

You can guess the rest. We shot hours of videotape of Richard repairing cars and working around the back of his house. We even had several days' worth of tape that showed him roofing the back portion of his house. He carried stacks of shingles up a ladder and placed them around the roof so they were available when he needed them.

One of Richard's alleged injuries was to his knee. We showed the videotape to one of his doctors, hoping she would say he was fit enough to go back to work. At one point, the doctor said that if we could show him climbing a ladder with a heavy burden, she would send him right back to work. Bingo. I pulled out the right tape, and there he was on the television screen, carrying a 50-pound stack of shingles up the ladder.

From that day until the day they closed, the Jacksonville Shipyards used my firm as its primary investigative resource. The company spent hundreds of thousands of dollars a year with us. An analysis of all the cases we worked for the Shipyards showed that we saved the company several million dollars each year in wages that would have been lost and in frivolous medical bills it no longer had to pay.

LEGAL TRAP

You have to know the rules of *right to privacy*. There's a difference between videotaping from an upstairs window of an adjacent building and climbing a tree to see into another person's bedroom. You can push right up to that line, but don't go over it, or your evidence will not be allowed in court. Worse, you'll be arrested as a Peeping Tom.

Looking Beyond the Flash: The Other Side of PI Work

Robert Bailey, a former PI and now author of PI novels, begins his novel *Private Heat* with PI Art Hardin this way:

> Everybody wants to be a detective, carry a big shiny gun, and be all the rage at cocktail parties. Nobody wants to get up at o-dark-thirty and drive ninety-three miles to see if Joe Insurance Claimant—who has been collecting a total disability check for the last three years—is also working for wages on the sly, but that's the kind of work that usually pays the bills, not the flashy stuff you see on the tube.
>
> —From *Private Heat*, by Robert Bailey. Used by permission of the publisher, M. Evans and Company, New York.

If you're looking for a career that's interesting and exciting, private investigation fits that bill. I can't think of anything more interesting than being a private investigator. But PI work also involves hour after hour of sheer tedium. The job requires a mountain of paperwork and documentation. If small details are your thing, the private investigative field may be for you. If you're not up for the paperwork—dotting every *i* and crossing every *t*—you'd better think again.

The Least You Need to Know

- Allan Pinkerton began the private investigating business in the United States in 1850.
- Many investigative niches don't require a PI license.
- Successful private investigators must be able to make intuitive leaps in reasoning, a talent that can be learned and practiced.
- Although working as a PI entails a lot of thrills, detectives must also do a lot of paperwork and be detail oriented.

The Path to the Professional PI

In This Chapter

- Honing your sleuthing skills
- Obtaining your PI license
- Considering your liability and insurance needs
- Peeping at privacy laws
- Marketing your business on the internet

A career as a professional private investigator can be emotionally rewarding and fabulously entertaining. I like to joke that it's much better than working for a living. But getting hired as a PI isn't a simple matter of filling out an application at Monster.com and hoping for the best. As with many other professions, state agencies often regulate private investigators, and in most states, you need the right combination of experience and training to get your sleuthing license.

If you've decided you want to be a professional PI, this chapter helps you get started so that you can begin collecting those checks. And collecting checks from clients is probably the only way most of us will ever get to have a Ferrari.

Getting the Experience You Need: Coffee and Donuts Optional

The approach you take to starting a PI business depends on your previous level of investigative experience. If you're leaving a position as an investigator with law enforcement, your years of running criminal investigations should give you a bit of a leg up in this business, at least at the beginning. Police experience is particularly helpful when you begin marketing your services.

If you've never cared much for coffee and donuts, though, don't worry: other occupations besides cop work can lead you down the path to PI-dom. Here are some of the most common routes:

- **Insurance claims adjuster:** Doing investigative work for insurance companies provides good background that can serve you well in the insurance end of the PI business.

- **Military intelligence:** Time spent in uniform can lead you directly into private investigative work.

- **On-the-job training:** You can get good training by working for another licensed private investigative agency.

In 41 U.S. states, you need documented experience such as the type I mentioned in the preceding list to get a PI license. For example, to qualify for a regular investigator's license in Florida, an applicant must have at least two years' investigative experience, or else a Bachelor's degree in criminal justice and one year of experience. Nine states don't require anything more than a business license; in those states, anyone can apply for a business license and hang out a sign as a PI. (I tell you which states require licenses and which don't later in this chapter.)

As someone who has run a PI agency for more than 20 years, I know that it's nearly impossible to find a job in this field without experience. Agencies have relatively few openings, and you can count on stiff competition for the slots that do become available. Thanks to the many books, movies, and TV shows about PIs, many people think of it as a glamorous occupation and want to try their hand at it. I don't blame 'em.

HIDDEN HINT

If you live in a state that allows interns to work toward their PI license, you can jump right over the hurdle of finding a job with an established PI agency by starting your own agency, even with no experience! Here's what you do: hire a fully licensed investigator to manage your agency, and have the manager serve as your mentor or sponsor. If you're in a state that has a state licensing board, check with them to see if this runaround works in your state.

On average, my firm receives three inquiries a week from folks seeking to intern. How do you compete with the crowd for the few openings out there?

Step back for a minute and think about the difference between skill sets and their application to specific jobs. If you already have good skills in one job, you can often quickly be taught how to apply those same skills to another job. On the other hand, if you lack any applicable skills for a job, you face a double whammy: you need double the training because you need to learn both the necessary skills *and* the right way to use them.

When looking for a job with a PI firm, emphasize the skills that qualify you to do the work. Over the years, I've learned that it's easier for me to teach a person how to be an investigator (applying the person's existing skills) than it is, for example, to teach him the photography skills and research skills that good PI work requires. Come to me already skilled, and I'll teach you how to apply those skills to this line of work. Here's your second investigative assignment: as you read this book, keep a running list of the skills an investigator needs. That ought to strip away some of the TV-induced glamour. Are you already good at each one? Can you take classes to learn or enhance the necessary skills? As an employer, my attitude toward a potential employee is favorably affected when a candidate shows initiative by taking steps to improve her qualifications. For example, if she can talk intelligently about photography, she significantly increases her chances that I'll hire her.

If you really want to impress me, walk in with a top-of-the-line digital 35mm single-lens reflex (SLR) like a Canon 5D Mark III (it shoots both 35mm full-frame and video). Show me how cool it is and demonstrate that you know how to use it. I'd probably hire you on the spot.

Make yourself attractive to the firm where you're seeking employment, and be persistent.

Consider this list of skills and experience you should acquire before applying with a PI firm:

- Experience in digital photography, both single-lens reflex (SLR) and video

- Knowledge of computer programs, especially Microsoft Word, Excel, and Apple operating systems because many agencies are leaving Microsoft and turning to Apple

- Excellent keyboarding skills

- Good knowledge of Internet search engines

- Knowledge of your local and county courthouses and the ins and outs of the clerk's office (see Chapters 5 and 6 for details)

If a person came to my office possessing all of these skills, I would hire him on the spot and create a position for him even if I didn't need another investigator.

HIDDEN HINT

Having your own surveillance equipment can boost your chances of getting hired. Most PI firms don't supply the high-tech camera equipment anymore; each investigator has to have his own. When you get the job, buy the equipment that your firm recommends. Be familiar with both digital video and single-lens reflex digital cameras. Learn the difference between physical zoom and digital zoom on video cameras.

Obtaining Your Licenses

Nine states don't specifically license private investigators:

- Alabama
- Alaska
- Colorado (a voluntary licensing statute allows you to obtain a license if you want one)
- Idaho
- Mississippi
- Pennsylvania (some counties issue licenses)
- Rhode Island (some cities and towns issue licenses)
- South Dakota
- Wyoming

Even in these states, you need a business license. In some of these states, individual cities might require a private investigator's license in addition to a business license. Many states require proof of training.

THE SCOOP

PI Magazine has a number of useful resources, including links to all the PI licensing divisions in the various states. Find out the requirements for your state by checking with the appropriate licensing authority (www.pimagazine.com/private_investigator_license_requirements.html) before you apply for a job with an agency.

Twenty-three states require PI applicants to pass an examination before granting a license. To pass the Georgia test, for example, you need to be familiar with the Georgia wiretap and eavesdropping laws, as well as the laws that apply to carrying concealed and unconcealed weapons. In addition, the test covers legal procedure, interview techniques, and basic investigative procedures.

Some states, including Florida, require you to possess at least two separate licenses: an agency license and a private investigator's license. Of course, you must pay a separate fee for each license. If you run a larger operation or have multiple sites, you may also be required to have what's called a manager-of-an-agency license.

If you want to carry a weapon while on or off the job in Florida, you need two more permits: a weapon license to carry while on duty and a concealed weapon permit to carry a firearm off duty. That adds up to as many as six different licenses and permits in the state of Florida if you want to be a PI.

Getting Reciprocity: Working Across State Lines

As your business expands, you may want to acquire licenses in states other than where your principal office is located. If you're working a case in your state and it leads you to a neighboring state, some states allow you to continue working within their borders as long as the case originated where you're licensed. Others won't. Always check the licensing regulations and *reciprocity agreements* between states before working a case in a state where you don't hold a license. Contact the state regulatory body before investigating where you're not licensed. (To find contact information for your state regulatory body, go to www.pimagazine.com/private_investigator_license_requirements.html.)

DEFINITION

A **reciprocity agreement** is an agreement between two states to honor licenses issued by either state, allowing license holders in one state to work in the other state, and vice versa. Usually reciprocity agreements between states are limited in time and scope.

Reciprocity is important. If a client wants you to travel from Georgia to Oklahoma, you need to know whether the two states have a reciprocity agreement. If not, you need to team up with a licensed investigator in the other state.

Florida has reciprocity agreements with the following states: California, Georgia, Louisiana, North Carolina, Oklahoma, Tennessee, and Virginia.

Check your state's reciprocity agreements and make sure you're legal before you pack your hiking gear to follow some guy and his girlfriend down the Grand Canyon in Arizona.

Protecting Yourself with Insurance or Bonds

Many states require a PI to carry a liability policy. Other states require PIs to be bonded. The requirements vary from state to state. Florida doesn't require PIs to carry liability insurance. California, however, requires $1 million in liability insurance if you're going to carry a firearm. Firearm-carry regulations for private investigators are often different and more harsh than for a simple concealed weapons permit. South Carolina requires a $10,000 bond, and Georgia requires a $25,000 bond or a liability insurance policy with a $1 million minimum. Check your own state before deciding how much liability insurance you need. Those states that require either a bond or insurance will want proof of coverage before issuing or renewing a license.

LEGAL TRAP

If you have serious doubts about the legality of any action you're about to undertake, get a legal opinion first—or don't do it.

The policies typically cover comprehensive general liability coverage for death, bodily injury, property damage, and personal injury coverage, including false arrest, detention or imprisonment, malicious prosecution, libel, slander, defamation of character, and violation of the right of privacy. I think the kitchen sink is in there, too, but at least they had the courtesy to leave out the toilet.

Even if your state doesn't require you to have liability insurance, consider getting it anyway. It's not unusual for corporate clients to require $2 million in insurance coverage and to be named as an additional insured on the policy. If you want to go after the big fish, you've got to use big hooks.

In nearly 30 years in the PI business, my agency has never been sued for any action that came out of our investigative effort (we have been sued for a couple automobile accidents). Despite that, in today's litigious society, only a fool would work as a PI and not carry insurance.

Pulling Back the Curtains on Privacy Laws

Surveillance is such a large part of many private investigators' practices that, to avoid being sued, you need to understand when people have a reasonable expectation of privacy and when they don't. The expectation of privacy comes from the U.S. Constitution, the Fourth Amendment protecting Americans from unreasonable search and seizure. (Many other Western countries have similar laws.) We have a reasonable expectation of privacy if a reasonable person would believe that other people will not hear or see what she says or does. How do you establish what is reasonable? Several factors of importance to the PI play out here, including the sophistication of equipment used to "invade" the private space and the vantage point from which the investigator is viewing or hearing. A general rule is, if the activity being observed can be seen from a public area, or an area open to the public, the subject does not have a reasonable expectation of privacy.

A couple kissing or making love in front of an open window that can be seen from a parking lot is fair game. How about a window with the blinds down? Many times I've sat in one of our surveillance vans and shot video of cheating couples through second-floor blinds because the miniblinds were shut in such a way that, from the ground-level parking area, I could see into the apartment. If you have miniblinds, play with the slat angles, and you'll see exactly what I mean.

Did that couple have a reasonable expectation of privacy? Some would say "yes," because they made an attempt to close the blinds. The fact is, I could observe and photograph the activity with ordinary, off-the-shelf photographic equipment. In my opinion, they may have thought they had privacy, but they didn't close the blinds properly. Their lack of proficiency in closing the blinds negated any claim they might make for an expectation of privacy.

The expectation of privacy can be applied to neighborhoods, surveillance, and crime scene investigations; in addition, a number of recent court rulings have addressed expectation of privacy in the workplace. As a PI, if you're conducting an internal theft investigation for an employer, you need to know what you can and can't get away with.

In Chapter 1, I told you about a Shipyard case in which I used a two-story apartment complex with a view over a subject's 8-foot privacy fence to video him working in his backyard. My subject never considered that a resourceful investigator could gain legal access to the apartment that had the view. But just because he didn't consider it didn't mean that he had a "reasonable expectation of privacy." If the apartment had been two blocks away and I'd had to use super-long lenses and digital zooms, maybe I would have crossed into his area of reasonable expectation to privacy. But then again, maybe not.

Always be alert to this privacy problem. It extends well into the information-gathering area, including not only physical, but also electronic and financial data. As I hope this example illustrates, privacy laws can be tricky. You need to know what the laws are in your state to avoid getting in trouble.

Finding Your Clients

Many agencies bill themselves as "full-service agencies." That's fine. Take whatever business you can get. A word of caution, though: it's difficult to be all things to all people. Successful agencies find a niche and then exploit the devil out of it.

When the Brown Group Inc. was marketing insurance surveillance work heavily, it was billing between $80,000 and $90,000 a month. This was in the early 1990s from a single location in northern Florida.

Sure, it did domestic work and some electronic countermeasure work, but its major market was insurance defense cases. The agency marketed that niche by staffing booths at workmen's compensation and insurance liability conventions, where it gave away promotional material and freebies to insurance adjusters and attorneys working insurance defense cases.

C. J. Bronstrup, a long-time private investigator and expert marketer in the PI industry has this to say about marketing:

> Beware: lack of "technical" knowledge is not the leading cause of failure. Many fine investigators with 20-plus years of law enforcement backgrounds go belly-up every year. The major cause of failure is not having enough business. Take the time to learn how to market your business. It can propel your agency from making peanuts to a steady six-figure income almost overnight.

Jimmie Mesis, editor-in-chief of *PI Magazine*, is known as the "marketing guru" for private investigators. He shares some of his key marketing points.

"Marketing yourself and your services is essential to survive as a PI. Those investigators who fail to market or advertise are doomed for failure," says Mesis. "It's unfortunate, because failure can easily be avoided with proper marketing and following a few simple steps."

Mesis alleges that success as a private investigator boils down to steady and aggressive marketing so that people will always remember you. "It's not who you know, but who knows you, and who remembers you when they need a PI."

Mesis goes on to say that investigators need to determine what investigative specialty niche they want to market, ideally a niche that they are good at and one for which there is a need. Finally, they need to identify the target markets that require that specialty. Or, as I like to put it: find your niche, and then market the heck out of that niche.

The typical PI customer base comes out one of the following sections of our economy:

- Attorneys
- Insurance companies
- Business (corporate)
- Consumers
- Other PIs

Each of these target markets must be approached in a manner unique to their specific investigative needs. Insurance companies will be more interested in your surveillance and video skills. An attorney will be more interested in your interviewing techniques, what kind of a witness you will make, and if you can put together a coherent written report that won't embarrass him in court.

In my own firm, we got tired of doing insurance defense work and moved away from that to skip tracing. For five years, we skip traced more than 2,000 people a month. Recently, I was able to sell the skip-tracing portion of my business.

The most important question you need to ask yourself is this: can this business be financially rewarding? The answer is yes, under certain circumstances. Here are three ways to make your PI business financially successful:

- Run the business yourself. Build it up until you have 6 to 12 investigators working for you. You will not make a six-figure income working cases by yourself. Do the math. If you work 40 hours a week, you'll be lucky to bill 24 of them. Twenty-four hours billed at, say, $85 per hour results in weekly billings of $2,040. Fifty weeks of those billings gives you a gross income of $102,000 a year. Subtract all of your expenses, and you'll be lucky to net 50 percent, or $50,000. It is very hard to succeed as a one-man operation.

  With six men whom you pay $30 dollars an hour, billing the same 24 hours a week, all of sudden you're bringing in about $396,000 a year after meeting your investigative payroll. Sure, overhead will increase, but you should still end up with a net well into the six-figure area.

- Use the "make-it-up-in-volume" strategy. Find a high-volume niche that needs little manpower, such as skip tracing or background investigations. Each case might only gross $50 to $100 dollars, but if the volume is high and the costs are low, you can make a nice profit. If the net profit on your high-volume, low-cost product is, say, $35, and you are processing 500 of them a week, the gross profit will be over $900,000 a year. Not too shabby, huh?

- You can make a six-figure income working high-dollar cases as long as the overhead is low. Consider due diligent adoption searches. The cost of working that type of case is practically nothing. Maybe $50 max per case, but you'll charge your client $750. A net profit of $700. If you do three a week, you're netting over $100,000 a year.

There may be other ways to make high dollars in the PI business, but these are three proven ones for me.

The Internet and Your Business

Much is made of marketing on the internet. Hundreds of books have been written on internet marketing. A whole new industry has sprung up dealing only with search engine optimization (SEO). A detailed discussion of internet marketing is beyond scope of this book, but here's some good advice from Mesis:

> A great website is not only essential for generating inquiries and assignments, but also for establishing yourself as an investigative professional. Your website must be search-engine optimized or no one will ever find you or your site. You also need to have a specific page for each investigative specialty that you're promoting. Do not create a dinner menu by listing all of your investigative services on just one page. When you promote one service on one web page, search engines reward you with a higher ranking, which means more traffic. More traffic translates into more phone calls and more assignments.

One of the main reasons PIs fail is they try to go the cheap route. They don't spend any time or money on marketing or advertising, yet they expect their phones to ring with cases.

HIDDEN HINT

The biggest mistake PIs make is building their own websites. Website design and optimization may look easy, but doing it well is difficult. You should leave it to professionals.

A full 30 percent of our new cases come from clients who found us on the internet. Usually they search "Private Investigator" and then the city where they want the work performed.

Those who ignore this advice may wake up one day to find their biggest client just got lured to another PI firm by some kid sitting at the kitchen table in his Harley boxers using a laptop computer.

I've had potential clients tell me that they are using a large national firm with an internet presence. How do they know this firm is large? All they see is the website, the toll-free number, and the claims on the website. It's not a large national firm. It's that damn kid in the underwear. Excuse me while I hit the stores in search of my own Harley boxers.

My agency had one of the original PI websites early in 1992. At that time, there were about seven private investigators on the web, and we were the only ones taking case assignments directly over the internet. Our bank, with whom we'd done business for years, would not give us a MasterCard and Visa merchant account because the internet was so new and they were afraid of it. We had to go elsewhere to set up our merchant account. Of course that sounds silly now, but that's how early our presence was on the net.

Even at that early stage, we were bringing in cases from all over the United States, and our bottom line began to increase because of our website. There's been a lot of shaking out in the industry since then, but a good, well-designed website can increase your business, even if you are working out of your kitchen. Don't be cheap.

The Least You Need to Know

- Becoming a licensed private investigator is a popular dream. Making it a reality involves acquiring certain skills.
- Forty-one states require PIs to be licensed. Twenty-two states also require a minimum passing score on a licensing examination. The test covers state laws on weapons, privacy issues, and general legal knowledge.
- States typically require liability insurance and bond coverage before issuing a PI license. Also, many clients require proof of insurance, often up to $2 million, before assigning cases to a PI.
- Surveillance is a big part of many PI jobs; to avoid getting into legal trouble, you need to be fully informed about privacy laws.
- Use a professionally designed web page to increase business. Expect 30 to 40 percent of your business to come through your website.

Tools of the PI Trade

In This Chapter

- Choosing a vehicle that blends in with your surroundings
- Focusing on the right camera
- Selecting computer equipment and peripherals
- Making a case with good binoculars
- Converting your video to DVD
- Recording what you hear

Private investigators sell a product just as surely as ice cream parlors sell ice cream to eager customers. As a PI, your "scoop" is information, not ice cream. In both lines of business, though, the scoop has to be pleasing to the eyes and satisfying to the tastes of your customers. Sometimes you want to package your information as a photograph or video clip; in some cases, you issue a formal written report; and other times you meet with your clients in person or on the phone to fill them in on what you found.

But no matter what kind of information you provide or how you deliver it, you need tools—tools to collect the information, to analyze it, and to deliver it to your clients. Some of the items in a private investigator's toolbox are digital, others are analog, and still others are good old-fashioned mechanical. Other PI tools are intangible, such as skills or techniques you gain as you get experience in the business. This chapter pokes around the PI's toolbox to give you insights into the many gadgets, devices, and tricks of the trade.

Getting Behind the Wheel

In the television show *Magnum, P.I.*, Tom Selleck plays the role of private investigator Thomas Magnum. Magnum drives a red Ferrari convertible—even while keeping subjects under surveillance. Now, I don't know about you, but if I saw a red Ferrari in my rearview mirror, I think I would recognize it when I saw it again a few minutes later, or even a few hours later. That's television for you. I know a lot of real-life PIs, and not one of them zips around in a Ferrari—or any other fancy sports car—when they're on the job.

Ideally, you don't want your subjects to see you at all. You want to stay far enough away from them that they can't get a good visual on you or your car. But if they do happen to see you, you definitely don't want them to notice you or your vehicle. To achieve these goals, choose a relatively high-horsepower vehicle that blends in with all the other automobiles on the road. More horsepower is better in surveillance vehicles so that you can linger a few blocks behind your subject but catch up quickly if you need to.

Your best bet is a four-door, eight-cylinder, gray or earth-tone auto. Such a vehicle blends into most parking lots and gives you room to take your clients to lunch. Pickup trucks and SUVs also make good surveillance vehicles, particularly in suburban and rural areas.

Avoid any vehicle that looks like a police car. Likewise, black vans with dark-tinted windows or no windows at all, sometimes called "kidnapper vans," make people suspicious. Also pass on driving a black SUV with tinted windows—they too closely resemble the vehicles driven by FBI agents on TV shows. And my final recommendation should go without saying, but I'll say it anyway: stay away from the flashy sport cars.

Shooting Your Subjects … with a Camera

A camera is a PI's best friend. Taking pictures is an important part of all aspects of the PI business, including domestic cases, criminal defense, insurance defense, nursing home abuse, homicide and suspicious suicide cases, and employee theft.

These situations, among others, call for a camera:

- **Providing a visual of the subject:** A lawyer might want to know what a potential witness looks like before deciding to put him on the stand; a wife might want to know the appearance of the person with whom her husband is having an affair.

- **Documenting injuries:** Bruises, cuts, and other signs of physical injury fade; take pictures of them for later use in trials or other legal proceedings.

- **Documenting crime scenes and locations important to an investigation:** These may include areas where a slip and fall occurred, the intersection of a traffic accident, or the place where a drug arrest went down.

- **Providing evidence of an affair or other suspected behavior:** Such photos can include a cheating spouse in a compromising embrace or two cars parked together in front of a motel or apartment.

About the only types of PI work for which you might not need a camera are cases that don't require you to leave your desk: skip tracing, diligent adoption and estate searches, and pre-employment background checks.

Except for the workers' compensation–type cases, which require video cameras (more on these in a bit), a quality digital single-lens reflex (SLR) camera is the most important tool in most private investigators' toolboxes. Admittedly, this type of camera is being challenged by the versatility and light-gathering ability of video cameras, but because you can change lenses with an SLR, it remains the standard bearer for most PIs. Buy the best 35mm digital camera you can afford. If you've got the bucks, get a Canon EOS 5D Mark III (Nikon makes a similar model) and use it for both still and video.

You can take as many pictures as your memory and battery life allow. And when you're writing your reports using a word processing program such as Microsoft Word, you can insert digital photos directly into the report and burn them to a CD to mail along with your report. Be sure to burn two CDs, one for the client and one for your file. Nothing sells your skills as well as a report with your photos inserted into it.

When shopping for an SLR camera, pay attention to these features:

- Number of megapixels

- Storage media

- Zoom capabilities

Because these features are so important, I devote a section to each of them.

Megapixels

A high-end digital camera has more than 20 million pixels, or 20 megapixels. Older and less expensive digitals have fewer pixels. Like everything else in the computer world, electronics get better and less expensive pretty quickly. Ten-million-pixel and higher cameras are pretty much standard issue now.

Storage Media

To access your digital photos, you have to transfer them from your camera to a computer. So before buying a digital camera, make sure that its magnetic storage media is compatible with your computer. Many older laptops have a PCMCIA card slot, which can accept memory cards. PCMCIA slots and cards have pretty much gone the way of the wooly mammoths. In today's world you want an all-in-one card reader, which plugs into your computer via a USB bus. These readers have slots that accept compact flash cards, memory sticks, SDs, and mini SDs. Pay the few bucks extra and buy one with a USB 3.0 transfer rate instead of the USB 2.0. Your current computer may not be up to USB 3.0 but your next one will.

All digital cameras allow you to download pictures directly from the camera to a computer via cables. The drawback to this method is speed: downloading pictures takes longer than inputting them directly from storage media.

HIDDEN HINT

You can use software to manipulate your photographs. Most computers come preloaded with photo-editing software, and digital cameras usually come with digital manipulation software. Some of these programs are excellent. For digital video, the Windows Media Player that comes with Windows is a pretty good program. Macs have their own easy-to-use photo and video software.

One more aspect to consider with magnetic media is that some media can record images faster than others. When you're shopping for still cameras, buy the media storage that allows for faster storage. You can take quicker shots and won't miss the critical photo while waiting for the camera to save the previous shot.

Zoom Capabilities

The more zoom power your camera has, the better it will serve you. When you've got a subject under surveillance (see Chapters 10 and 11), you want to be able to remain as far away as possible while still getting good shots. The catch-22, of course, is that the greater the distance to your subjects, the more difficult it is to get good pictures. A high-power zoom lens can help tip the balance in your favor.

Most PIs use a 100 to 300mm zoom lens. You can add a doubler between the lens and the camera body to get an effective focal length of 600mm. If you want a lens any more powerful than 600mm, you'll need to zoom in on a business loan to pay for it. The more megapixels your camera has the farther away you can be, because you can use photo editing software to blow up the area of interest and not have a fuzzy-looking photo.

How far away can you be? Well, you want to be able to see your subject in the viewfinder from the top of his head to the soles of his feet. Zoom into that point and you're good to go. If you've zoomed in all the way and have a lot of sky over his head, you might want to consider moving in a bit closer. Obviously, clear facial recognition is important.

Up to this point, I've been talking about optical zooms. Optical zoom is how long of zoom the lens has. Depending upon the camera, a 40 mm lens gives you a view of about what the naked eye sees. A 100 mm zoom lens will bring your view more than twice as close. Both digital still and video cameras may have a digital zoom feature. The digital zoom works very well, up to a point. Digital zoom works by magnifying the size of the image on the receptor chip in the camera. But since it's a digital magnification and not an optical one, it reaches a point where the picture becomes fuzzy or grainy. When deciding on a camera, all other things being equal, go first for the camera with the highest optical zoom, and then consider the power of the digital zoom.

For your photographs to be effective in court, the subject must be identifiable. This means you have to get good, clear, well-focused shots. At 600mm, you'll need a tripod to steady the camera to avoid blurring the picture. A fast shutter speed also helps prevent blurred pictures, but with a super-long lens on the camera, the amount of light that enters the lens is reduced, so you may need to use slower shutter speeds. With a good image-stabilized lens (these pricey devices digitally correct for motion blur, giving you a sharper image) you can probably get your shot.

Taking Pictures or Video in Low or No Light

When you need to take pictures at night or in dark venues but don't want to use flashbulbs or spotlights, you have two options:

- **ISO speed of 3200 or 6400:** A good camera set to a processing speed of 3200 or 6400 should get you a useable photo in low light. You might have to manually set the shutter speed to 1/30 or 1/15.

- **Infrared:** Sony offers infrared night shot capability on many of its video cameras. It works pretty well at close range, and you can buy an optional infrared light that should work up to a hundred feet. The night shot feature on many Canon cameras isn't infrared, but it increases the gain on the receptors in the camera. It works well, but if the subject is moving, the image will blur and be streaked.

> **THE SCOOP**
>
> One good site for comparing digital still cameras is www.dpreview.com. It has reviews of all the cameras, plus ratings. The site also has a pretty good learning center, where you can look up unfamiliar terms.

When purchasing a video camera, find one that has a viewfinder that you look through with one eye and not one that has a small screen viewfinder that flips out to the side of the camera. Why? Because if you're sitting in your vehicle at night, when you turn on the video camera the screen lights up the whole interior of your car, and anyone a block away can see you.

For digital video cameras, I suggest going right to the manufacturers' websites to read and compare the specifications on the cameras. Then go to your local electronics store for a hands-on feel of the camera and personalized answers to your questions. Now, where can you find the best price for the camera equipment you want to purchase? Sounds like a question for an aspiring PI to solve. Shop around, though, because most of the brand names have a street price considerably lower than the suggested retail price.

Lights, Camera, Action: Putting Your Camera to Work

It was 11:30 at night on Friday, May 10. The lights in the apartment I'd been watching had gone out about a half hour before. My client's husband, Jonathan, from whom she was separated, had taken their 3-year-old son with him for the weekend. Part of the separation agreement was that Jonathan wouldn't cohabitate or spend the night with other women while he had custody of the child.

I'd followed Jonathan to his girlfriend's apartment complex and watched him and the little boy enter. His SUV was parked in front of the apartment, and the girlfriend's car was parked next to his. I walked up to the vehicles and, using a large, black, permanent felt-tip marker, I drew an inverted V on the sidewall at the very top of the right rear tire on both cars. If the vehicles departed and then later returned, I would know it by checking the position of the V. It would be nearly impossible for the V to be in the exact same position relative to the fender as when I drew it.

Next, I backed off a ways behind the cars and took out my trusty Canon digital SLR that allows me to set the aperture for low-light situations. I took three shots of the two cars and the front of the apartment. My objective was to record both vehicles and the address in the same photo. Then I scooted out of there. Back at the office, I added the date and time onto the face of the photographs. I printed two high-quality prints of the photographs, one for my client and one for her attorney.

At 7 the next morning, I was back at the same apartment complex. Both cars were still there. The inverted V was in the same position I'd left it. Dew was on both car roofs and front windshields. I felt the grille area on both cars, and both were cold. My conclusion? Neither car had moved since 11:30 the previous night, indicating that Jonathan had spent the night with his girlfriend, son in tow.

I shot two more photographs of both cars and hustled back to my office. This time, I added "May 11th 7 A.M." to the prints. After three or four weekends of this, we had what the client wanted. The case went to court, and Jonathan's attorney agreed to the facts in my report without me having to testify. The client told me that, of all the money she'd spent going through the divorce, the most productive use of her money was what she'd spent with my firm.

Choosing the Right Computer

You can't run a successful PI business today without a good computer and a fast internet connection. If you're not computer literate, don't hang out your shield until you are. Even if you want to handle the financial and administrative aspects of your business on paper, you need a computer to access the databases for researching your cases. Check out Chapters 4, 5, and 6 for a rundown of the various types of information available to PIs through the internet.

Your computer should have the fastest processor, the largest hard drive, and the most memory (RAM) you can afford. Why does it have to be so powerful? Thirty days after you've bought your new state-of-the-art computer, it'll be outdated, and a newer, faster, larger computer will be on the market. By starting with the best product *du jour*, you'll get about four good years out of it before you need to start thinking about replacing it.

If you're going to skimp at all, skip the hottest processor and get the day-old version. You can sometimes save a considerable amount of money by buying the second-fastest processor on the market. The sometimes slight differences in performance aren't that big. Never skimp on the hard drive or the memory.

Computer programs get larger and require more RAM every time companies issue a new version. If you're having stability problems, programs are crashing, or the computer is locking up, try adding more RAM to your computer. Increasing RAM can solve a whole host of problems.

Stocking Up on Peripheral Equipment

You can buy plenty of bells and whistles for your computer—just don't tell your spouse that *The Complete Idiot's Guide to Private Investigating, Third Edition* suggested the high-quality soundcard with the subwoofers. Not true. But you do want these add-ons:

- **CD/DVD burner:** You can duplicate your photographs or video right onto a DVD and make copies for your file, your client, and your client's client.

- **External hard drive:** Use it for backup and additional nonessential storage, like copies of subpoenas and affidavits that you'll probably never need again after the return of service has been made.

- **Color printer:** A high-quality color printer, using premium photo paper specifically designed for color printers, will give you prints nearly indistinguishable from those made at a photography shop.

Harnessing the Latest Tablet Computer Technology

If you already own a laptop computer, you may have a hard time justifying the expense of the latest iPad or other brand of computer tablet. Maybe this story will help you see how valuable one can be as an investigative tool:

A few months ago, I was making the late night/early morning runs on yet another child custody case. This time, the ex-husband hired me to find out if his wife was cohabiting with a man when she had their son with her. My client, Robert, called me on Saturday and said his ex-wife and the boyfriend were going to be at the apartment complex pool with his son. He wanted documentation of the boyfriend hanging around his 4-year-old.

I could have sat in a car and tried from a distance to get photos or video of them playing in the pool, but that would have been very difficult. Instead, I took my drink, my pool towel, and my iPad. I pulled up a chaise lounge in the pool area and sat there "reading" on my iPad. Well, not really. Instead, I was taking photos with the iPad of the ex, the new boyfriend, and my client's son frolicking in the pool. Nobody paid any attention to the guy who was engrossed in his ebook. I got the best pictures ever and could not have done that with any other type of camera. My iPad is a regular part of my surveillance toolkit.

Looking into a Good Pair of Binoculars

A good pair of binoculars will make you a more productive investigator. Binoculars come in a variety of sizes and types, but you can't go wrong with a pair rated 7x50 (the first number indicates the optical magnification; the second number is the aperture of the light-collecting lenses in millimeters). At that power and that size, the image doesn't "bounce" around too much.

Get the most expensive pair of binoculars you can afford. The difference between an inexpensive pair and an expensive pair might not be noticeable when you're inspecting them in the store, but the light-gathering aspects of binoculars vary significantly, usually in proportion to the price tag. On a nighttime surveillance, quality binoculars will gather more light and make it easier to see your subject's activities. A good set of binoculars is filled with nitrogen or some other inert gas injected into the binoculars between the lens and the eyepieces. This prevents moisture and dirt from getting into the binoculars.

Some binoculars have a compass built into the viewfinder. Knowing where north, south, east, and west lay is very handy. If you're in radio contact with another investigator and your subject is on the move, you can tell the other investigator exactly which direction the subject is moving or toward which direction the activity is shifting. It's a lot clearer to say, "The subject is moving east around the end of the shopping center" than to say, "The subject is moving toward my right, around the end of the shopping center." The other investigator probably doesn't know which way you're facing and will be unsure of which direction he should be looking.

Converting Video to DVD

In surveillance operations, probably 95 percent of private investigators use video. This is because, by far, the largest customer market in the PI business is the insurance company checking on claimants to be sure that they're injured and their claimed disabilities are genuine. When shooting video that might need to be used in a courtroom as evidence, you need to keep one point in mind: having the time and date on the video screen is very important when showing a video in court. Unfortunately, many video recorders record the time and date on a different track than the video itself, and when you transfer the video from the recorder to your computer to burn onto a DVD, you often lose the date and time track or your computer doesn't recognize it. If you burn a copy of the video without the date and time stamp, you're essentially rendering the video useless as evidence.

According to Mitch Davis of TSCM/Special Operations Group of Nashville, Tennessee (www.tscmusa.com), the key is to avoid changing file formats. Instead, burn your digital video directly to disc using a standalone DVD burner. These devices are inexpensive and simple to operate.

There is a rule of evidence called "next best evidence." Among other things, it means if the original piece isn't available, but a photocopy is available, then the photocopy can be entered into evidence. This applies to making copies of your video for use in a courtroom. If your video is on the hard drive of your camera, then a DVD with a copy of it will suffice.

The problem comes in making the copy. As many PIs know, when copying a video from the camera to a computer hard drive, the date and time stamp on the original on the camera is lost in the downloading to your computer. So to avoid this problem many PIs use a program like Dazzle, which enables you to add the date and time. However, this means that you have altered the original file format because you have to tell Dazzle what time to start with.

The better option is to copy the video directly from the camera to a standalone DVD burner. This transfer to a DVD burner will create an analog copy of the High Def (HD) original, but will also capture the original time and date stamp. If you do it any other way, an astute attorney can ask you if you've altered the video in any fashion, and you'll have to say "yes" because you reinserted the time and date. "What else have altered?" the attorney will ask. "Did you take out where my client was limping so badly he could hardly walk?" And on and on.

Use the simple, straightforward approach. Use cables and the analog output of your camera to burn your copies directly to a DVD burner. No muss, no fuss, and you can honestly say you have not altered the video in any way.

Sometimes we get caught up with "high tech" stuff and think we have to show an HD video because it was originally shot in HD. Not so. Neither the judge, the jury, nor the attorneys will even notice, and most likely the TV or monitor used in the courtroom isn't HD anyway.

While producing or obtaining video for clients, remember your goal is to use that video to show an irrefutable act or incriminating activity performed by the subject. The video will look the same whether in HD or not. If the images you obtain demonstrate their intended purpose with minimal question, you've done a good job, and you'll have a satisfied client.

Recording the Facts

A private investigator's clients see only the written or photographic results of our work. They don't see the gallons of sweat on the floor of your car after a hot afternoon surveillance. They don't feel the fear of a near collision on the freeway when your subject exits suddenly and you have to jump three lanes of traffic to stay behind him. To them, your product is your report. That's all they'll see—that and any evidence you collect.

Because your written report represents all the work you put into an investigation, you need to make it look professional. I talk in greater length in Chapter 20 about formatting your reports. Here, I discuss the process of getting the facts down so that you don't lose them or forget them. The quality of your report reflects directly on you as an investigator. And when clients are impressed with the product, they become repeat customers.

Some surveillance investigators handwrite their surveillance logs. That works, but it is tedious. A better way is to dictate the surveillance into a digital recorder as you go along. With that method, you can capture all the details—license plate numbers, right and left turns, and the rest—as they happen. Down the road, those little details that you record may become important. People really are creatures of habit, and as you work a subject, his patterns will develop. If this is all laid out in your surveillance logs, the next guy working him will have the benefit of your experience.

Keep a pen and paper ready for quick notes. Always jot down any important license plate number as you see it; sometimes we transpose numbers when dictating. Plus, you may need to call in the tag to your office and have the registration run. You don't want to have to listen back through your entire surveillance log to find a tag.

As long as we're on the topic of surveillance logs, here's one piece of advice you won't find in any other book. Back at the office, watch the surveillance video you've just made on a monitor. Dictate while the tape is running. In your dictation, note the times of significant activity. When the claimant picks up that 50-pound bag of fertilizer, note that in your log. You don't have to mention every bend and each motion of his body, but do enter into the log the time of any activity you think is important.

When you show these tapes in court, the judge won't want to watch the entire thing. After a few moments, he'll ask you to fast-forward the tape to the "good parts." With the time and date on the tape, and the same time and date in your typed log, you can go right to the good parts and skip over the long, boring, and unimportant parts.

If you're just beginning a business, you might not have a secretary. I suggest not hiring one until you find that the volume of report typing you're doing is actually keeping you from working on cases. At that point, hire a part-time secretary, and you'll become more profitable.

> **HIDDEN HINT**
>
> Use a digital recorder while in the field. With a digital recorder, you can download the dictation directly to your computer and burn copies to a CD. You can use voice recognition software like Dragon NaturallySpeaking to transcribe the dictation without anybody actually keyboarding it in. The best way, however, is to email the audio file to a secretarial service that will type it for you for about $15 an hour and email you the Word document in a day or so.

The importance of producing a high-quality product cannot be stressed enough. The candy maker's fudge must first look good enough to eat. To keep clients coming back, the fudge has to taste even better than it looks. Likewise, your product should look professional, and as the client reads through the report and views the photographs, the contents should be even more pleasing to him.

In one of the examples in this chapter, I talked about a subject named Jonathan, whom I had under surveillance for spending the night with his girlfriend while having his 3-year-old for the weekend. Who do you think his wife, or her attorney, is going to recommend the next time somebody asks for the name of a good private investigator? In fact, his attorney, recognizing my good work, now regularly refers clients to me. Even better than that, last year Jonathan, recognizing good work when he saw it, called me to work on a case for him and his now new soon-to-be ex-wife. Success, in this case, is sweet and just keeps building on itself.

The Least You Need to Know

- Buy a car that is practical for both conducting surveillance and carting clients to lunch.
- Three important tools of the trade are a digital SLR camera, a digital video camera, and a good pair of binoculars.
- You can't run a PI business without a computer. Buy a computer with a recent processor, a very large hard drive, and as much RAM as you can afford.
- Use a good-quality digital recorder to dictate during a surveillance instead of handwriting a surveillance log.
- Convert your video to DVD by using a DVD burner instead of your computer.
- A high-quality finished product will please your clients and fatten your bottom line.

Getting the Scoop

Now that you've decided exactly what you're looking for, it's time to find it.

In this part, I tell you about the sources of information PIs use around the country to get the scoop on the subjects of their cases. You learn how to skip trace on the web and prowl the courthouses to access to federal, state, and local records. I also show you how to log on to those special private databases that professional PIs use.

Skip Tracing

In This Chapter

* Determining where to begin your search
* Deciphering the name game
* Mining social networks for information
* Contacting neighbors and relatives

There's a big difference between looking for somebody you've lost contact with over the years due to moves, job changes, and other life events, and looking for somebody who doesn't want to be found. Old high school friends would probably like to find you as much as you'd like to find them. They're not hiding their identity. They haven't put their phone in somebody else's name, and their mail goes to their home address, not some private mailbox at The UPS Store.

PIs refer to people who don't want to be found as *skips*, meaning people who are intentionally hiding—perhaps from creditors—or who have some other reason to keep their whereabouts a secret. *Skip tracing* is the process of tracking down those individuals through whatever means possible. When searching for skips, PIs often search public and private databases; contact the skip's friends, family, neighbors, and employees; and even use social networking sites such as Facebook to glean information about them.

If a person is really on the run, it's highly unlikely you'll find his current whereabouts on free internet sites such as Whitepages.com and www.411.com. Professional pay sites may turn up the information you need, but even they may lag months behind. In this chapter, I delve into the fascinating world of skip tracing, cluing you in on the tricks that PIs use to ferret out people who would just as soon have their location remain a secret.

Misconceptions abound concerning the effectiveness of using the internet to track down skips. If you want to learn about Great Black-backed Gulls, you can probably find all you'll ever want to know about them online. But if you want to dig up the maiden name of your husband's mistress because you want to check her criminal record, and she's been married three times, you're much less certain of getting the info you need on the web.

Zeroing In on the Right Search

The first thing you need to do when searching on the web for somebody is to narrow your search as much as you can using the information that you have. If you're trying to track down a skip named Joe Schmoe, an initial search might turn up thousands of Joe Schmoes. So that you don't have to spend the next six weeks making thousands of phone calls in the hope of finding *your* Joe Schmoe, you need to refine your search. You can do this by using the subject's date of birth, his last known residence, or the name of his spouse, or through a number of other techniques. Refining your search in these ways seems elementary, I know, but you'd be surprised how even seasoned investigators have a hard time narrowing the focus of their search to the right party.

Playing the Name Game

You have to know whom you're looking for before you can begin searching. But you may not have a complete name. If you have a partial name and a complete date of birth, you're a long way toward your goal. In the United States, a country of over 300 million people, you'll find a lot of duplicated names. So unless a name is very uncommon, it isn't sufficient data by itself to perform a thorough locate.

For instance, my first and last names—Steven Brown—are fairly common. If you do a criminal background search on that name, you'll find that Steven Brown has been arrested in almost every jurisdiction in the United States. If you add my middle name, Kerry, and search for Steven Kerry Brown, you narrow the search significantly, but you still have some sorting to do. For instance, one Steven Kerry Brown in Oregon has multiple arrests. (I'm happy to report that yours truly isn't the same guy.)

THE SCOOP

Criminal records, which I talk more about in Chapter 18, rely almost entirely upon name, sex, race, and date of birth. They rarely involve a person's Social Security number. And if you're not sure of the sex or race, the person's name and date of birth probably suffice.

Okay, so you have the name, but most of us don't know our old friends' dates of birth. Shoot, I sometimes can't even remember my own kids' dates of birth. So what are we to do? Let's start with what we have. The name.

Knowing What Names to Use in Your Search

Most Anglo-Saxon names have a first name, a middle name, and a last name, which is usually taken from the child's father. But not all cultures structure their names this way. Hispanic names, for instance, include a first name, a middle name, a last name taken from the child's father, and a second last name, or fourth name, which is taken from the child's mother's maiden name.

THE SCOOP

When I was assigned with the FBI to the San Juan, Puerto Rico, office, my name was Steven Kerry Brown Bellamy—Bellamy being my mother's maiden name. I still have credit cards from down there that read "Steven B. Bellamy." I once had fun explaining that to a clerk in a department store when he wanted to compare my driver's license, last name Brown (hence the B in the credit card), with the credit card showing Bellamy as the last name.

Most databases have only three fields for names: first, middle, and last. Such databases make it very difficult to do a search for Hispanic names. Don't believe me? Try searching the Puerto Rican court system. You need to have the mother's maiden name (the fourth name) to search it. When clients request a criminal check in Puerto Rico, the first thing I ask for is the subject's fourth name. According to the latest Census Bureau data, 16 percent of the U.S. population speaks Spanish, so a savvy investigator needs to know how to search for people with Hispanic names.

Getting to the Root of Nicknames

Another potential problem is that many people are known by their nicknames, and you might not even know that it's a shortened version of their names. For instance, I wanted to find a Peggy from high school. Did you know Peggy is short for Margaret? Or Jack can be short for John? This one will throw you for sure: in the 1950s, many male children were named Carroll. The nickname for that? Charlie. If you're not absolutely sure of the person's full or correct given name or how it's spelled (Steven or Stephen?), thumb through a name book at a local bookstore or the library before you begin your search. This one clue might save you hours of fruitless searching.

Relying on Family and Friends for Info

The absolute easiest way to find a skip or a lost love is to ask someone who knows your subject and knows where he is. You'd be surprised how many hours PIs waste on internet searches and telephone directory calls when they could just pick up their phones and ask where the subject is.

I had a client hire me to find a skip. The client was an attorney, and his client wanted him to sue the subject for $500,000. They had no idea where the subject had gone. They'd heard rumors he was living on a sailboat in Florida. I tracked down the rumors, which were about a year behind the subject, and found the owner of the boat that the subject had been living on. But the subject had moved to locations unknown by then.

So I had the attorney subpoena the subject's cell phone records. Frankly, I was hoping that the records would show us a new billing address that we didn't already have. But no, as luck would have it, the cell service records we'd subpoenaed showed that the service had been disconnected six months earlier. I searched multiple PI databases but didn't turn up any new information. Even the most expensive pay databases available (I get into those in Chapter 6) didn't disclose any newer addresses.

I did track down the subject's parents and tried several different pretexts to glean from them his current whereabouts, but they didn't fall for any of my ruses; they merely claimed they didn't know where he was.

Where in the world was this guy? Most private investigators would have stopped at that point. If you have the time, sometimes stopping is a good move. Wait a few months, and one of the data suppliers might pick up a fresh scent. But I didn't have the luxury of waiting. We needed to get this guy located and served right away. So I picked up the phone and starting calling numbers that showed up more than once on the subject's cell phone bill. These were old numbers he'd called a year ago. On the second number I dialed, I found a friend of the subject in New York City. In about 15 seconds, I had the subject's new cell number, out of San Diego, and his address in Cabo San Lucas, Mexico. Plus, the friend told me where he was working in Cabo. The next knock on the subject's door in Cabo wasn't the tortilla delivery man, but the process server. Surprise!

Without those cell phone records, I wouldn't have found that subject. Those records can lead you to your subject's friends, relatives, acquaintances, and neighbors, who might just have the information you're looking for.

Telephone directories, internet search engines, pay databases—none of them keep up with people's movements as well as relatives and close friends. If you can't find any relatives, drive around the old neighborhood and knock on a few doors. If the doors you need to knock on are across the country, there's a way to do that, too: via social networking sites like Facebook and LinkedIn.

> **HIDDEN HINT**
>
> People are disconnecting their landlines at an astonishing rate and using only their cell phones. But many older people still maintain their landlines. Even more important for PIs, most commercial establishments keep their traditional phone lines. Why is that important? If your subject is renting a house or an apartment, you can call the landlord and verify that he is indeed in apartment 405. Likewise if your skip is working someplace, a carefully prepared pretext call to the employer's human resources department might net you the department he works in and the shift he's working.

Harnessing the Social Network

Anytime a new technology or social media comes into popular use, a clever private investigator can find a way to use it.

A while back, I was doing an adoption diligent search (see Chapter 19 for details). Thomas, the missing father who was delinquent in his child support payments, hadn't been seen or heard from for more than a year. I spoke with his mother, but she claimed to have had no contact with him for a year. After filing the appropriate forms with the post office (see Chapter 19 for details), I was told that it didn't have a forwarding address for him. Every indication I had was that he'd moved from Florida to a western state. Instead of packing up my car and heading west, I logged on to my Facebook account and searched for him. And there he was, profile photo and all. His page was fairly open, so I sent him a message via Facebook with my phone number. Because I wanted him to respond, I didn't say anything about the back child support. Instead, I said that I needed to talk to him about his son. That got his attention, and he called me.

Another client contacted me from the Federal Penitentiary he was serving time in. He wanted me to interview a witness, Justin, for an appeal on his case. The witness was living somewhere in the New Orleans area. I had access to Louisiana motor vehicle records through one of my data suppliers. So I ran Justin's driver's license and found vehicles registered to him. I then hired a Louisiana PI to drive by those residences several times, but he never saw Justin's truck. Finally, the PI knocked on the door and was told that Justin had moved. I began searching the social network sites. Sure enough, there he was on MySpace. He mentioned on his MySpace page that he worked in a hotel in New Orleans. Before I sent my subcontractor PI to the hotel,

I called the hotel to make sure Justin was still working there, and through a friendly conversation, I discovered he was working a 4 P.M.-to-midnight shift.

I had another client who had heard that her soon-to-be ex was traveling to the Caribbean with a girlfriend. She wanted some coverage and documentation of the trip. She assumed he'd be staying at a first-class resort and traveling by private plane. The evidence would help her in her divorce case.

I had the girlfriend's name and went searching on Facebook. I found her, but her privacy settings made it difficult to get any information about her. However, Facebook did list some of her friends. I looked through the list of friends and noticed that she'd friended a page of a deceased young woman. Using my wife's computer, I friended the same page. Next, I sent a friend request to the soon-to-be ex-husband's girlfriend telling her we were friends through this deceased mutual friend. Okay, so it was a lie and, yes, we were taking advantage of some poor deceased woman's Facebook page. But it worked. Pretty quickly, she friended us back and our subject was posting about her trip: when they were leaving, where they were going, photos of her and her boyfriend together. Through her Facebook page, she gave me just about everything I needed to hand a nice fat report to my client.

The bottom line: I search social media pages almost every day doing research for my clients. The best part about it? It's free.

THE SCOOP

Not everybody you find on a social media site will respond to your friend requests or messages. I've sent messages to a missing mother in a diligent adoption search, to her relatives, and even to some of her more recent friends, but none of them ever contacted me.

Getting to Your Subjects Through Their Spouses

If your subject has an uncommon name, consider yourself lucky. A database search by name may well turn her up. But if you're looking for Steven Brown, you're going to need a middle initial and some other data to help you filter the thousands of Steven Browns to the one you want. But you have other ways to narrow your search. For instance, many free searches list the phone in both spouses' names. If you know that Steven Brown married Melanie Brown, you might find a listing for Steven and Melanie Brown. There's a good chance you've just found your subject.

If you still can't find your subject, stop looking for him. Instead, track down his girl-friend, spouse, or relatives. Remember, the girlfriend, the ex-spouse, and the relatives probably know where he is. They may not tell you, but they'll know—and often they will lead you right to him. More than once, I've been looking for a skip, called a relative, and had the skip answer the phone.

Searching Free Public Databases

Not everyone owns real property, but if your subject does, you have a good shot at tracking him down. That's because his contact information may be in the property appraiser's records for the county in which he owns property.

> **HIDDEN HINT**
>
> As an investigator, for profit or just for yourself, you need a variety of tools in your toolbox. Using the right tool at the right time marks the difference between an apprentice and a true craftsman. This book is designed to raise your level of craft from apprentice to artist. Experience by itself won't get you there. You'll need a mentor. And this book can be your mentor.

A while back, an experienced investigator called me for some help. The investigator and the client's attorney wanted to fly to Jacksonville, Florida, to interview a potential witness in a case. The witness had previously lived in another mid-Southern state, and the investigator found some evidence that the witness had relocated to my area. He'd searched some of the pay databases that I tell you about in Chapter 6, but he couldn't find a definite address for the witness. He asked me to search the Florida driver's license records by name and date of birth to see if the missing witness had a Florida license.

While we were talking on the phone, I brought up on my computer a public database that's open to anyone who has access to the internet. I found my client's witness in less than 30 seconds. By the time our brief conversation was over, I'd told him where his witness lived, how much his new house was appraised for, how much the witness paid for the new house, and the fact that he'd purchased it about six months ago.

This seasoned investigator said to me, "Man, you're fast." He might be right, but that's because I knew which database to search. I knew I could go online to the county property appraiser's website and search property ownership records, which are available to the public for free. The investigator who hired me had spent his time searching fee-based databases.

HIDDEN HINT

Many investigators rely solely on fee-based databases for searches. As you discover in Chapters 5 and 6, searching public records is the key to a successful investigation.

I always follow up on what I find online. For instance, in the aforementioned case of the missing witness, I went to the Department of Motor Vehicles to see what cars were registered to the subject and drove by the house to make sure he was actually living there. But I was able to solve the big mystery of his location quickly, and I looked like a superstar to the out-of-state investigator who'd hired me.

I bookmark all of the Florida property appraiser's websites so that I can access them quickly. How do you find the local county property appraiser's website? Go to any major search engine and put in the criteria for the search: "Property Appraiser [Your County and State]," being sure to fill in the appropriate county and state you're searching for. Don't click the top search result; usually the returns at the top of the page are paid listings. Instead, look at the URLs on the returns lower on the page. You want to click the listings that end in .US, or .gov, or .[state name].US.

Most property appraisers' websites offer searches. Not all county property appraisers' search sites are created equal, though. You can almost always search by name, but sometimes you must have the parcel number. Usually, you can search by property address as well. Some websites are updated daily, some monthly, and some only annually. Normally, the website tells you this; if not, then call and ask. Searching property appraisers' records is also a good way to find the landlord of your subject, if you need to. If you can't find your subject there, well, at least it has cost you nothing.

The other great public record search, which I talk more about in Chapter 5, is a search of the official records. Official records contain property deeds, liens, judgments, and other documents. Even if the property appraiser's records aren't up-to-the-minute, the official records (OR) are, and many clerks of the court offer free OR searches from the couch in front of your television.

As I mentioned in Chapter 1, if you're going to be a do-it-yourself PI or become a professional PI, you have to think outside the box—or "sideways." When attempting to locate someone, most folks think only of telephone directory information, whether it's on the internet or on the telephone dial. Due to so many telemarketing campaigns and a growing desire for more privacy, having a nonpublished or unlisted phone number—or no landline—is becoming more popular.

HIDDEN HINT

Want to find out who a nonpublished number belongs to? Try SkipSmasher.com, masterfiles.com, or Tracersinfo.com.

Wanted Dead or Alive—Searching the Death Master File

If the person you're seeking is a birth parent of an adult client or someone who's elderly or whose age you're unsure of, she might be deceased. Before you spend too much time tracking down the individual, first make sure she's still alive.

Fortunately, you have a good tool at your disposal for finding out who has died. The Social Security Administration maintains a Death Master File with information about deceased individuals who had a Social Security number, and it sells its death data to search databases. Some of those sites let you search the data for free. Others, of course, want you to pay. As in any database search, you need to know exactly what records are being searched and when they were last updated.

A client hired me to locate an elderly cousin of his that he hadn't heard from for several years. He had her last known address and telephone number, but he couldn't locate her through directory information or find anything current using the free white pages searches on the internet.

I quoted him a minimum price of $250, which he agreed to, and set about searching for her. First, I called the number he'd given me. Sure enough, it was disconnected. At this point, I could have spent hours tracking down her friends and relatives, looking up her last place of employment, or even stopping by her last-known address to ask old neighbors about her whereabouts. But since he'd told me she was elderly and lived alone, I first checked the Death Master File.

She was listed there. The Death Master File gave me her Social Security number; the day, month, and year of her death; and the county of her last known residence. I waited a few days to get back to the client because I didn't want him to think it had been too easy. Then I called and related the sad news. He could have saved himself $250 if he'd bought this book instead of calling me.

Keep in mind that the Social Security Death Master File search isn't without its flaws. For example, its coverage of deaths listed before 1980 isn't nearly as comprehensive as with deaths from 1980 to the present. For instance, my father, who died in 1975 and had a surviving spouse, is not listed. My mother, who died in 1988 and didn't have a surviving spouse, is listed. Like any database, this is not a definitive resource. If the person you're looking for is listed in the database, he's probably deceased. But if his name isn't listed, you can't be certain that the subject is alive—all you know is that he's not in this particular database.

You can buy access to the Social Security Death Master File directly from the National Technical Information Service that handles the distribution of this data from the Social Security Administration. A password for unlimited searches costs around $1,000 a year. Ouch! Or you can buy 1,000 searches for a mere $600.

Don't need 1,000 searches? Just type "Death Master File" in the search box of a search engine such as Google, and you'll get a list of websites that will run the search for you. Some sites charge as much as $49; most charge $5 to $15. Others, including many genealogy websites, let you search for free.

You can search for free on sites like these:

- FamilySearch (https://familysearch.org/search)

- Genealogy Bank (www.genealogybank.com/gbnk/ssdi/)

- Family Tree Legends (www.familytreelegends.com/records/ssdi)

- American Ancestors (www.americanancestors.org/search.aspx)

Note: FamilySearch displays the subject's Social Security number as well as death data; the rest of the sites on this list block all or part of the Social Security number.

Searching the databases is fairly straightforward. The more exact information you have, the better. With that said, too much information can hinder your search. For example, try searching for my mother, Brookie Bellamy Brown. If you search her full name, you won't get any hits. However, if you search for Brookie B. Brown, using just the initial for the middle name, you get a hit.

HIDDEN HINT

Be persistent when searching for people on search databases. If one of the search sites doesn't give you the information you desire, don't give up. Try different combinations of the name you have on every site until you get a hit. First try searching for full first, middle, and last name. Then try searching for just first and last name. Then try with a middle initial.

Any information that you get from databases, whether they're free or ones you paid big bucks for, must be looked at with a broad view. Sometimes the information is exactly right, but just as often, the "facts" returned may have part of the truth, but not necessarily all of it. For example, my mother's last residence is shown as Tempe, Arizona. That's not exactly right. While she did maintain a residence there, that isn't where she was residing at the time of her death. Just as a good mariner doesn't rely on only one source for his navigational data, a good investigator checks the facts through multiple sources before testifying that they are accurate and complete.

The Social Security Death Master File also returns the correct date of birth and often—drum roll, please—the complete Social Security number of the deceased individual. Why might you want that? Well, suppose you're doing an estate search and need to find the relatives. Plug in the Social Security number of the deceased into one of your pay, PI-friendly databases, and you'll get the past residences of the deceased, plus a list of individuals who shared those various residences with her. And you'll get a list of possible relatives.

Curing the Plague of Social Security Truncation

In 2004, ChoicePoint, a major data supplier, was scammed by several small clients. The clients were crooks and took thousands of identities from ChoicePoint data and used it, yep, you guessed it, for illegal gain. As a result, ChoicePoint and most other major data suppliers now truncate the Social Security numbers of their listings. Instead of reporting the complete nine-digit number, they report only the first five digits, like this: 123-45-XXXX.

Why do you need the SSN? You can search Steve Brown across the county by name and date of birth, and you'll find me and a few thousand other Steve Browns. Then you'll have to do some more searching to figure out which one is me. And suppose you don't have my complete date of birth. You're dead in the water. But if you search for me using my Social Security number, you'll nail me the first time out. Probably.

I say *probably* because it's not unusual to see others associated with my or your Social Security number. How can that be? My son's credit file is sometimes mixed up with mine. Someone might be using my SSN for nefarious deeds. Or some clerk might have mistyped my SSN when I bought a car.

So what's the cure for the plague of truncation? The good news is that solutions exist, and you don't even have to be a licensed PI to use some of them:

- **The Death Master File:** This works only if your subject is deceased.

- **Official records in your county clerk's office:** These still have complete biographical data: name, date of birth, and SSN. However, note that many clerks redact the SSN from the more recent records that are publicly viewable on the internet. You may still visit the clerk's office personally and view the complete record.

- **PI-friendly subscription databases that don't truncate:** These include www.tracersinfo.com, www.skipsmasher.com, TLO.com, and findmyskip.com.

- **Driver's license data:** If you are a licensed PI, you fall under the exemptions provided by the DPPA and can go to your local DMV and see what's on file for your subject. Usually the DMV has the driver's SSN. Sometimes the clerk at the DMV doesn't want to give it to you, though, so be prepared with a copy of your state law that regulates the release of that information. Some DMV clerks don't know about the PI exemption in the DPPA. Many states have passed legislation that is similar to the DPPA with the same exemptions. Save yourself a second trip to the DMV by taking with you a copy of that state statute that allows PIs access to DMV info.

- Cobble together the number using two different sources that truncate the number differently. The Public Access to Court Electronic Records database (typically just called *PACER*; www.pacer.gov.) is a federal government database that I describe in Chapter 5; I mention it here because it uses a different truncation method than other databases. PACER lops off the first five numbers and provides the last four, as in XXX-XX-6789. You can obtain the first five numbers from almost any other database, search PACER, and if your subject has any sort of federal record (civil, criminal, or bankruptcy), you get the missing four numbers.

Sending a Message via the SSA or IRS

Both the Social Security Administration and the IRS may forward a letter to an individual for humanitarian reasons or to inform someone that she has money owed to her. Write the letter to the individual, place it in an unsealed envelope with first-class postage on it, and then place that envelope in a larger one addressed to either

Internal Revenue Service
Office of Disclosure Operations
1111 Constitution Avenue NW
Washington, DC 20224

or

Social Security Administration
Office of Public Inquiries
6401 Security Boulevard
Baltimore, MD 21235

If you're sending it to the Social Security Administration, include a check for $3. I wouldn't hold my breath, but let me know if it works for you. Read on for another method of obtaining a military person's location.

Looking Behind Bars: When Your Skip Is a Jailbird

One of the unpleasant things you have to consider when searching for someone is the possibility that your subject has been incarcerated, whether in a federal facility, a state prison, or a county or city jail.

To find a federal prisoner, go to www.bop.gov, the Federal Bureau of Prisons website. On the left side of the screen, click Inmate Locator to perform a search by name. If you're at your computer as you read this, just for fun, search for John Gotti or Martha Stewart, and see what comes up. Have you ever wondered how old Martha Stewart is? Now you know.

THE SCOOP

In June 2012, more than 217,000 inmates were housed in about 100 different federal detention facilities. The federal prison system houses only individuals convicted of federal crimes. According to the U.S. Department of Justice, Bureau of Justice Statistics, as of June 2011, about 236 persons for every 100,000 of population were confined in local jails.

These records not only show you everyone who is currently incarcerated, but also list their anticipated release date, the institution where they're housed, the institution's address, and its telephone number. The database records date back to 1982 and should show anybody who has spent time in a federal prison since 1982, even if that person has since been released, like Martha Stewart.

I searched my own name and found 11 Steve Browns and 50 Steven Browns (and no, I've never spent the night in a federal prison). I even found one Steven K. Brown who at one time was incarcerated in the Middle District of Florida, where I live, but is now deceased. Nope, not me. So be sure to search all possible name variations for the person you're skip tracing.

Note that this database won't show what crime sent the subject to the federal penitentiary. I show you how to track down that information in Chapter 18.

If you're pretty sure the subject is in jail, but he doesn't show up in the federal prison database, you can start searching the state prisons and county jails.

The first place to check is www.VINElink.com, the website of the National Victim Notification Network. Most states subscribe to the service (you can view a map on the site for details), so you can do a fairly thorough search of most state offender databases with just one click. If you find your subject, you can register with VINElink to be notified when there's a change in that person's status. VINElink doesn't disclose what people are in custody for. If you need to know that, keep reading.

Another site you can try is www.corrections.com. On the menu bar, hover your mouse over Resources, click Inmate Locator, and choose from the links to the various state prison databases, as well as the records for Los Angeles County.

Many states allow you to search for individuals on *probation* and *parole* in addition to folks who are still locked behind bars. By adding parolees and probationers to your search, you're considerably expanding the number of people in these databases, so don't overlook these options. The databases usually have a separate search or a button to click to include the probation and parole populations.

Most states' web-based inmate locators work well. Some states allow access only to sex offenders; other states let you search their entire prison population.

DEFINITION

Probation indicates that a person was convicted of a crime, but rather than sentencing him to a jail term, a judge allows him to remain out of jail on condition that he not violate the law, stays employed, and follows any other terms stipulated by the judge. **Parole** means that an individual was sentenced to jail and actually spent time behind bars, but was released earlier than the original sentence called for. If the individual violates any conditions of parole, he might be sent back to prison.

Using Military Locators

Currently, no websites run by the military allow the public access to the military locator databases. You can determine whether your subject is in active-duty military, though. Go to www.dmdc.osd.mil/appj/scra/scraHome.do and put in the information requested. You need your subject's complete Social Security number.

If you're a family member of someone in the military and have an emergency, you can call the numbers that follow, and a representative of the specific branch will find your family member for you. If you're a private investigator or nonfamily member, or a family member without an emergency, you can write to the following addresses, include a check for $3.50 (a fee set by Congress), and give the individual's name, Social Security number, and as much information as you have. (Family members do not need to pay the $3.50.)

The current exceptions to this method are the Coast Guard, the Army, and the Navy. The Coast Guard might respond over the telephone and doesn't charge a fee. Due to current security considerations, the Navy will not respond, but will forward mail to the individual. The Army has discontinued this service altogether.

Air Force
HQ AFPC/MSMIDL
550 C Street West, Suite 50
Randolph AFB, TX 78150-4752

Coast Guard
Send an email to ARL-PF-CGPSCCGlocator@uscg.mil

Marine Corps
USMC–CMC
Code–MMSB–10
2008 Elliott Road
Quantico, VA 22134-5030

Navy
Navy Personnel Command
PERS–312F
5720 Integrity Drive
Millington, TN 38055-3120

Putting It All Together

Here's your final exam. Like all the examples in this book, it is true and from my case files. Now is your chance to test your knowledge of skip tracing.

In 2004, Mariah Sue needed a new place to live. She had two small sons, was working, and was making a pretty good living. Mariah found an attractive one-bedroom condominium that was clean, had a community swimming pool, and was close to work. The owner—let's name her Peggy Ferrar—owned several of these condos and rented them all.

Mariah Sue gave Peggy a check for $2,100 as a deposit to hold the condo for a few days until she could decide whether she wanted it. Peggy agreed and said that if Mariah Sue didn't want the condo, she should call her and let her know within seven days.

Three days later, Mariah decided that a one-bedroom condo was too small for her and two boys and called Peggy. Peggy wasn't home, but Mariah left a message informing Peggy of her change of mind and requested that she tear up the deposit check.

Fast-forward to 2006. Two sheriff's deputies showed up at an old address of Mariah's to arrest her on a worthless check charge of $2,100. The people at the old address knew Mariah and called her, but they didn't tell the deputies where she was.

Mariah checked with the district attorney's office by telephone and verified that there was a warrant for her arrest, and she needed to bring either the $2,100 plus costs to the office or a receipt from Peggy Ferrar showing the amount paid.

Mariah tried desperately to reach Peggy, but the number had been disconnected. She tried the telephone directory information but couldn't find a listing for her. Peggy was an older lady, and Mariah wondered whether she was dead. She called the State Bureau of Vital Records and paid $30 plus a $25 rush fee to search the death records for the last three years. The site promised to mail her the search results within two weeks. Meanwhile, Mariah sat waiting for the sheriff's ominous knock on her front door.

Okay, now you have the facts. Using what you've learned, how would you find Peggy Ferrar?

As we learned at the beginning of this chapter, there is a quicker and free way to determine whether Peggy has died, unless it happened within the last few months. First, you'd search the Social Security Death Master File.

Let's say you search the Death Master File, and it's negative. Okay, what next? In the county where Mariah Sue lived, she could have gone online to the county property appraiser's website and searched by address for the ownership of the property she was going to rent. That's what I did.

The property records showed the address was owned by Frank Ferrar and June M. Ferrar. I presumed that the middle initial "M" in June's name probably stood for Margaret. And as you learned above, Peggy is a nickname for Margaret.

I went to my favorite white pages listing pay service, www.masterfiles.com, and searched for Frank Ferrar. I found a listing for him at an address close to the condo Mariah was going to rent. Just for fun, I went back to the property appraiser's records and checked the ownership of that address as well. It showed that Frank and June M. owned that property, too.

In less than 30 minutes, I'd found Peggy for Mariah Sue. The total cost was one search at www.masterfiles.com. Again, for giggles, I searched the free white pages listings on the internet and found the Ferrar family also listed in the free sections. So it could have been a totally free search.

As it turned out, in case you're interested, Mrs. Ferrar was not about to forgive the debt and insisted that Mariah Sue bring the money to her right away. That was an expensive lesson for Mariah, but it could have been a little less expensive if she'd read this book first.

The Least You Need to Know

- Query old friends and associates to gather information on your subject before you begin your search.
- County property appraisers' websites usually allow searches by name and can be a quick way to locate somebody.
- Make social media sites a priority when conducting searches.
- The Social Security Administration has maintained a database of deceased individuals, known as the Death Master File, since 1980.
- The Federal Bureau of Prisons has a prisoner locator database, and some states have websites that allow you to search the inmate, parole, and probation populations.

Prowling the Courthouse

In This Chapter

- Locating property transaction records
- Navigating the lower and higher court systems
- Searching for local and federal criminal records
- Accessing bankruptcy court files
- Cancelling alimony obligations

Christine called me one day. She and her boyfriend were getting married soon. Problem was, he wasn't yet divorced from his first wife. They'd been separated for four years, but no divorce—hence, they'd never agreed to any formal alimony or child support settlements. The soon-to-be ex-wife was asking for more money than Christine thought she was entitled to. Christine, being no dummy, knew that money out of her fiancé's pocket meant less money for her.

She wanted to know how much the ex-wife was paying each month in mortgage payments. Christine thought the ex-wife had grossly inflated the figure to bump up the child support payments. Proof of a lower mortgage payment would result in lower support payments.

I actually was kind of rooting for the kids in this case, but I don't make up the facts—I just report them. In Christine's case, I shrugged my shoulders and took her American Express credit-card number over the telephone. She could have saved herself $225 if she'd read this chapter. All she'd had to do was make a quick trip to her local courthouse.

Going to Court: Accessing Courthouse Records

Need other reasons to read this chapter? Have you ever bought a house? Or might you buy a house in the future? If so, and if you're smart, you will want to know how much the seller paid for it and how much he still owes on his house before you make your offer. You don't *have* to know those facts, but knowledge is power. Your realtor either won't know or won't think to tell you. If you know that the seller has a gazillion dollars' worth of equity in the house, you can submit a lowball offer, and he may just accept it. If you know that the house is free and clear, you may ask the seller to finance the house for you instead of using conventional financing. You can get all this information from your local courthouse.

Have you ever thought about going into business with a partner, a buddy from work maybe? Before you sign those partnership agreements, you'd better find out whether he has any judgments against him. You can get that information from your local or state courthouse, too.

> **THE SCOOP**
>
> State courts bear a tremendous load when it comes to handling cases. Approximately 30 million cases a year are filed in the U.S. state court system. For comparison, about 2 million cases were filed in 2010 in the federal system. Of those federal cases, about 70 percent are bankruptcies, 20 percent are civil cases, and 10 percent are criminal cases.

Or are you paying alimony to an ex-spouse? In most cases, the alimony is supposed to end upon remarriage of the spouse. She's been dating the same guy for a year and moved in with him, but you're still shelling out the big bucks each month. Ex-spouses remarry all the time without telling their former spouse. And they cohabitate without remarrying, thinking that they can continue to collect the alimony without recourse as long as they aren't legally wedded. Well, surprise! Many states have laws that allow for the reduction or withdrawal of alimony if the receiving spouse cohabitates and receives substantial sustenance from her common-law husband. Want to take a guess at where you might be able to find the information you need to put a stop to your monthly financial obligation to your ex? If you answered, "The courthouse," you're right!

The Local County Courthouse

County courthouses have four main areas of interest for investigators—and that's not counting the courtrooms where you may be called upon to testify (for details on testifying, check out Chapter 21). Here are the four main areas:

- Official Records
- Property Appraiser's Office/Records
- Civil Files
- Criminal Files

Different courthouses may call the areas different names, but every county has them. I describe each of these areas in the following sections.

Making the Official Records Speak

Searching official records seems to confuse a lot of my investigator interns. I think they feel it's a waste of time—they would rather be out on the street following somebody. But a good private investigator knows the courthouse, and all of its nooks and crannies, inside and out.

Don't just think databases and restrict your courthouse searches to the computer. You need to understand how the record system works in the courts where you're doing the research. Pay databases are great, but you need to develop calluses from flipping through files to really know your local court system.

Official records are records that are recorded at the courthouse for all the public to see. By *recorded*, I mean that the document is entered into the official records in a particular book and on a certain page. In the precomputer era, a notation was handwritten into a large ledger-type book saying, for example, a certain mortgage from such-and-such lender was recorded against a particular piece of *real property*.

DEFINITION

Real property is anything that's not personal property; it's anything that is a part of the earth or attached to the ground and that can't be easily moved. Think dirt, houses, and barns.

The existence of this mortgage was physically entered into a book on a particular page number. An index was made somewhat alphabetically, and you could hand-search those indexes by year to see whether a mortgage was recorded. As the pages of one book were filled up, the county recorder's office began a new book. The books were numbered, and hence you would find a legal description of a mortgage, noting that it was recorded in such-and-such book and on that particular page number.

Anybody who may have a claim or want to establish a claim or lien on or to any particular piece of property is free to search these official records. You'll find notations regarding other mortgages, liens, or judgments (or satisfaction of mortgages, liens, or judgments) that might pertain to a particular person or piece of property.

When you purchase a piece of real property, a deed is recorded in the official records of the county. If you borrowed money to buy the property, most likely the mortgage company or bank also recorded the mortgage. The lender does this as a sort of notice to all the public that it has the first mortgage on that property. If it wasn't recorded, and you borrowed some more money on the property, the next bank would record its mortgage, and it would have the first mortgage recorded. If you failed to pay the mortgage on the second loan, the second bank could foreclose and the first bank would just be out of luck. This is why, when you buy a piece of real property, you should always hire a professional to do a title search to make sure all the mortgages and liens recorded on that property have been paid or satisfied before you take title to the property.

THE SCOOP

I hear people complain all the time about our public servants. I disagree whole-heartedly. I've searched for information in courthouses all across the United States, and I've never found a more helpful bunch of people than at local county courthouses. They've always been more than willing to show me how to do the search I need—and if I act pathetic enough, they might even do it for me.

Now, why should you care about all of this? Remember Christine, at the beginning of this chapter? The house the ex-wife lived in belonged to her father. All I had to do was go into the official records and search his name to find the mortgage on her house. In fact, I found out that the house had been purchased in 1979, and a mortgage had been placed on it. I found a satisfaction of the mortgage recorded in 1989, and another mortgage had been placed on it. That mortgage had been satisfied in 1999, and another, higher mortgage had been placed on it at that time. On this last refinancing, it looked like she had pulled some cash out of it and refinanced it for

15 years. The mortgage was for $72,000. Unfortunately for my client, since this mortgage was for only 15 years, her payments were higher than for a 30-year mortgage.

Using a financial calculator, I figured out what her payments were for principal and interest based on a $72,000 loan for 15 years. I had to guess at the interest rate because the promissory note wasn't recorded with the mortgage. But it wasn't too hard to go back three years and see what the average 15-year loan was going for in April of that year. Principal and interest came to about $607.58.

Christine needed to know the amount of the mortgage payment. Now I had the first piece of the puzzle, the principal and interest payment.

The Property Appraiser

I went across the hall to the property appraiser's office. (Actually, that's a fib. In our county, as in most counties now, the property appraiser's records are online, and before I went to the courthouse, I looked up the latest appraisal on the website.)

The appraiser's office showed the value of the property, the type of construction (which was brick), and this year's current tax amount. In this case, the property taxes were about $1,200 annually. This meant the ex-wife's mortgage company would have added about $100 per month to the principal and interest payment for the property taxes.

I called my insurance agent to see what a typical homeowners insurance policy cost for a brick home. He gave me a figure of about $485, which is about $40 per month. (That was before the parade of hurricanes that hit Florida, so insurance rates are higher now.) Add the three figures together (principal and interest $607.58, taxes $100, and insurance $40), for a total of $747.58.

Bingo. In 30 minutes, I had the information Christine wanted. Let's see, Christine paid me $225 for a half-hour's work—that's $550 per hour. Better than minimum wage, for sure.

The State Civil Court System

Court systems in most states are divided into higher courts and lower courts. Some states have other civil courts, like water courts, traffic courts, and magistrate courts. These miscellaneous courts are almost always lower courts dealing with less serious infractions or lower financial amounts. You may have to do a little research in your city of interest to see what the courts are called there.

Higher Civil Courts

The higher courts and the lower courts have different names in different states. In Florida, they are called *circuit courts* and *county courts;* Arizonans call them *superior courts* and *justice courts;* New Yorkers call them *supreme courts* and *county courts.* Let's forget the names and just call them higher and lower courts.

The higher courts deal with more important cases. *More important* usually means more money.

Civil actions such as divorce, malpractice, libel, and other suits are likely to involve amounts over $15,000 and are heard in the higher courts. Petty actions like residential rent disputes are typically handled in the lower courts. Everybody has heard of small claims court. In most jurisdictions, small claims refers to damages sought that are less than $15,000. (In some states it's even less.) In lower court cases, people frequently don't use the services of an attorney and represent themselves.

My client, Mary Beth, whom I'd known on a personal basis for a long time, called me. She said her husband was in jail on charges of spousal abuse (toward her), and she had a restraining order against him. He'd blackened her eyes, dragged her around the house by her hair, and beat her with a clothes hanger.

Mary Beth had been married to Lionel for just under a year. She wanted to know whether he'd had physical altercations with any of his previous three wives. Where do we go to look? To the office of the clerk of the higher court.

I reviewed all three of the previous divorce files. One restraining order in one of them alleged physical brutality. I found the personal data on the ex-wives and tracked them down. Each of his ex-wives told me Lionel had been physically abusive to her. In fact, he had been arrested multiple times for abusing each one. (Lionel's relationship with his second wife was a little different: she told me they used to beat each other up. Now that was a new one for me.)

If Mary Beth had come to me before she'd married Lionel, she would have known about his propensity for violence and perhaps been prepared to diffuse it or even not marry him at all. At least now she knows it wasn't her fault. It amazes me, though, how few people do any sort of prenuptial background investigation, especially when it's a second, third, or fourth marriage. This was Lionel's fourth marriage and Mary Beth's fifth. I also checked the criminal records for Lionel, and I talk about what I found there later in this chapter (in the section on criminal courts).

By the way, Mary Beth is still married to and living with Lionel. He goes to anger-management classes every Tuesday night. I told her to lock up the clothes hangers, but she didn't think it was funny.

Lower Civil Courts

I conduct background investigations for a local landlord. This fellow rents high-dollar furnished homes located in a golfing community; almost all of his leases are short term. One of the checks he insists on before renting a house to a prospective tenant is to search the lower court records from whatever county the renter previously resided in. He's been involved before with tenants who pay the first month's rent and then begin some kind of action in small claims court, and end up living rent free month after month until he can finally get them evicted. If we find any previous litigation in which a prospective tenant was the *plaintiff*, he refuses to rent to her. If the person was a *defendant*, he wants the details of the suit and then makes a decision.

DEFINITION

Legal actions require a minimum of two parties. The **plaintiff** is the party who initiates the action or lawsuit. The **defendant** is the person on the receiving end of the action.

This client figures that even though it costs him a little bit more to have us run a civil records search, he saves big bucks in the long run in attorney fees and loss of rent.

In most court actions, the plaintiff's name is listed first on the complaint. The defendant is being sued or arrested by the plaintiff. In criminal cases, the plaintiff is the government and the person being charged with the crime is the defendant. Usually you see a criminal case listed as, for example, *the State of Florida* v. *Brown*.

Cases are indexed in the state court system by the plaintiff's name and cross-referenced by the defendant's name. In *Kramer* v. *Brown*, Kramer is the plaintiff and Brown is the defendant. In a court index, you might find the notation *Brown* adv. *Kramer*. "Adv." stands for *adverse*, the reverse of *versus*. In that case, Brown is still the defendant and Kramer is still the plaintiff. Some states use the abbreviation "ats" instead of "adv.", as an acronym for "at the suit of." In cases that use "ats," generally the defendant's name is the first listed.

HIDDEN HINT

Lower court records are also at the county courthouse. Large counties may have annexes or subcourthouses in different locations around the county, for the convenience of the taxpayer. Usually the annex has computer links to the entire courthouse system so that you can run a check from any annex. When in doubt, ask whether a search at an annex will search all the records in the entire county. If not, go to the main courthouse. In smaller, less computerized counties, you probably have to go downtown to the county courthouse to get the information you need.

The clerks working in the clerk of the courts office can direct you to the records you're looking for and show you how the system is organized.

State Criminal Courts

State criminal courts, not including the appellate courts, are divided into higher and lower courts, just like the civil courts. The criminal courts usually carry the same name as the civil courts. In Florida, they are the circuit court (higher court) and county court (lower court); Arizonans call them the superior court (higher court) and justice court (lower court).

THE SCOOP

Cases in the state criminal courts are usually prosecuted by attorneys working for the local or county government. They are sometimes called state's attorneys, district attorneys, or county attorneys. They are, in fact, attorneys for the state, district, or county, which is the plaintiff in criminal actions. These are often elected positions, and the attorneys are usually involved in prosecuting cases that originate with the local police or sheriff's office. Most states have a state attorney general's office that may get involved in prosecuting cases that originate with state law enforcement bureaus.

Remember Mary Beth and her abusive husband, Lionel, from earlier in this chapter? Well, had Mary Beth paid a visit to the courthouse and checked the criminal records on her husband-to-be before she married him, she would have found that charges against Lionel were still pending, even as she walked down the aisle at her wedding.

I can't stress enough the value of checking criminal records on your husband- or wife-to-be prior to getting married. You have all the tools right here in this book to do it yourself. If you grew up with your intended spouse, high school sweethearts and all, maybe you know all there is to know about the person. And those who meet the love of their life online really need to do their homework before committing to this new person.

But do you know your sweetheart's money-management habits? Has he ever written a bad check? You'd be surprised by how many people have 3, 5, or sometimes as many as 15 bad check charges against them. Often there are even warrants out for their arrest for insufficient funds checks, and they don't know it. They should know it. They probably received a letter from the prosecuting attorney's office but never responded. Hence, the warrant is issued. Usually the sheriff is not going to beat down your fiancé's door (or, if you're married, *your* door) at midnight to arrest him. But don't be surprised when he calls you from jail because he got stopped for speeding, and the policeman found warrants outstanding for the insufficient funds checks. Happens all the time. A 10-minute search through the court records will alert you if your spouse-to-be has this problem.

I know one woman who wrote a bad check for her wedding dress. Imagine her husband's surprise a year later when he had to pay her bail and pay for the wedding dress, too. When he asked me to look at it, I found that she'd had numerous other bad check charges against her, all dismissed because she'd paid them before the wedding.

Especially if you're from different towns and states, spend the few dollars or whatever it takes and find out for sure. If you don't want to do it yourself, hire me or another PI to do it for you.

No magic bullet can guarantee a long, peaceful, and happy marriage. We all know that. But you can sure improve the odds a lot by doing your homework before you wed. Mary Beth wouldn't be wearing sunglasses today to cover her black eyes had she taken the trouble to check into Lionel's background. It's not hard.

Federal Civil and Criminal Courts

The federal judicial system breaks down a little differently than the state systems. Excluding the federal appeals court and the United States Supreme Court, the three basic federal courts are the federal civil courts, federal criminal courts, and bankruptcy courts. I talk about the criminal and civil courts in this section; bankruptcy courts are covered in the next section.

Other than walking into the nearest federal courthouse, you can usually find the answer to your question in the PACER (Public Access to Court Electronic Records; www.pacer.gov) system. All 94 district courts participate in the system.

THE SCOOP

Each part of the United States, (including the U.S. Virgin Islands, Puerto Rico, Guam, and the Mariana Islands) is broken down into federal districts. There are 94 federal districts in the United States. Districts don't cross state boundaries. The districts are also broken down into divisions along geographic and population lines.

To access PACER via the internet, all you need to do is register; you can do so for free, but you have to wait about two weeks to receive your system password by mail. The government will not email or fax it to you.

PACER charges 10¢ per downloaded page. The government will invoice you every three months for usage of the system. If your bill for using the system is less than $15 per quarter, the government will forgive your debt and not expect payment. (It would most likely cost more than that to physically bill you.) Each court maintains its own database, so they are all a little different.

After registering for PACER, be sure to check out the PACER Case Locator, a national index of all of the district court cases that is updated nightly. By utilizing this index, you can conduct a nationwide search for federal court cases involving whatever individual or entity you are interested in. If you find a case that piques your interest, you can go to that file and view the contents.

The PACER Case Locator is a great tool if you don't know for sure where a particular case may have been filed. In addition to civil cases and bankruptcy cases, you can search for *federal criminal cases.*

DEFINITION

Federal criminal cases are cases brought by the Federal Bureau of Investigation; Drug Enforcement Agency; Bureau of Alcohol, Tobacco, and Firearms; the Secret Service; Homeland Security; and other federal agencies when they allege a violation of federal law.

By searching the PACER Case Locator, you can basically perform a national federal criminal conviction and national federal civil and bankruptcy search. Don't confuse this with an NCIC (National Crime Information Center) rap sheet. I talk about rap sheets and the NCIC in Chapter 18.

Bankruptcy Courts

Filing for bankruptcy is a federal matter. Personal and business bankruptcies all fall under federal statutes and are handled in federal court. The bankruptcy law was designed to give insolvent individuals and businesses a fresh start by restructuring their debt or forgiving their loans altogether, depending on the type of bankruptcy involved. Bankruptcy courts are organized differently than the other federal courts, have their own set of rules, and actually trace their origin back to a different part of the Constitution.

Searching the records at bankruptcy court is similar to searching the district courts. Most of the bankruptcy courts are on the PACER system. To understand the records you review, you need to know that bankruptcies are filed under four different chapters:

- Chapter 7, *liquidation*, for individuals and businesses

- Chapter 11, *reorganization*, for larger corporations

- Chapter 12, reorganization, for family farmers

- Chapter 13, reorganization, for individuals and smaller businesses

DEFINITION

Liquidation means all the assets (with some allowable exceptions) are disposed of and all debt (with some exceptions, like debt to the government) are discharged. **Reorganization** stops collection activity on the part of creditors and gives a business or individual a chance to work out a plan of action in coordination with a trustee appointed by the bankruptcy court.

I get requests to perform due diligence searches all the time. This can be a check of an individual, but more often it's of a company's reputation, ability to perform under contract, and verification that no liens or judgments have been filed against it. A good due diligence search also encompasses any lawsuits, pending or potential, or other current or potential areas of liability, such as a pending bankruptcy. Some private investigative agencies do only due diligence searches.

Most clients request a bankruptcy check as part of a due diligence to determine whether the person with whom they are going to be doing business has filed for bankruptcy in the past or is in the middle of a bankruptcy now.

HIDDEN HINT

If you're thinking about doing serious business with a company or individual, check the appropriate bankruptcy court before signing any contracts.

Reducing or Eliminating Your Alimony Payments

So you were the breadwinner and your jerk ex-husband sued for alimony after he left with the new girlfriend. How are you going to get that bum out of your life and off your payroll?

Ralph went to his attorney and posed that question. Florida has a law that allows for the cessation of alimony (Florida Statute 61.14 (1)(b)), which states:

> (b)1.The court may reduce or terminate an award of alimony upon specific written findings by the court that since the granting of a divorce and the award of alimony a supportive relationship has existed between the obligee and a person with whom the obligee resides. On the issue of whether alimony should be reduced or terminated under this paragraph, the burden is on the obligor to prove by a preponderance of the evidence that a supportive relationship exists.

In plain English, this means that if your ex-spouse is in a "supportive relationship" with another person, your attorney can petition the court to reduce or terminate your obligation to pay alimony. My agency has recently successfully completed a number of these cases. So how do you show the supportive relationship?

If the ex is living with another person, before you pay a lot of money for surveillance, check the public records. See who is paying the utility bill. Find out who owns the house they're living in. In Ralph's case, I didn't know who the boyfriend was or where Ralph's ex was living. So I put a two-man surveillance team on the ex-wife, Carolyn, and followed her home from work. Not rocket science. In about an hour, the boyfriend showed up. We got the tag off his car and called it quits; we planned to return at 5 the next morning (not my favorite time of day) to document that she'd spent the night there and was living with this guy.

I decided to do a little background on the boyfriend, to see who he was. Did he have a criminal record? Did he own the house where Ralph's ex, Carolyn, was now living? Carolyn owned another house in a different county that she'd been renting out since she'd moved in with the boyfriend six months previously.

I searched the official records in the other county and found that, three weeks earlier, Carolyn had refinanced her old house and pulled more than a hundred thousand dollars in cash out of it. On the new mortgage, she declared she was a single woman.

In looking through the official records in the new county, I saw that—guess what?—one week after Carolyn refinanced her old house, she and the boyfriend closed on the purchase of the house where they were now living together. And as a sweetener, on the deed and the mortgage, they declared themselves to be husband and wife, even though she kept her old married name.

So somewhere in that week, between the refinance of the old house and the purchase of the new one, they'd gotten married. She hadn't told her ex and she hadn't told her children, but who did she tell? The clerk of the court and the entire rest of the world. Ralph's alimony agreement, like many, included an agreement that the alimony would cease upon Carolyn's remarriage. Slam dunk, and only one afternoon of surveillance and a quick trip to the courthouse.

The Least You Need to Know

- Real property transactions such as sales and mortgages are recorded in the official records of the county and are public records that you can review.
- State court systems have higher courts that deal with more important cases (think higher dollars) and lower courts, which handle less important cases (think lower dollars).
- The criminal divisions of the state court system are nearly identical to the civil divisions. Higher courts handle felonies, and lower courts deal with misdemeanors.
- You can conduct a national search of the federal court system by using the PACER Case Locator.
- Some states allow for the reduction or cessation of alimony payments if the ex-spouse is in a supportive relationship with another person. Searching public records can help establish the relationship.

Professional PI Databases

In This Chapter

- Making sense of credit reports
- Reading credit headers
- Using credit reports in asset searches
- Choosing the right database

The single major aspect of investigative work that separates the true professional from the amateur is the professional's access to proprietary databases. These databases aren't generally open to the public. If you're serious about a career in the private investigative field, you need to get up to speed on the kinds of information you can access through proprietary databases and how to go about doing so efficiently.

Professional PIs subscribe to a variety of data brokers, also known as information brokers. These individuals or companies have access to specialized sources of information or use advanced techniques to gather information and then resell that information to PIs. Each data broker has strengths and weaknesses. In this chapter, I examine several of the more popular providers that serve the professional private investigative industry.

Getting the 411 Quickly and Efficiently

An attorney client called me as I was writing this chapter. A female friend who was trying to get a divorce had spent all her money on one attorney who'd skipped town. My client/attorney wanted a favor. Before she sent divorce papers to be served on this woman's soon-to-be ex-husband, whose last known address was in Upland, California, she wanted to make sure that the address her client had was still accurate. Could I do her a favor? *Pro Bono?*

DEFINITION

Pro Bono derives from the Latin *Pro Bono Publico,* or "for the public good." Usually it's shortened to just "Pro Bono" and means legal work undertaken without expectation of payment.

I had his name, date of birth, Social Security number, and last known address. How hard could this be? The name she'd given me wasn't very common. Let's call the soon-to-be ex David Morph. I went to my favorite telephone database, www. masterfiles.com, and searched for his name in Upland. No David Morph listed.

I used the telephone database again and did a reverse search. I searched the address I'd been given to see if any telephones were listed at that address. The address was a large apartment complex, and there was one listing for a Jack Morph, but not a David. The telephone companies in their directory listing don't give apartment numbers, so I wasn't sure whether this was the right phone number.

Not including my time, so far I'd spent maybe 40¢ on this search. My client/attorney had referred some pretty large cases to me in the past and was a continuing source of referrals. Still, because I wasn't getting paid for this locate, I didn't want to be out of pocket a lot of money.

My next step was to run a Social Security trace, which is the process of using a Social Security number to gather other information about the individual. The search normally returns residence addresses connected to your subject. I went to one of my favorite PI databases, IRBsearch (www.irbsearch.com), and plugged in the subject's Social Security number. In 30 seconds, and for the cost of $1, I verified the current address for the subject: the same address my client had given.

The nice thing about these databases is that often you get a date that the information was reported, so you have a pretty good idea of how current the information is. In this case, the address had been reported to the database the preceding month. But because the phone number was in a different first name, I wasn't 100 percent certain that this was the primary residence of my subject. It could have been his father's or some other relative's, and he was just using it as a mailing address.

I needed to call and be sure that this was a good address, enabling my client to have him served. I made the call and asked for David. He answered and confirmed this was his residence. I did not use a pretext because they'd been separated for two years and by 3,000 miles; I figured this guy would probably be just as happy to get the divorce over with as would his wife. I told him outright why I was calling. He seemed fine with that and indicated we could serve him at that address.

My total cost for the locate was $1.40, for 30 minutes of my time. The key to efficient locates is using the professional databases and fee-based telephone look-up sites I tell you all about in this chapter.

THE SCOOP

Databases glean address information from a variety of sources, including credit headers, telephone company records, public records, and forwarding records from the post office. When people are intentionally trying to hide their whereabouts, are traveling extensively, or are students, they often list family members' addresses as their permanent residences. They may also have mail sent to a private mailbox or P.O. box. So even though a database provides you with an address for an individual, you still need to do some legwork to ensure that your subject actually physically resides there.

Treat these databases as tools. Just as there are different types of hammers for different jobs, there are different databases you want to use, depending on the job requirements. You wouldn't use a sledgehammer to put up a tack; you'd lose all your profit repairing the hole in the drywall. Likewise, if you use your most expensive data provider for a $25 case, you won't last a year in this business.

Knowing What's in the Data Mix

Although many databases buy their information from the same sources, some are stronger in some areas of data than others. In addition to credit bureau data, here's what else might go into this stew:

- Magazine subscription lists, with addresses and names
- Telephone directory information
- Postal change of addresses
- Licensed drivers
- Book club lists
- Registered vehicles
- Boats and trailers
- Cell phone users
- Uniform Commercial Code (UCC) listings

- Corporate officers and registered agents
- Internet search engine results
- Pizza delivery names, addresses, and phone numbers
- Public postings of liens and judgments
- Public notices of bankruptcy and foreclosure
- Names that appear in newspapers and magazines
- Public professional licenses
- Traffic accidents
- Criminal charges
- Social media pages
- Email addresses associated with the name

When you combine all the preceding information—and there's more I'm sure I've omitted—with a good algorithm and a fast computer server, it's amazing how much information these agencies can correlate and report on one individual.

The computer doesn't always get it right, especially with common names, but just think about this. Take your last known addresses. They're in the computer data mix somewhere. Throw in the time frame when you were there as reported by your credit-card company, and then ask the computer who else shared that address with you during that time frame. That's how these databases generate reports that show relatives and roommates, by comparing addresses with time. Then expand that exponentially to show current addresses on those relatives and former roommates, and pretty quickly the PI can find your mother or brother or former roommate, to perhaps get a lead on your whereabouts.

Researching the Big Three: The Credit Bureaus

A lot of information that goes into private databases is derived in some way from credit bureau files. These are the three main credit bureaus:

TransUnion (www.transunion.com)

Equifax (www.equifax.com)

Experian (www.experian.com)

Credit bureau files contain information about payments on credit accounts, in addition to a lot of other useful data. Negative information stays in a credit file for 7 years, with the exception of bankruptcy, which remains in a credit file for 10 years after the discharge date.

> **LEGAL TRAP**
>
> Private investigators aren't usually in the position of granting credit to clients and normally don't have a permissible purpose for pulling a subject's credit report, unless they're working judgment collections, tenant screening, or pre-employment. Be aware that credit-reporting agencies monitor and audit their accounts to ensure that reports are pulled for permissible purposes.

Credit bureaus provide a variety of reports, which they tailor to the needs of their customers. A credit report run for pre-employment purposes usually doesn't include the individual's *credit score* because the prospective employer isn't issuing credit. The credit score is a key piece of information included on credit reports for home financing or car purchasing.

A resourceful private investigator will have developed credit bureau sources and be able to pull credit reports for permissible purposes. *Permissible purpose* refers to 1 of 11 (depending on how you count) legal purposes for pulling a credit report, as defined by the Fair Credit Reporting Act last updated by Congress in 2010. You can download a copy of the act at www.ftc.gov/os/statutes/031224fcra.pdf.

Although some private investigative companies offer the types of services deemed permissible under the Fair Credit Reporting Act, most private investigators don't provide those services and don't have access to credit bureau reports.

When to Look

When might an investigator get a request for or need a credit check? I regularly get requests from ladies who are dating men in a relationship that's turning serious. Is this a permissible purpose? Well, yes and no. The Fair Credit Reporting Act (FCRA) governs access to credit information. You can read the act at www.ftc.gov/os/statutes/031224fcra.pdf.

LEGAL TRAP

Pulling premarital credit reports probably doesn't violate the restrictions of the FCRA. And if more people pulled their prospective spouse's credit report before they got married, there'd probably be fewer divorces. But the FCRA doesn't take that into account. Two reasons exist for PIs not to pull premarital credit reports. First, an inquiry will show on the prospective spouse's credit report, and your client might have to explain to her fiancé why she doubted him. Second, there's a very good chance the credit bureaus will yank your access if they find out you pull premarital credit reports, because they may not agree that it falls within the permissible purpose rules of the FCRA.

Basically, two reasons might qualify, although I doubt you'll find universal agreement in the credit or PI industries:

> (E) Intends to use the information, as a potential investor or servicer, or current insurer, in connection with a valuation of, or an assessment of the credit or prepayment risks associated with, an existing credit obligation

> (F) Otherwise has a legitimate business need for the information

Is marriage not a legitimate business need? Certainly, it's governed by civil laws and involves financial transactions between the two parties. Still, I doubt that you'll want to ask your fiancé for a release to pull his credit report. If that's the case, what can you do?

What You Might Find in the Credit Report

Other than the credit score, most credit reports include the following information:

- Information for each creditor, including account number, date the account was opened, high credit limit, remaining balances, past-due amounts, payment history, and current monthly balances

- The subject's current address and previous addresses

- The name and date of birth associated with the SSN queried

- A profile summary of subtotals of all accounts, broken down by installment accounts, revolving, real estate, and other

- Any negative public records in the credit bureau's file, such as *judgments*, tax liens, and bankruptcies

> **DEFINITION**
>
> A **judgment** is a final determination by a court of competent jurisdiction setting forth the rights and liabilities of the parties in a lawsuit. Usually the term refers to a financial judgment in which the court may decide that a plaintiff is owed money by a defendant in a case. These judgments are recorded in the official records at the clerk of the courts office and are generally public records. Credit bureaus review these records on a regular basis and include them as part of their credit report.

Okay, now that you know what the credit report is, how can you, as a PI, use it? You can use it in asset searches for the purpose of collection of judgments. But keep in mind that although the credit report shows who your subject owes money to, it doesn't show any of his assets, like bank accounts or real property. So how does that help you find his assets?

I thought you might ask that question. If your client has a judgment, there was or is a court case. You then get your client's attorney to subpoena the records of your subject's creditors. Be sure to include in the subpoena the application for credit that your subject completed.

Generally, when people apply for credit, they make themselves look as solvent as possible, so they list their bank accounts, their equity in real property, and other assets they hold. Bingo! As soon as you get that information, you've got the location of your subject's bank account; your client's attorney can then arrange to garnish those accounts, as well as place liens on property and even have the sheriff seize vehicles and boats.

When subpoenaing bank loan records, in addition to requesting the application, don't forget to ask for copies of checks and bank transfer records (both transfers in and transfers out), as well as copies of all deposits. Wire transfers and cancelled checks can tell you a lot about a person's finances, as well as facts about his life, like personal travel and payment for a girlfriend's rent, which may be germane to your family law case.

> **HIDDEN HINT**
>
> The technique of subpoenaing credit applications and then following the leads to bank accounts and other assets works particularly well in family law cases, when your client (one of the spouses) doesn't really know what assets the other spouse has. You don't need to have a judgment to subpoena credit applications—an ongoing civil case, like a divorce, will do. Start with one bank or credit card that the spouse is aware of and go from there.

Credit Headers

Even though the credit bureaus won't sell their data directly to private investigators, they are in business to sell data, and they do possess data that isn't governed by the FCRA because it isn't directly related to people's credit. This information is called *credit header information,* and because credit bureaus are in business to make a buck, they sell this information to data suppliers—who, in turn, sell it to private investigators.

Credit header information includes these details:

- Name and previous names, or "also known as" (a.k.a.)

- Date of birth

- Social Security number

- Current and previous addresses

- Current and previous employers (sometimes)

- Telephone numbers

- Relatives

Credit header information is valuable for private investigators because the credit bureaus update it regularly. Current information helps PIs tremendously when searching for individuals. Every time you apply for new credit or call your credit-card company, mortgage company, or any other creditor, they verify your address and phone number. Your creditors report any changes, and even if there aren't any changes, they report the date of last verification. So the information can be fairly current.

Logging On to Subscription Databases

Here is a list of databases that market to the PI industry. Many of these grant a PI firm a free trial period. If you're a professional private investigator, I encourage you to try as many as possible before narrowing your subscription.

- Enformion (www.enformion.com)

- FMS Research (www.FindMySkip.com)

- IRBsearch (www.irbsearch.com)

- Locate Plus (www.locateplus.com)

- Merlin (www.merlindata.com)

- PallTech (www.pallorium.com)

- SkipMax (www.SkipMax.com)

- Skipsmasher (www.skipsmasher.com)

- TLO (www.TLO.com)

- Tracers Information Specialists (www.tracersinfo.com)

Many of these databases have what are called *no hit, no fee* searches. When you input the name, Social Security number, or other data, if the database can't locate any records on your subject, it might not charge you. Then again, it might. Be sure to compare this feature when looking into which databases you want to subscribe to.

Another feature that bears examination is the monthly charge. Some databases have a minimum monthly charge. Some charge the minimum only if you use the database, and some charge it even if you don't use the database during the month. Some databases don't have a minimum charge, so give those a good look. And to complicate matters a bit, some give you an unlimited amount of basic searches (usually of older data) for a flat fee.

HIDDEN HINT

A factor to keep in mind with these data providers is that generally they began as suppliers of data in different regions of the country, and many of them continue to be stronger in some regions of the country than in others. The geographic coverage areas of a potential data provider can make a significant difference in the effectiveness of your work and your bottom line. How do you know their strong areas? Look to see where their corporate headquarters are; that's a good indication of the section of the country where they have the most depth of data.

I usually find it beneficial to subscribe to at least two, and usually three, databases at any one time. Each has different strengths. Some truncate the Social Security numbers, and some don't. You need to have at least one that doesn't truncate because, let's face it: most of the identifying data is more easily sorted by Social Security number than any other way. Just think how many Steven Browns there are in the country. Several may even have my same date of birth. But there's only one Steven Brown with my Social Security number. Of the databases in the preceding list, the following don't truncate the Social Security number: www.findmyskip.com, www.skipsmasher.com, www.tracersinfo.com, and www.TLO.com.

In the following sections, I describe some of the searches that these different databases make available to private investigators, collection agencies, and law enforcement. Generally, the database companies require you to show proof of investigative licensing. However, they do sell their product to non-PIs and other companies for collection purposes and human resources department needs.

Most of these pay databases offer similar menus. However, they each perform differently in different searches. Like the credit bureaus, they may have similar records, but they're not all searching the same records. They offer searches such as the following.

Public Records

Subscription databases are a great way to access public information in a single place. But don't use them as your only public record search. These databases don't search every county in every state. Here are some of the types of information you can expect to find:

- Bankruptcies, judgments, and liens
- Drug Enforcement Administration registration
- Fictitious business names
- U.S. aircraft
- U.S. vessels
- U.S. air pilots
- Professional licenses
- Hunting and fishing licenses
- Concealed weapons permits
- Voter registration
- Federal firearms and explosives licenses
- Court records
- Traffic accidents
- Marriages and divorces
- Uniform Commercial Code searches
- Official records
- Social Security Death Master File

Proprietary Data

Proprietary data is any information that isn't public; in other words, this information is owned by various businesses or individuals, who sell it or otherwise make it available to the subscription databases. Although by no means an exhaustive list, here's an overview of the kinds of proprietary data held by subscription databases:

- People-locator searches
- National phone directory
- National property searches
- Phone directory—real time
- Cell phone subscriber information
- Social Security number verifier
- Employment searches
- Internet domains
- Dun & Bradstreet reports
- Delaware corporation search

- Motor vehicle tag registration information

- Driver's licenses

- Patriot Act search

- Sexual offender search

LEGAL TRAP

Some data providers are located beyond the territorial boundaries of the United States, to avoid the prosecutorial jurisdiction of the U.S. federal government. You can read between those lines to figure out what this means in terms of the legality of their data.

The Least You Need to Know

- The credit bureaus don't normally sell their data directly to private investigators or attorneys, but they do sell their credit header info to private database companies, who, in turn, sell it to PIs.

- The Fair Credit Reporting Act (FCRA) governs the release of credit information. Sometimes a PI needs a credit report that falls within the purview of the FCRA.

- Database information that includes credit header data usually has a date that the information was reported, and it often is fairly current.

- Private databases use algorithms to match addresses with people and dates. They can often report current addresses for relatives and previous roommates of your subjects.

- The data in the private databases includes credit header data, public record data, and other proprietary data.

Telephone Secrets You Need to Know

In This Chapter

- Outflanking the telephone company's defensive line
- Slashing directory information costs in half
- Finding the people behind the telephone numbers and the numbers behind the people
- Determining a pay telephone's location
- Giving caller ID the runaround
- Using smartphones to outsmart your subjects

The telephone is a tool. I know, all this time, you thought it was a voice instrument used primarily for ordering pizza. Surprise, surprise, it's really the most basic tool in the private investigator's toolbox. A competent PI can find out more information using the phone than any database can possibly provide. You may not always have access to your computer, but you should be able to lay your hands on your smartphone.

This chapter examines the ins and outs of using the telephone to enhance your PI career. To make the best use of the phone, sometimes you have to outwit the person you're calling, and frequently you have to outsmart the telephone company itself.

Verifying Nonpublished Numbers

In the private investigation business, sometimes knowing where your subject lives is just as good as knowing his telephone number. If you want to conduct surveillance on an individual, you don't necessarily need the telephone number, but you do need the address so you can get out of bed well before dawn, venture out into the cold while every sane person is still sleeping (isn't PI work fun?), and set up the surveillance on the residence before the subject leaves for work.

You've already run the subject's name in one of your databases and found an address for him, but you're not sure whether the address is current. The databases are not infallible, and they may have out-of-date information.

Next, you check directory information, where you can get a phone number as well as an address. If you call 411, the recording and the live operator might both report the listing as *nonpublished*. What do you do? You certainly don't want to get out of bed and go to the wrong address. You could run all of the other checks I tell you about in Chapter 5, but there's an easier way to verify the address when your subject has a nonpublished number.

DEFINITION

A **nonpublished number** is one that the subscriber has requested that the phone company not release or publish in phone directories. The telephone company won't give the number to you willingly.

With a possible address in mind, and knowing that the subject's telephone number is nonpublished, mumble your way through the 411 computer until you get the live operator. Next, tell the operator you'd like her to check a listing for you. Tell her that you think the number is nonpublished but that you'd like to verify the address.

Operators don't get this request very often because most people don't know that you can verify an address on nonpublished numbers. Be prepared to have her say she can't give you the address. When she says that, tell her that's okay; you already have the address, you just want to verify it. Give her the address where you think the subject is living. Either she'll confirm it or she'll tell you it's a different address. She might not be willing to give the address to you, but she does have it in front of her on the screen, and there's a good chance that she will verify it for you if you give it to her first. If you've got the right address, set the alarm for about 4 A.M. and go to bed early. Although this doesn't work for all telephone companies, I've found that it does the trick 99 percent of the time.

THE SCOOP

Area codes seem to change within some states every week. If you need an area code, just Google "area codes," and you'll get a half-dozen sites where you can search by area code or geographically.

Breaking the Number

Obtaining a *telephone break* can be one of the most challenging and exasperating problems facing a private investigator. A wife may come to you with a telephone number she found in her husband's billfold or coat pocket. The wife suspects the number belongs to her husband's mistress, and she wants to know for sure.

DEFINITION

A **telephone break** is the process of using a telephone number, with no other identifying information, to obtain the subscriber information, including name, the service address if it's a landline, or the mailing address if the number rings to a cell phone or pager.

In obtaining a telephone break, you have to first satisfy yourself that the client means no harm to the subscriber. The last thing you want is to find that, by breaking the phone number, you've enabled your client to go to the subject's address and attempt to physically harm that person.

Next, arrange the price with your client. On a listed number, the price should be about $30. It's hardly worth the paperwork if you charge any less. For a nonpublished number or a cell number, charge about $150.

Start with the easy checks. If you subscribe to Skipsmasher.com, go there; otherwise, go to www.masterfiles.com or www.555-1212.com and run a reverse search on the number. There's a good chance that the number will be a regular listed number, and you will have just turned a 25¢ search into an extra $30 in your pocket.

If those searches come back as "no record," it's more than likely either a nonpublished number or a cell number. But some other possibilities exist. For example, if the client picked the number off her caller ID instead of finding it in her husband's billfold, it could be a trunk-line number, such as a T1 line, from a commercial establishment. You can do a simple, free search to find out what kind of line it is: go to www.phonevalidator.com and enter the number to find out whether you're dealing with a cell number or a landline.

If you find out that it's a cell number, see the section later in this chapter on cell phones.

If you find out your number is a nonpublished landline, you may want to use one of your favorite telephone information brokers to break the number for you. You can expect to pay around $50 for the service. But if you're not a licensed PI, most of these data brokers won't deal with you.

LEGAL TRAP

Some data brokers use illegal means to obtain the data their clients request. Recent changes in state and federal laws make it illegal for anyone to use pretext to obtain cell or phone call records that don't belong to them. But more important for you, it is also illegal to *possess* such records. Don't bury your head in the sand; if you suspect that a data broker uses illegal methods, don't work with that company.

Another option is to use one of my favorite techniques, a pretext call, which works most of the time. Actually, in my 20 years in the business, I don't recall it ever having failed. In Chapter 12, I talk at length about the do's and don'ts of pretext telephone calls. You need to read that section before attempting this particular pretext call.

LEGAL TRAP

Pretext is really another word for a lie. Didn't your mother tell you never to lie? Well, pretexts are sometimes the heart and soul of the methods private investigators use to obtain information from people in such a manner that they freely divulge the information when they might not have so freely given it otherwise. Licensing agencies in various states recognize that PIs can't always identify themselves as such and successfully obtain the information they need. So at this time, there is no push to make "pretexting" illegal. However, stay abreast of the laws. Remember, pretexting a telephone company to obtain phone records is illegal.

The pretext goes like this. You spoof your caller ID so it will show the name of the pizza company you claim to be from. Be specific—use the name of a pizzeria in your local area. Call the number. Identify yourself as a representative of that pizza home delivery company. Tell him that if he answers three quick questions, you'll send him a coupon for a free large pizza.

Here are the questions:

- Have you ordered home-delivery pizza from (insert the name of the company) within the last three months?

- If so, how many times per month do you call for home delivery? If never, do you know where the closest home-delivery outlet is?

- Are you familiar with Sicilian-style pizza, and have you ever ordered that?

Now, you don't give a hoot about the answers to the preceding questions, so just get through them as quickly as you can. Next, thank him very much for his time. Tell him you'll send him a coupon for a free large pizza, and thank him again for his participation in this survey. To what address should you send the coupon? If he's gone this far with you, he'll always give you his address. And what name should you address it to? Bingo, you've got his name and address. If he wants it to go to a P.O. box, take the box information (it might come in handy later), but tell him that these coupons can't be mailed and the delivery folks will drop one off, so you need the street address and apartment number, if any.

Finding Other Sources for Nonpublished Numbers

Just because a telephone number is nonpublished doesn't mean you can't get it. *Nonpublished* simply means the telephone company won't give it to you willingly. Fair enough.

What I find, however, is that although the subscribers have made that request to the telephone company, they violate their own instructions by giving it to the cable company, the electric company, the water company, the pizza delivery company, the newspaper for home delivery, service and repair companies of all kinds, the credit bureaus, their employer, the schools their children attend—the list of folks who have the nonpublished number goes on and on and on.

In many locales, the utilities are publicly owned, and so are their records. All you have to do is go to the source, examine the records, and find the nonpublished number.

If the utility records where you live aren't public, look at your list of friends and see if any of them or their spouses work at the cable company, the newspaper, or any other place where your subject may have given out his number. If you think of someone, ask that person to get the number for you. But you don't want to ask this favor of anybody you know who works for the telephone company. First, it is a violation of the telephone company rules for employees to divulge proprietary information. Second, it could be considered theft of information. The likelihood of either you or your friend being prosecuted for it are nil, but still, your friend could lose her job.

If you can't find a friend who can get the nonpublished number for you, go to your favorite broker of telephone information and pay to get it.

Tracking Down the Location of Pay Phones

My client's 16-year-old son ran away. Anybody who has dealt with a teenager would think my client should be ecstatic. The kid's finally out the door. But no, the client wanted him back. And the kid didn't even take the family car with him. Go figure. This particular runaway is someone I've picked up and returned to his family four times in four years, so I knew the kid's friends and haunts pretty well.

This time, the boy apparently headed south to a city 200 miles away. The girlfriend cooperated with us to some degree because she was more mature than the boy and was genuinely concerned for his safety, although she wouldn't rat out the kid entirely. She never told us exactly where we could find him. She did say he would routinely call her from pay phones, and she would call him back because he didn't have any money.

We got the incoming phone numbers from the girlfriend's cell phone bill. I then ran a reverse search on the numbers. After running the reverse search, it was pretty easy to figure out which numbers were pay phones and which weren't. That's because pay phones frequently have repeating numbers or a successive series of numbers in their phone number, such as 305-768-9999 or 305-768-3456. (However, that's not *always* the case, so don't count on it.) Next, we needed the physical address for the phones because we wanted to stake them out to find the boy. (For more details on finding runaway kids, check out Chapter 15.)

Sometimes taking the direct and honest approach works just as well as being sneaky. Although the locations and phone numbers to pay phones are not published in the telephone directories, they're not a secret. In this case, I called the telephone company business office and told them I was a private investigator. I explained the facts of the case, and in a few minutes, after the customer service representative checked with her supervisor, she gave me the street address where the phones were located.

I plotted the street locations on a city map. They all fell within about a three-block radius in West Palm Beach, Florida. You have to read Chapter 15 to see if we found the runaway boy, but now you know how to find the location of a pay phone if you have the number.

Cell phones are rapidly putting pay phones out of business. And smartphones are slowly but surely replacing traditional cell phones. PIs can mine cell phones and smartphones for a great deal of information. You just need to know what you're looking for and how to get it. To find out how, keep reading.

Giving Caller ID the Runaround

Part of being a clever and successful PI includes knowing how to keep your subject from seeing that your call originates from a private investigative office. It's a growing challenge, since caller ID comes standard on almost all cell phones, and many, many residential telephones are equipped with it as well. An astute investigator has to assume that every telephone number he dials is going to show the recipient the calling telephone number and probably the name. It's a fact of life that the private investigator has to deal with and be prepared to circumvent when necessary.

In the following sections, I show you some ways to circumvent caller ID.

Dial *67 Before Dialing the Phone Number

Most landline telephone companies allow a person to dial *67 before dialing the phone number. Dialing *67 blocks the transmission of the caller ID information to most telephone numbers. A *67 blocked call is reported to the receiving party's caller ID as a "private call." Usually no additional charge is levied for this service if it's available within your area.

Another service phone companies provide is automatic number identification (ANI). (Some telephone companies call it automatic identification number [AIN] instead of ANI.) ANI is typically used with toll-free numbers, 911 emergency operations, and large companies, but anybody willing to foot the expense can have the service. ANI sends different data over different lines than caller ID, and you can't block it by dialing *67 first. However, with spoofing technology, you can spoof a toll-free number if the spoofing service allows it. Technically, it can be done.

If you call any subscriber to the ANI service, he or she will be able to see your number. Not all ANI subscribers have "real-time ANI," which gives the recipient the caller's phone number at the time of the call; 911 relies on real-time ANI to locate callers. Toll-free subscribers usually get their list of callers at the end of the month, along with their bill. However, if they have caller ID service on their lines, your phone number will appear on their caller ID screen at the time you make the call. ANI service is usually combined with more sophisticated telephone equipment and lines such as a T1. Expect to pay more than $1,000 a month to get it started.

You can dial *67 from your cell phone, too. Before entering the phone number you want to call on your cell, enter *67. Your number will show up on caller ID as a private or restricted number. Note that *67 doesn't work for toll-free numbers or anyone subscribing to ANI; they will see your real number on the caller ID screen. You'll end up as naked as the emperor in his new clothes.

When someone phones my agency using a toll-free number and refuses to identify himself, or if my staff or I need to know who a particular caller is, we write down the date and time of the call. When the toll-free bill comes, we compare it to our list of suspect calls by date and time, and we usually can identify the caller. If the unknown call is particularly important, we can wait one day before calling our toll-free provider, who can then provide us with the phone number for the call.

Use a Spoofing Service

Spoofing a caller ID is a technique in which numbers are substituted in the caller ID data stream so that the "real" originating number is not shown, but "fake" numbers appear, or seem to appear, on the caller ID screen. You can find several companies that offer spoof searches online simply by typing "caller ID spoofing" into your favorite search engine. Your search should turn up several vendors. If you plan on doing a lot of spoofing, you might want to look at Rapidvox.com, which works with a lot of PIs.

Note that you cannot dial 911 through these companies' spoofing systems. They may also block some toll-free numbers, and they can block whatever numbers they feel are appropriate. They also won't tolerate "misuse of their system." The spoofing works in North America and Canada, but it probably won't work in Hawaii because of the long-distance rates or any place where you have to dial a country code first.

LEGAL TRAP

Some suppliers of spoofing software cooperate fully with law enforcement and respond to law enforcement subpoenas.

The Fair Debt Collection Practices Act prohibits "the use of any false representation or deceptive means to collect or attempt to collect any debt," which means that debt collection personnel cannot spoof their telephone numbers. Other than that, I know of no law that requires the calling party to provide to the receiving party the calling party's phone number.

In addition to spoofing services, many spoofing companies offer services that change your voice from male to female and vice versa, and also record the call. In some states, implementing the recording feature could be illegal, but in "one party" states it may be legal (see Chapter 16 for details).

An attorney recently hired me to track down a passenger in a vehicle accident. I called the young man's family, and they said he no longer lived there, but they would pass along my message. No return phone call. A few days later, I called the family again. Once more, they said they'd pass along my request to the witness. No return phone call. I called the family again, and this time got the father, who, when I asked, gave me the young man's cell phone number. The lesson there is, if you don't ask, you won't receive.

I called the cell phone and left a message. No return phone call. I called the cell phone again and left a message. Yep, you guessed it, no return phone call. Okay, maybe I'm a little slow, but I finally figured out the kid didn't want to talk to me.

I called the number one more time, but this time I spoofed my caller ID. I could have blocked it by dialing *67 first, but it would show up on his cell phone as either restricted or private. I didn't want that, so I spoofed it. Now, think for a moment. What number did I want to insert as a substitute that would show up on his cell phone instead of my real number? I wanted a number that he would see and be sure to answer.

I had his family's home number. Right. I spoofed my number to look like the old homestead was calling him. Mom was calling to invite him over; the meatloaf would be ready soon. And guess what? He answered the phone, and I had him. In my mind's eye, I could see him sitting there scratching his head wondering why his cell phone had said it was his mom calling, but instead it was me. But he never thought to ask. I set up an appointment to meet him the next day and took a recorded statement from him. It wouldn't have happened if I hadn't been able to spoof my caller ID.

LEGAL TRAP

The Truth in Caller ID Act of 2009 was signed into law in December 2010. Its major provision is to make it illegal "to cause any caller identification service to transmit misleading or inaccurate caller identification information, with the intent to defraud or cause harm." Take note and use caller ID spoofing only for legitimate purposes, or you might find yourself before a federal judge.

The Myth of the Untraceable Prepaid Cell Phone

You can walk into almost any stop-and-shop market or a discount store like Wal-Mart and, for less than $30, buy a prepaid cell phone with 10 minutes of airtime on it. You can buy time to add to your cell phone at the same store for less than 20 cents per minute. Using the "throw-away" cell phone is a favorite ploy of mystery writers. The kidnappers use them for ransom demands because they're "untraceable." Right? Well, yes, no, maybe, maybe not.

To understand whether these phones are untraceable, you have to define what you mean by *untraceable*. Let's take a closer look.

You can purchase these with cash and don't have to reveal any personal identifying data. So in a sense, you can make anonymous calls on them, and only the cell phone number assigned to your phone will show on the receiving party's caller ID.

If you make some illegal or threatening call, can law enforcement trace that call back to you? Think like an investigator. First, assume that whomever you called will have the phone number of the prepaid phone. That's a given. And even if they don't have caller ID, law enforcement (LE) can get the numbers that called that person's phone, and your cell phone number will be there.

Now, how is law enforcement going to trace the phone back to you? These phones are sold by various companies in numerous stores. But each phone has an *electronic serial number* (*ESN*) programmed into it. The prepaid cell phone company certainly keeps track of which phones went to which retailer. So it's not too difficult to see how, once law enforcement has your particular cell phone identified, they can trace it to the retail outlet that sold the phone. The phones require activation at the time of sale, so the exact time of the sale is recorded.

DEFINITION

ESN is the acronym for **electronic serial number**, which is the unique number that identifies a single particular cell phone. The phone continuously broadcasts the ESN to the cellular network to let the network know where you are when your cell phone is turned on and which cell towers to utilize to transmit your calls.

When you're buying a prepaid cell phone, look around. Do you see yourself on a video monitor somewhere? Bingo. Now they not only have your phone identified, but they also have a photograph of you buying the phone. And if they have your photograph, how far away do you think you are from being identified?

Also, since they know your ESN, every time you switch that phone from off to on, it is possible that law enforcement will know which cell tower you're close to. If the phone is GPS equipped, you can be located within a few yards—or, at least, to the nearest cell tower.

Not to give away all of law enforcement's secrets, but if the stakes are high, they'll have a list of all the phone numbers you called using that cell phone. If you called your mom, she'll identify you from the photo they show her.

So are those prepaid cell phones untraceable? Well, you decide. However, if you want to use one just to side-step caller ID rather than engage in illegal activities, I think they're a pretty good product for that.

Mining Cell Phones and Smartphones for Data

Landlines are slowly but surely losing ground to cell phones and *Voice Over Internet Protocol (VOIP)*. As a PI, you may find yourself dealing with cell phone communications in a number of ways.

> **DEFINITION**
>
> **Voice Over Internet Protocol (VOIP)** is a popular and cost-effective method of making telephone calls via your broadband Internet connection rather than normal telephone wires.

Breaking the Cell Number

You can use a couple neat tricks to break a cell number. Instead of calling the number, go to Skipsmasher.com and use the Voice Mail Probe; if you don't have a PI license, try Spydialer.com, which is free. With either of these features, you enter the cell number in question, and a computer calls the number. The computer call bypasses the cell phone's ringer and goes right to voice mail. Within a minute or less, you will be able to hear the voicemail message belonging to that phone.

HIDDEN HINT

Spydialer has a free version and a subscription version. I prefer the subscription version because the call can't be traced back to you. You can also download and save the recorded message and play it for your client or other people to see if they recognize the voice. It's really slick and works well.

Another option is to use masterfiles.com. This company offers reverse cell number searches and charges you (about $5) only if it gets a hit. Finally, you might try Patrick Baird, at pdjservices.com; if he's convinced you have a real need for the information, he can help you. Patrick has always treated me fairly and is reasonably priced.

The next easiest way for a PI to get a break on a cell phone number is to pay the information broker. It's quicker for me to send the number to my phone guy and get a response from him the next day with the information I need. The client is footing the bill anyway.

If you're not a PI and you don't have a "phone guy," you can call the number and pretext it. You can use the same pizza pretext that I recommend for the nonpublished number earlier in this chapter, with a few changes in the questions. Start like this: "We know we've called you on your cell phone, but this will take less than 60 seconds, and we'll send you a coupon for a free large pizza from (name the pizza company) if you answer two questions for us:

- Have you ever used your cell phone to order a pizza from us?

- Have you ever used your cell phone to order any other type of carryout food so that it would be ready when you got there? If so, what type and how often?

Then say, "Thank you very much for your time. To what address should we send you the coupon for the free pizza? And what name should we address it to?"

I've had pretty good success with this pretext for cell phones. It's not unusual for the person answering to say he doesn't have time to talk right then. If he says that, ask if it's okay to call later. There's no gimmick, and you're not trying to sell anything, so most people are willing to cooperate.

Three FAQs about Cell Phones

If you work in the investigative business for long, you'll find that clients frequently ask three questions about cell phones. I answer each of these pressing questions in this section.

Who does the cell phone belong to?

First thing to do is check PhoneValidator.com to make sure the number is a cell number. Next, try SpyDialer.com and listen to the voicemail message, if there is one. If that doesn't reveal the owner, try using your favorite search engine and just putting in the phone number as the search parameter. I haven't had much luck with that, but some people swear it works. Try the pay databases or the pretext I outline in the preceding section, or use a phone data researcher like PDJServices.com, who will dig it up for you for $50.

Where is the cell phone located?

You can track a cell phone so that you know where it—and, hence, the user—is. (Some underhanded companies will try to sell you cell phone pings. They charge about $400. Don't fall for them.) Smartphones have useful apps, such as iPhone's Find My iPhone app. I've had dozens of clients install that app on their spouse's phones so that we could follow them easily. The app won't tell you who they're with and what they're doing, or take photos of what they're doing (which is why PIs are still needed), but it will tell you the phone's location. Smartphones also cache their GPS locations, and you can view or download this cache of information.

 LEGAL TRAP

> Be aware that if your client is the owner of the cell phone and has installed an app to report the phone's location, you're probably on the legal side of the law. However, if the wayward spouse is the owner of the phone and your client installed the app, you might be in violation of the Telephone Records and Privacy Act of 2006.

Can I install spyware on my spouse's phone?

Some companies sell technology that you can install on a cell phone. It allows the installer to dial a silent call to the cell phone, which activates the phone's microphone and turns the handset microphone into a room microphone. This is patently illegal and violates federal and state eavesdropping and interception of communication laws. (However, the U.S. government uses this technique and does not require direct physical access to the phone. It performs a system update, and the software is installed. So if you're planning something illegal, turn off your phone.)

THE SCOOP

Smartphones may be smart, but their users are sometimes not so smart. You've probably been "butt dialed," when someone calls you accidentally because your number was the last number called or was on speed dial. I recently had a client who was in New York on "business." He was talking to a prostitute on his cell phone and accidentally conferenced his wife in on the call. It made for an interesting conversation when he returned home. They're now divorced.

Examining Cell Phones for Other Data

Cell forensics is the process of recovering deleted text messages, images, audio recordings, and more from cell phones. It can also involve obtaining call detail records, which are generally obtained through the carrier; these contain call records and tower data. Tower data can be extremely useful in placing a cell user within or away from certain proximity of a cell tower.

Cell forensics has become widely known in the private sector, having established itself as a hot commodity for prosecution and defense alike. For obvious reasons, criminal defense attorneys either love or hate cell forensics. Either way, to get good data that will stand up in court, you need to find a skilled expert to examine the phone and associated records. It takes a trained eye, acquired skill, and patience to perform a competent exam of a cell phone. The "sticks" many PIs use will help perform a cursory exam but are not qualified for forensic examination use.

I went to Mitch Davis of tcmusa.com for a few tips about cell forensics; I share that information with you here.

Today's cell phones are divided into two categories: standard and smart. Popular smartphones include Blackberry, iPhone, Android, Symbian, and Windows mobile. Popular standard phones include the Casio Rock, Samsung A460, and Motorola Razr.

The type of information that's recoverable depends on the device's capabilities, the carrier (Sprint, T-Mobile, AT&T, and so on), and the technology used by the carrier. The device and/or technology used for cell forensics plays an important part in what you can recover.

HIDDEN HINT

AT&T and T-Mobile are known as GSM phones. GSM stands for Global System for Mobile Communications and is a standard set for digital cellular networks used by mobile phones. Most of the other carriers in the United States, including Sprint, Verizon, and ALLTEL use CDMA, which stands for Code Division Multiple Access. All GSM phones use SIM cards. CDMA phones don't have SIM cards unless they are set up for international use; in that case, they use CDMA and GSM technology.

What can be recovered from a cell phone depends on the type of acquisition performed on the phone:

- A **logical examination** provides information that is readily available on the phone, such as text/MMS messages, photos, call history, phonebook, sometimes voicemail, and other simple information.

- A **physical acquisition** recovers all the information provided by a logical examination *plus* flash memory data, raw coding, full and partial deleted text, the last location the phone was at outside its normal roaming area, and more. Often enough useful data can be discovered within raw text files inside a device.

SIM cards can contain text messages, phonebook info, subscriber info, security information, and carrier data. SIM cards in iPhones do not contain user-friendly data. Useful data from an iPhone can be found inside of the backup file located on the user's computer, if they have backed up their phone to iTunes. We have recovered data from iPhones that were never backed up or updated. The phone data stored on the actual device went back to the day the phone was placed into service.

HIDDEN HINT

If a client gives you a phone for recovery and the phone is password protected, don't attempt to decode the password. Some phones, including iPhones, automatically delete everything and set the device to factory default if the password is entered incorrectly too many times.

Performing cell or handheld forensics requires many hours of formal training and is always subject to scrutiny when used in court. Considering that a new phone is introduced into the market every three to six days, it can be challenging to keep up with new devices. A PI taking a phone-in request from a client must get a signed authorization to perform the exam, as well as understand what to do and what not to do with a handheld device that is to be examined. Cell forensics is a valuable tool for civil and criminal cases, but you need to handle it with care!

The Least You Need to Know

- Directory assistance operators will verify a nonpublished address if you give them the address, but they will not give you the address outright.
- Phone numbers and cell numbers can be broken by use of pretext phone calls.
- Nonpublished numbers can be found in public record information and retrieved from sources other than the telephone company.
- Bypass caller ID by dialing *67 before the number, using a pay telephone, or using a prepaid calling card.
- Caller ID spoofing can be an effective tool if used for legitimate purposes. It might be illegal to use it to defraud or with intent to cause harm.
- Cell phone forensics can reveal text messages, voicemail, photos, and deleted texts.

On-the-Job Training

In the previous part of this book, I showed you how to search the public records and the private databases. Now it's time to learn actual investigative techniques.

In this part, you learn how to conduct successful surveillances. You uncover the tricks PIs use to get nonpublished numbers, reverse cell phone numbers, and obtain subscriber information. I teach you step-by-step methods of conducting investigations that generate proven results on your own cases. You learn how to conduct an interrogation and how to use GPS-equipped tracking devices—and stay on the right side of the law in the process.

Techniques of Interview and Interrogation

In This Chapter

- Preparing for the meeting
- Getting the most out of a witness
- Outsmarting suspects for a confession
- Taking notes
- Recording interviews

Obtaining information from people is typically the largest part of a private investigator's job. Attorneys ask investigators to track down witnesses and take statements from them. Insurance companies want PIs to look into accidents. Businesses ask investigators to solve internal thefts. Parents want their runaway teenagers returned. Criminal defense attorneys will hand you a list of witnesses to interview. Each of these types of cases involves interviewing witnesses and potential witnesses, and interrogating suspects.

A witness is an individual who may have testimony pertinent to an investigation. A suspect is an individual who may have committed or aided in the commission of a crime that is under investigation.

In this chapter, I examine some techniques and methods that aid you in extracting information from witnesses and make it possible for you to get those suspects who have the most to lose—the guilty ones—to reveal the details of their crimes.

Making Preinterview Preparations

The best advice I can give you for debriefing a witness or interviewing a suspect is to be prepared. Before beginning an interview, make sure that you're completely familiar with all the facts of the case.

HIDDEN HINT

Even though attorneys and insurance companies usually call with a new case assignment or fax or email the assignment to you, it's a good practice to go to the client's office and review the entire file concerning the case before you begin the investigation. I made a practice of this whenever possible, for two very good reasons. First, you're the investigator. You know better than your client what will help you locate your witness. You may be able to squirrel out nuggets of information in those files—such as license tags, phone numbers, dates of birth, and Social Security numbers—that your client doesn't even realize are important.

In making your preparations for the interview with your witness or suspect, write a list of the topics you need to cover. Sometimes the interview takes an unexpected turn; the witness reveals some information you were unaware of, and in the heat of following the new lead, you forget to ask everything you need to ask about the facts you had to begin with. That's why you should always make a list of the topics you want to cover. If the interview gets really exciting for some reason, be sure to go over your list before you leave the witness and cover any topics you originally intended.

A while back, I sent one of my investigators to a small town, a three-hour drive away, to interview a witness. When I went over his report, I saw that he'd forgotten to ask some really pertinent questions. He hadn't made a list before he left, as I'd taught him to do, so he had to drive six hours round-trip to redo the interview on his own time and at his own expense.

HIDDEN HINT

Going to your client's office and reviewing the file gives you an opportunity to meet face-to-face. I can't tell you how many additional cases I've picked up by going to an attorney's office and walking past other attorneys in the practice. They see me going down the hall and invariably I hear, "Well, since you're here, I've got a case I could use some help on." It never fails. Even the attorney or claims adjuster you originally came to see will frequently find additional work or other files for you to review. Whenever it's feasible, go to the client's office.

Getting Witnesses to Talk to You

In conducting interviews, you have to give the person you're interviewing a reason to tell you what you need to know. Logical reasons why the witness should cooperate are actually the least effective. Emotion works better than reason. One of the best emotional reasons for your witness to cooperate is because your witness likes you and wants to help you.

If you're interviewing a driver who witnessed a car accident, she really doesn't care about helping some attorney win a case in which the attorney is going to take 30 or 40 percent of the settlement. Most people don't like attorneys anyway. And she certainly isn't interested in helping a big insurance conglomerate save a few bucks at the expense of some poor old guy who ran into another person's car accidentally. So why should she help you at all? The answer is to make her like you. You want her to think of you as a friend—and to think of your relationship as something that she's willing to invest time and emotion in.

When you knock on the door, greet her with a smile and genuine warmth. Once inside, survey your surroundings immediately, for two reasons. First, you want to make sure that there is no danger present—nobody hiding behind the couch or the front door, for example, with a weapon. You may think this is a paranoid thing to do, but you just never know what was going on in that house or apartment at the time you knocked on the door. You could be walking in on a drug deal or a violent domestic dispute, and the couple stopped to answer the door. Better to err on the side of caution.

A second reason for taking in your surroundings has to do with building a relationship with the individual. People surround themselves with what's important in their lives. Look around to find some common ground or an interesting hobby that your witness has. If you can discover her passion, what really motivates her and makes her life worthwhile, then you are on the road to making a new friend.

Find a common element with her life. If you're a sailor and she has a picture of a sailboat on the wall, talk sailing. If the woman you're trying to interview is busy cooking dinner and the kids are screaming, pick up the screaming baby and keep her occupied while you talk to the mother. If you can make friends with the child, the mom will be your friend, too.

The quickest way to the emotional center of many people is through their kids or pets. If the children or the dog like you, your interviewee will like you. I can't tell you how many times I've had to spend five minutes on my knees getting a dog to warm up to me, and then the witness says something like, "You know, I've never seen that dog warm up to strangers before."

I like parrots. Last year I went into a home to conduct an interview and this couple had a scarlet macaw walking around on top of the couch. Macaws are large parrots with formidable beaks. As I began talking to the bird and then picking it up, I saw the couple both eyeing each other and then the bird. I think they thought he was going to bite me. Soon the bird was giving me kisses and we were best friends. When we finally settled down to the business of the interview, they had warmed up to me as much as the bird had. They didn't give me any kisses, though.

Talk to the witness about her problems, her life, what interests her. Be charming and witty, if you can. Once she's told you what is going on in her life, you've succeeded in subconsciously tying yourself to that part of her that makes life worth living. Now, instead of being an outsider, a representative of one of those "damn insurance companies," you're a real person with a tie to the better part of her life. And most important, she's now emotionally involved with you, even if she's not actually aware of it.

After you've established that bond of trust, the witness will tell you everything you want to know, as long as your questions don't break that bond.

At one time during my career with the FBI, I was assigned to the Phoenix division. I had a road trip that covered three Indian reservations: the Pima, the Maricopa, and the northern part of the Papago. Early every Sunday morning, I'd receive a telephone call from the tribal police indicating that some federal crime had been committed, typically burglary, rape, assault with a deadly weapon, or homicide. I'd leave my bed and travel to the reservation. Generally, by midmorning, the crime would be solved, the perpetrator arrested, and the prisoner handcuffed with his hands behind his back and strapped into the front seat with the seatbelt where I could keep a close eye on him. I'd transport the prisoner a two-and-a-half-hour drive back to the Maricopa County jail in Phoenix.

The suspect's rights would have been read to him, and usually he would have waived those rights, signing a document to that effect. During this drive to the jail, I'd engage him in conversation. Invariably, we'd talk about his life on the reservation and his frustrations with life in general. Before the trip was over, he would have told me how some part of his life had made him commit the crime I'd arrested him for. It was never his fault—some outside force or inner demon made him do it—but he always confessed to the act itself. Because of the ironclad confession I obtained during the drive to the jail, I never had one of those cases go to trial. Every one of them pled guilty.

There was no rubber hose, no coercion—just concern for the suspect's troubles and his life. You know, some of these guys committed the most heinous of crimes—brutal, body-mutilating crimes, sometimes against their own mother. But during that drive, I always found a redeeming side to each one of them. I never arrested a man I didn't grow to like during that ride back to Phoenix. And I think the feeling was mutual.

Interrogating Suspects

Do private investigators ever get involved in criminal investigations? Absolutely. Some PIs make a career out of working criminal-defense cases. Our firm usually has some criminal cases ongoing at any given moment. Frequently, in the defense of a *premise liability* case, we investigate rapes and assaults that were alleged to have occurred on our client's property.

DEFINITION

A **premise liability** case involves the allegation that a property owner was negligent by not curing some default in the premise or real property owned or managed by the defendant, and this negligence led to the harm of the plaintiff. An example of this could be the plaintiff alleging that the defendant failed to provide adequate exterior lighting, and the ensuing darkness caused a rape or assault inflicted upon the plaintiff.

When interviewing suspects in criminal cases, it may not be easy to establish a bond of trust. Most criminals are street smart and believe in their hearts that they're smarter than you, the investigator. For certain, they may have more street smarts than you do. But a good investigator can turn the criminal's "smarter than you" self-image to her advantage in interrogating the suspect.

After a high-speed chase through downtown Phoenix, I arrested Daniel Black for interstate transportation of a stolen motor vehicle and assault on a federal agent. He'd assaulted my partner and fellow FBI agent who'd accompanied me to interview Black concerning his attempt to obtain false identity papers.

A week or so later, Daniel called me from the county jail and requested I come down to talk. He claimed concern for his wife, who'd escaped during the chase, but whom we later identified and charged as well. Previously, he'd had shoulder-length hair, but when he entered the interview room, I noticed he sported a completely shaved head. I ignored the change in his appearance and listened to his stated concerns about his wife, who'd made bail for herself, leaving him in jail. I think he actually called for the interview (he was represented by counsel, but since he'd initiated the contact, I could talk to him without his attorney present) to try to find out how much we knew about his numerous and varied criminal activities.

After a few minutes, he couldn't stand the fact that I'd asked nothing about his shaved head. To show how "smart" he was, he admitted he'd shaved his head so that when he was put into a lineup, his appearance would be radically different and the witnesses wouldn't be able to identify him. That statement constituted an admission of guilt, and I used it at his trial to convict him. He got eight years in the federal penitentiary because he just had to demonstrate how much smarter he was than the young FBI agent.

Whatever the case, if you can figure out what motivates your suspect, you can successfully interrogate him. A client who held a fairly high political office called me a while back. His home had been burgled three days previously, and a safe containing more than $40,000 in cash had been stolen.

THE SCOOP

Occasionally, a case lends itself to some sort of a percentage for recovery instead of an hourly rate. In most civil cases, private investigators are prohibited from working on a percentage because they are supposed to be "finders of fact"; if their fee is dependent on the success of the case, it could lead to a conflict of interest. This is especially true if the investigator will be a witness in the case. Some states, like New York, prohibit PIs from working on any type of contingency basis.

The facts were as follows: my client and his wife (I'll call them the Smiths) had returned home one evening to find a glass panel in the front door broken. A baseball bat lay on the front stoop. Wisely, instead of entering the house, they called the police. The officers arrived and found the door locked. They reached through where the broken pane had been and opened the door. When the police entered the home, the burglar alarm sounded. The police inspected the house and found that the burglar was not present. The Smiths entered the home and discovered that the safe, which had been in a hall closet, was now missing. They reported to the police that the safe had held $20,000 in cash, but they insisted to me that the figure was really closer to $40,000.

Who had committed the burglary? After interviewing my clients, I was convinced that there had indeed been a burglary, the Smiths were actual victims, and this was not just an attempt at insurance fraud. The facts of the case and the burglar alarm being armed when the police arrived gave me three good clues to the identity of the thief. Can you guess what they are?

- Whoever broke in and took the safe knew the alarm code, turned it off when he entered, and reset it when leaving with the safe.

- The burglar took the entire safe because although he knew the alarm code, he didn't know the combination to the safe and, hence, couldn't open it on the spot.

- The psychology behind rearming the alarm when he left indicated to me that the burglar had concern for the Smiths and didn't want anybody else to burglarize the house while the Smiths were out—or else the burglar set the alarm out of habit.

Evaluating those three reasonable deductions, I decided that the thief was a regular visitor to the house and probably a family member.

We can make other deductions based on the facts I've given you, but those are the important ones. I went through the list of possible suspects with the Smiths and narrowed it to their 21-year-old unemployed son, Luke.

Luke lived in a trailer park with his girlfriend, whom the Smiths did not approve of. I went to the trailer park to interview the prime suspect. Luke was a thin white boy who was unsuccessfully trying to grow a mustache. A bare whisper of straggly dark hair grazed his upper lip. I showed my private investigator's identification to Luke and asked him to open the trunk of his car. He didn't balk at the request and didn't ask why. I knew then he was good for the burglary because if he'd been innocent, he would have protested. Protesting wouldn't have necessarily made him innocent. A guilty man might have protested, too—maybe even more—but not protesting, combined with the other facts, certainly convinced me he'd done it. When he opened the trunk, I also knew the money wouldn't be in there, or he never would have opened it so readily.

I went through the motions of searching the car, just in case he'd left some of the money hidden there. Nothing. Luke told me his girlfriend was pregnant, but his folks didn't know about the pregnancy. Luke appeared vulnerable, and I knew he wouldn't fare well in the state penitentiary.

I asked him whether the police had been there yet. They hadn't. "The police are coming," I told him. "They'll be there shortly." I explained to him very graphically and in great detail what life in prison is like for young men of his slight build and complexion. Next, I put myself in a position to help him, to become a friend with his best interest in mind. I told him the only way for us to keep him from that fate was to get the money he'd stolen and return it to his parents before the police got there. Once the police had him, there was nothing his parents or I could do to help.

After my clear description of prison life and his alternatives, it took Luke about 30 seconds to step to the side of his trailer and begin digging with his bare hands. In a few minutes, he'd dug up a plastic container filled with bills. We took it inside and counted it together. I photographed him with the money, wrote out a receipt, and had him sign it. Together we took it back to his parents.

The police had a three-day head start in solving that burglary. It took me a little over an hour. Why was I able to solve it when they couldn't? First, I used a little deductive reasoning. Second, I was able to read what would motivate Luke into confessing. Lastly, I was more motivated than the police because I needed results to justify my rather large bill to my client. The police get paid whether or not they solve the crime. It's not unusual in a case like this to use *results billing*.

DEFINITION

Results billing is the practice of charging more than a standard hourly rate if the results achieved justify a higher bill or a higher hourly rate.

Taking Copious Notes

When interviewing witnesses or suspects, always take copious notes. You should have a yellow legal pad or other type of notebook; record as much as possible of your interview. It's not necessary to write down the questions you ask the witness, but you should record in a personal shorthand or scribble how the witness responds.

Always initial your original notes, date them, and, after using them to write your report, place the original notes in the case file.

There are three good reasons for this:

- **Memories aren't perfect.** The interview will be absolutely clear in your mind when you leave the witness, but it may be a day or two until you can write or dictate your report. In the intervening time, you will forget some of the facts the witness related to you. Your detailed notes of the interview will refresh your memory and make the report you deliver to your client more accurate.

- **A witness will change her story.** Anywhere from a few months to several years later, you may be called upon to testify about your interview with that person. The witness also will be called to testify. Her memory of the accident will have been colored by what she's read, or seen, or been told by other people. Sometimes a witness changes facts intentionally; sometimes she just can't remember.

- **Your attorney, the opposing counsel, or the judge will ask you to produce the original notes.** Your original notes are considered documents produced in the normal course of business. As such, they are admissible into court. They carry considerable weight in our judicial system. When the witness's story, four years later, conflicts with your reporting, your attorney or the opposing attorney may ask you to produce your original notes. If your notes have been dated and initialed and are clear on the point in question, your testimony will be considered factual. When a case is won because of your professionalism, charge the client more. You deserve it, and he will pay it.

A successful resolution to a case makes the client happy and the attorney happy, and you should be happy, too. The attorney who hired you will usually suggest that you get your bill to him right away so that he can submit it to the client for prompt payment. If the case was a big win for the client and you don't have a signed contract with him, you might at that time want to bump up your rate a notch. Nobody will balk because you're worth it. You may have just saved your client a million dollars. If you're a successful PI and produce winning cases for your clients, consider raising your rates anyway.

Recording the Interview

Attorneys use investigators to locate potential witnesses and interview them because it's cheaper for the client to pay the investigator than it is to pay the attorney. It makes no sense to have the attorney running around interviewing folks who may or may not have any information about the case.

After an investigator finds a witness that has information germane to the investigation, the attorney may schedule a *deposition* for the witness. Depositions are expensive and time-consuming and require that a court reporter be present to record the questions and answers. Also, the opposing counsel is present. An attorney doesn't want to depose everybody on the block where the accident occurred; he wants to depose only the folks who actually witnessed the accident and who will help his case.

> **DEFINITION**
>
> A **deposition** is a statement made under oath by a witness, usually written or recorded, that may be used in court at a later time. If there is the likelihood that the deponent will not be available later—for instance, due to illness—it is not uncommon for the deposition to be videotaped. The deponent is the witness being deposed.

For instance, you, the PI, might find a woman who can testify that the driver of one of the vehicles involved in an accident you're investigating was drunk when he left a party. Later that driver caused the accident. Although the witness didn't see the accident, she could testify to the driver's condition shortly before the accident when he left the party.

You, the investigator, need to get all the facts, good or bad, to your client. But your client—the attorney, in this case—doesn't want the opposing side to know there is a witness out there who will hurt his case. If he deposes a witness harmful to his case, the other side will be at the deposition and obviously know it.

> **LEGAL TRAP**
>
> Unfortunately, the law in civil cases isn't always about truth as much as it is about which side can present its view of the truth most effectively. As a PI, you shouldn't take sides in a case. Instead, you should report the facts accurately. If the facts are not good for your client, that's too bad. Report the facts, and let the chips fall where they may. If you start skewing the facts, you will tarnish your reputation and lose clients. If information out there is going to hurt your client's case, he needs to know about it, because you can be sure the other side will bring it up. At least your client can be prepared for the worst.

To make sure you have all the facts and don't omit anything from your report, consider recording the interview. We talked in Chapter 3 about the advantages of a digital recorder. Whether you're using a dedicated digital recorder or a smartphone, you have to get the witness's permission to record the interview.

Getting permission isn't always easy. One approach that often works is to tell the person you're interviewing that recording the conversation would really save you the trouble of taking handwritten notes. Would she mind? Don't make a big production out of it. If your approach is low key and you make it sound like it's the normal thing that you always do, most people won't object. But if you make a big production out of setting up the recorder, the witness may change her mind.

Once you have the witness's permission to record, you need to record four items at the very beginning of the interview:

1. State your name and occupation.

2. State the date and location where the interview is taking place.

3. State the witness's name and indicate that she has given you permission to record this conversation. "Mrs. Brown, you are aware that we are recording this interview and I have your permission, is that correct?" Make sure the witness verbally says yes to that question. A nodding of the head can't be heard on the tape when you produce it in court two years later.

4. Indicate the subject matter of the interview: an accident that occurred on such and such a date at a certain intersection.

Some clients ask for the original tape (if you're still using tapes). Give them a duplicate. Besides violating the chain of custody on the evidence (see Chapter 20), attorneys are notorious for losing things. Produce the original tape when you go to court. With interviews in digital format, save a copy on your computer hard drive and make two CD copies—one for your file and one for your client. Hard drives crash and the material on CDs doesn't last forever. Redundancy in backing up data is the best way to go.

The Least You Need to Know

- Never go to an interview unprepared.
- The best way to gain a witness's assistance is to befriend her. Have the witness invest in your mutual relationship, and then you'll have her help.
- Successfully interrogating a suspect requires outsmarting her and figuring out what will motivate her to confess.
- During a witness interview, take complete notes and retain the original notes, as they may be called into evidence later at a trial.
- With permission, recording a witness interview is a good idea. Make a copy of the recording on a CD and maintain it in your file.

The Neighborhood Investigation

In This Chapter

- Searching for the know-it-all neighbor
- Weaving neighborhoods with liability investigations
- Fibbing to the neighbors
- Checking out the dirt … literally
- Finding other crimes, other times

At some point in your work as an investigator, you'll inevitably have to perform a neighborhood investigation, usually referred to in the trade as just a "neighborhood."

If you're investigating a burglary, for instance, and you're going to "do a neighborhood," you knock on every door in the immediate area and interview the neighbors. If you have the time and the budget, you should check with neighbors up to several blocks away. Why? Because burglars don't usually park their cars in front of the home or business they're burglarizing. If you want a description of the burglar's getaway vehicle, it's not going to come from the guy across the street from the victim.

A neighborhood investigation can be one of the best investigative techniques a professional can use, yet inexperienced PIs or lazy law enforcement detectives frequently overlook it. This chapter gets you up to speed on doing neighborhoods by introducing you to them and showing you several techniques you can employ when conducting them.

Neighbors Know More Than You Think

In almost every neighborhood, you can find someone—perhaps a little old lady or gossipy man—who knows what's going on all the time. It's not unusual for that type of person to be peering out her window to see what the fellow across the street is doing.

At one point in my PI career, we were moving the office from one rental space to a newer one. While waiting for the new space to be readied, I ran our operation out of my home. My wife, who worked in a medical facility, had to leave for work by 6:30 every morning. A female assistant, who drove a little red sports car, would come to the house around 9. After about six weeks of this, my next-door neighbor made a point of asking my wife if the cleaning lady who drove that little red car and came to our house every day was any good. She needed somebody to clean her place, too, but not as often as we did. My wife, of course, knew we didn't have a daily cleaning lady, and it took her a minute to realize whom my neighbor was referring to. My neighbor was just doing her neighborly duty, making sure my wife knew that after she'd gone to work, some strange woman came to our place and always left before my wife got home.

The FBI is big on neighborhood investigations, and so am I, because they work. Sure, they're manpower intensive, but they can produce good leads.

While I was still with the bureau, I was doing a neighborhood because I had an interest in some people at a certain address. I went to the residence and noticed that the house stood vacant. The mailbox by the front door was stuffed with letters. Don't tell the postal inspectors, but I thumbed through the mail and wrote down the return addresses. After walking around the house and not seeing anything of further interest, I began knocking on doors and interviewing neighbors. Eventually, in doing this neighborhood investigation, I arrived at the house directly across the street from my subject's residence. I'd noticed that, at this house, the drapes were drawn. I didn't think anybody was home, but there was a car in the driveway. As I started up the walkway, I noticed the drapes in the front window move a little.

I rang the bell, and a little old lady came to the door. I identified myself and showed her my credentials. She opened the door and invited me in. Next to a chair by the front window was, no kidding, a pair of binoculars. When she saw my glance toward the binoculars, a sheepish grin spread across her face. After explaining the interest I had in her former neighbor's comings and goings, she produced a lined pad of paper. On it she had written 45 license plate numbers. These 45 cars had all visited her neighbor across the street during the last month the house was occupied.

I've never found anybody that nosy, or that conscientious, since. But I have found a lot of very good neighbors who write down license plate numbers of suspicious cars they see in their neighborhood.

I have developed many, many excellent leads and solved numerous cases by executing the laborious and tedious task of a neighborhood investigation. If the circumstances warrant it, there is no better investigative technique.

The Mechanics of Investigating a Neighborhood

A neighborhood investigation can entail a number of investigative techniques, but by far the most important part of the work is to knock on doors in the neighborhood where the accident took place, the home was burglarized, or the child was kidnapped. You should do this as soon after the inciting incident as possible. If the case is a kidnapped child, chances are, the police will have beaten you there. If it's a runaway teenager, the police probably won't be involved at all. If your case does have police involvement and the police have already done a neighborhood, do it again.

THE SCOOP

In a number of jurisdictions, the police won't respond to a home burglary if the items taken amount to less than $5,000.

In addition to knocking on doors, you want to try to track down the vehicle the suspect used to flee the scene of the crime. I delve into both of these facets of any good neighborhood investigation in the sections that follow.

Knocking on Doors

Your goal should be to talk to every person who was home on the day and at the time of the incident.

HIDDEN HINT

Take good notes while you're talking to the neighbors. Keep track of whom you've talked to, what they saw, who was home at the time of the burglary, and who wasn't home at the time you knocked on their door. If a wife tells you she wasn't home when the burglary occurred, but her husband might have been, make a note of it. You're going to want to go back and talk to that husband, even though the wife says the husband didn't see anything.

Let's take burglaries as an example. Chances are, when the PI arrives on the scene, it is going to be some time after the burglary occurred. Remember the son in Chapter 8 who stole the safe from his parents? The police didn't do a neighborhood investigation in that case. Had they done one, they might have found that the neighbor across the street had seen the young man at the home during the time of the burglary. We'll never know, though, because the police didn't ask. (I didn't do one either, in that case, but I would have come back and done it if the son hadn't confessed to the crime.)

Obviously, you have to narrow the time frame of the offense. You do this by interviewing the victims, their family, and the immediate neighbors to get a fairly specific idea of when the burglary occurred.

When you've established the approximate time, try to figure out the point of entry and exit. These two points aren't always the same. If the burglars entered through the back door and there are neighbors across the back fence, theirs should be the first door you knock on—not because they're suspects (although you need to keep an open mind), but because they might have noticed someone cutting through their backyard and climbing the fence to get into the victim's yard.

The only way to do a thorough neighborhood is to talk to each and every neighbor—not just a representative from each home, but every person in every house who may have been home at the time of the burglary. That's a lot of work and requires multiple trips through the neighborhood.

HIDDEN HINT

You can cut a corner in a neighborhood investigation by getting the phone numbers of each home visited. Then instead of going back to the residences to speak to those who weren't home on the first visit, you can call and conduct the interview over the phone. A face-to-face interview is better, but your budget may not allow for repeated trips back to do the neighborhood.

Don't forget to talk to the neighborhood kids. Kids are typically all over the place, riding bikes, walking to friends' houses, and just hanging out. Kids notice strangers and strange goings-on.

Finding the Getaway Car

Most criminals use some sort of transportation to flee the scene of their crime. Certainly, if it's a planned crime, getting to and from the scene of the crime is an important part of the plan. Now, we all know that criminals are not always the smartest folks, but usually they try to think a little bit ahead. In solving burglaries or property crimes, the PI has to put himself into the mindset of the criminal. If you were a not-very-bright criminal, how would you make your escape? Where would you have parked the getaway car?

Examining the list of items stolen can give the PI an idea of how far away the getaway car may have been. If the burglars stole a big-screen television, they didn't carry it very far. If they took only jewelry and small items, the car might have been several blocks away.

Why do we care about the getaway car? In movies, the getaway car is always stolen and not traceable back to the criminal. In real life, most getaway cars belong to the criminal or an associate. If you can identify the getaway car and run the license plate, you'll probably catch the criminal.

After you've identified where the getaway car might reasonably have been parked, you know how far out to conduct the neighborhood investigation. It's possible that a neighbor spotted the getaway driver, sitting in the car with the engine idling, and wrote down the license number. If so, you just hit the jackpot.

Working Premise Liability Cases

Premise liability cases always involve an allegation of negligence on the part of a property owner and some sort of injury to the plaintiff. The underlying incident that starts the whole case rolling may be an assault, a rape, a homicide, or something as simple as a slip and fall on a banana peel or a dog biting a neighbor.

If the inciting incident of a premise liability case is a slip and fall in a grocery store, you obviously don't need to do a neighborhood investigation. You can only hope that the store manager took down the names of customers and store employees who witnessed the accident. However, in most premise liability cases that take place outside a commercial establishment, such as in a parking lot or an apartment complex, a neighborhood investigation is definitely warranted. Keep in mind that, for our purposes, the neighborhood does not have to be residential. Employees of neighboring stores make good witnesses.

One such case I worked involved the alleged abduction and rape of a young girl from her residence. It was in the heat of a southern July day, at about 2:30 P.M. Julie, a 15-year-old girl living with her mother in a large apartment complex, was brought into the hospital emergency room. She had been beaten about the face, and her bottom lip was swollen and bloody. She was alleging rape. Physical examination confirmed her allegations, and the sheriff's office began an investigation.

Julie stood only 4 feet, 10 inches tall. Her mother had gone to the store for cigarettes and told her daughter not to let anyone into the apartment while she was gone. Julie said that while her mother was out, someone knocked on the door. She thought it was her mother returning. She went to look through the peephole installed in the door, but the hole was too high for her to see through, even standing on the tips of her toes. She opened the door, and an unknown male grabbed her by the hair, dragged her through the apartment complex to a wooded area behind the apartments, and proceeded to rape her.

Her father and mother, as her guardians, were suing the apartment complex, alleging that the peepholes were installed at such a height as to make the apartments unreasonably unsafe.

The crime scene in the wooded area indicated a struggle may have taken place there, and articles of the girl's clothing were still there, along with a packet of spilled cigarettes. At the time we were called in, nearly six months after the incident, the crime was still unsolved.

I began interviewing neighbors and came up dry. Nobody had seen or heard anything. Several of the people I talked to had been home at the time of the assault. It seemed unusual that the girl had been dragged, kicking and screaming, past the swimming pool, through the apartment complex, and down a hundred yards or so through an asphalt parking lot, and nobody would admit to having heard or seen any of it. Perhaps this might happen in New York City, but I found it unlikely in this southern town.

Some of the people I talked to had been at the swimming pool but were not there continuously. They had gone inside to get drinks and such, so the girl's story could have been true. Nonetheless, I smelled a rat.

In talking with the apartment residents, I had several tell me they knew the girl had been friends with a couple of boys who hung out at a certain corner market. They gave me a good description of those boys. I spoke with the manager of the market. Of course, the boys weren't there, but the manager said they came in every afternoon between 2 and 5 P.M. It was already after 5, so I went back the next afternoon at 2 and waited. Eventually, two boys came in who matched the description I'd been given.

I spoke with the two youths, and they admitted that they knew about the assault. In fact, those two and a third boy had been in the woods smoking pot with Julie at about 2 P.M. the afternoon of the rape. The third boy, let's call him Leroy, had wanted to have sex with Julie for a long time. When Leroy began putting the moves on Julie, these two told him to leave her alone because they knew she was underage.

Julie seemed mildly cooperative, but my two informants didn't want anything to do with that particular scene, so they departed, leaving Leroy and Julie alone smoking more pot.

It's apparent that Julie probably got scared and changed her mind, but Leroy was determined and finally beat her and raped her. It was a terrible crime, but it didn't happen because the peephole was too high in the apartment door. It happened because Julie had some questionable friends.

The rape didn't actually occur on the apartment grounds, so my client, the owner of the apartment complex, was off the hook. I provided a copy of my report to the sheriff's office, and Leroy was eventually charged with the crime. Why was a PI able to solve this case when the sheriff's office couldn't do it with all its manpower and forensic evidence? Because the investigating detectives didn't perform a thorough neighborhood investigation. Remember, I did my neighborhood investigation six months after the incident, and I still got a good lead from it. Suppose I'd been able to do it the day of the rape or the following day. Had the sheriff's office executed a proper neighborhood investigation, they probably would have found Leroy hanging out at the corner market still bragging about what a good time he'd had.

Being Discreet with the Neighbors

Interviews are successful if you build the bond of trust with the person you're interviewing. Part of that bond of trust is that the interviewee is confiding in you and expects you to exercise discretion with the information he entrusts to you.

Almost without fail, during an interview, the subject will say something like, "Well, I don't really want to get involved. I have to live in this neighborhood, even after your case is over." And that is very true. He knows that if he rats out the lady across the street, she may try to get even with him at some point. That's a very real fear people have. You'll be long gone, but he's still living across the street from her.

If you promise the subject that what he says is "just between you and me," he won't believe it and he will know you've just lied to him. If you say that, you've just broken the bond you've worked so hard to build. He knows you've got to report the results of your interview to your client. He knows that a lawsuit or criminal investigation is going on, and he may end up in court testifying.

How do you handle that situation? By being completely honest—well, almost—with the interviewee. Tell him that most of these cases never go to trial. Ninety-nine percent of the time, these types of lawsuits are settled out of court. Of course, you have to share the information that you get from him with the attorney for your client, but you will not share it with anyone else. Unless the case actually goes to court, the other side will never know what your interviewee says. If it does go to trial, he will likely be subpoenaed and will have to testify anyway. By cooperating now, he might help settle the case, which would prevent him from going to court and testifying.

Keep in mind that some people might enjoy going to court and testifying. Your interviewee may get a big kick out of saying what he has to say about his neighbor across the street and doing it in front of her. If that's the case, play on that. Encourage him to tell you all he knows now; if it's good enough, you can practically assure him of his day before the judge. To be successful, evaluate whom you're talking to, determine what motivates him, and manipulate him accordingly.

Recently, I had a child support case. The delinquent father, let's call him Ralph, produced a receipt for his rent to the judge, hoping to establish that he could no longer afford the burden of child support. The receipt looked funny to me, so I went to his supposed landlord. Yep, Laura confirmed that the receipt was a complete forgery.

Ralph and his girlfriend had at one time lived in the rental house but had been evicted months before the date on the phony receipt for not paying their rent. To justify them being three months behind in the rent, they claimed the leaking roof had made the house uninhabitable. Of course, that didn't prevent them from living there for three months.

Ralph and his girlfriend called the building and zoning department to prove that the house wasn't inhabitable. They showed a ceiling fixture with water pooled in the bottom. The department condemned the house for rental until a new roof was installed. In reality, Ralph had poured some tap water in the fixture before the house was inspected. The landlord had to put the new roof on at considerable expense. In the child support case, Laura said she would be delighted to testify against Ralph and the forged receipt. She kept calling me asking when she should appear to testify. Sometimes you find witnesses who can't wait to testify.

On some occasions, the interviewee's information might get reported back to the client even if the case doesn't go to trial. In the settlement process, a case might go to *arbitration*.

DEFINITION

Arbitration refers to a process in which the plaintiff and the defendant in a civil lawsuit meet with a third party, known as a professional arbitrator.

If your report contains some really hot stuff, a smart attorney will use those statements as leverage to encourage a better settlement. It's possible that those statements might be reported to the subject of the investigation, the neighbor of your interviewee, even though the case is settled before trial. It's not likely, but it's certainly possible. So the neighbor might find out what your interviewee said.

Keeping an Eye Out for Other Trouble

One final major factor to consider in conducting neighborhoods is the "other crime" aspect. Be aware of your surroundings and what the folks you speak with are telling you. You have to be intuitive and sensitive to the meaning behind their words. Many times people try to tell you something but are afraid to come right out and say it, so they allude to it instead of being direct. You need to have your antennae up all the time.

By listening carefully, you may become aware of other factors that have a bearing on your case. Remember Daniel Black from Chapter 8? He was the fellow who shaved his head in an attempt to fool the witnesses at a lineup. We later obtained a search warrant and conducted a search of his home. In his garage, we found, in addition to the stolen motor home he was driving when we arrested him, a stolen Volkswagen and a stolen Porsche. In talking to his neighbors, they all mentioned that some items around their homes had gone missing. We were able to return bicycles, a lawn tractor, numerous personal items, credit cards, and traveler's checks, all belonging to the neighbors. Daniel was a thief. And it didn't matter to him whom he stole from.

As a PI, most of your neighborhood investigations will involve some sort of criminal or fraudulent activity. You might be talking to neighbors about an insurance fraud case. Most investigators don't consider performing a neighborhood in those cases, for two reasons:

- They don't think of it, or they don't know how to do a neighborhood investigation.

- If they do consider it, they're afraid that the neighbors will alert the subject to the investigation, and this will spoil any chance they have of getting "good" video of the subject's activities.

We spent a lot of time trying to catch a man who was the subject of a workmen's compensation fraud case. We knew he was physically capable of working and had been told that people saw him performing all sorts of physical feats that he'd told his employer he could no longer do, yet we rarely saw him leave his house.

We decided to do a neighborhood investigation. We talked to his neighbors on either side of his house and the ones across the street. Those interviews didn't turn up any information. Finally, I went around the block and spoke to the family that shared the back fence line. It seems they would see him through the fence nearly every morning chopping firewood. You can guess where I was the next morning with the video camera.

In working any case, you have to use your judgment on whether a neighborhood investigation might bear fruit. Put the neighborhood in your toolbox and put it to use when appropriate. A well-done, thorough neighborhood investigation, although possibly labor intensive, is a good technique. If the FBI is fond of it, you know it has its merits. Most investigators don't like doing them because they don't want to spend the effort or have never been taught how. Now you know more than they do.

The Least You Need to Know

- Conducting a neighborhood investigation can further your leads on a premise liability case, rape, assault, or slip and fall.
- Every neighborhood has residents who know everything going on in the area. Find those people and interview them. In addition, talk to everyone in the neighborhood who was at home when the crime occurred.
- Try to find out what how the criminal entered and exited the crime scene so you can track down his escape vehicle.
- Be honest with the people you interview. If they feel you're lying to them, they will not be forthcoming. You can promise them anonymity only to a certain degree.

Stationary Surveillance

In This Chapter

- Choosing the site
- Planning your cover story
- Handling the nosy neighbor
- Staying cool if you're busted by the cops
- Keeping your secrets to yourself

If there's one technique that most people associate with the professional PI work, it's surveillance. Your entire practice may be criminal defense work, which almost never requires surveillance. But if you're introduced as a private investigator at any cocktail party or business luncheon, one of the first questions you'll hear is something like, "I suppose most of what you do is following husbands and wives, that sort of thing, huh?" Depending on your clientele, that may or may not be true. Many PIs do spend a good deal of their time doing surveillance. For example, workmen's compensation fraud cases are 99 percent video surveillance, with maybe a little judicious neighborhood investigation thrown in.

In this and the following chapter, I prepare you to conduct a successful one-man surveillance without being noticed and help you most effectively utilize additional manpower, if it's available. The focus of this chapter is stationary surveillance, in which you spend most of your time in a fixed location watching your subject. I tackle mobile surveillance in the next chapter.

Picking the Site

PIs use two methods of stationary surveillance:

- Fixed surveillance

- Fixed-mobile surveillance

In a fixed surveillance, the location the surveillance team uses is usually an apartment or house that has a clear view of the subject or the subject's property. In a domestic case, the PI is more interested in what the subject does after she leaves her house than her activities at the residence—unless the boyfriend is making house calls, which boyfriends sometimes do. In that case, you might set up a fixed-surveillance site some distance from the subject's location, but along the path of the subject's egress, to alert mobile units that the subject is on the move.

By far the most common type of surveillance in the PI business is a fixed-mobile surveillance. This is a surveillance set up in a temporary fixed site, such as a surveillance van or other vehicle. In this case, although the surveillance takes place from a mobile vehicle, the purpose is to gather evidence at one specific location.

The key to obtaining successful surveillance video is to get as far away from the subject as your video equipment will allow and still get good-quality video. The client, and possibly a jury, has to be able to recognize the claimant's face in the video. If you get too close, you'll *get burned* every time. Amateurs always begin a surveillance too near to their subject. You can always move closer, but once you've been burned, the jig is up. Explain to a client how he paid for round-trip plane fare to Grand Cayman, only to have you get burned on the first day.

DEFINITION

Getting burned means the same thing as *getting made:* the subject has become aware of the surveillance. One clue that you've been burned is to see the person you're following give you the finger.

Fixed Surveillance

An attorney for a department store chain contacted my agency and explained that a man who claimed to have slipped and fallen in one of its stores had filed a lawsuit. Because of the fall, the man allegedly hurt his neck and couldn't work. The plaintiff was a commercial underwater diver by profession. He'd been working on drilling rigs off the Louisiana coast. It was a coincidence that the slip and fall had occurred about the same time the oil drilling business hit a new low and the diver was scheduled to be laid off.

The diver was supposed to be living temporarily with his folks. I spent a little time watching the parents' house but never saw the guy there. I called the man's father and, using a pretext, learned that the diver was flying out the following day to Grand Cayman to work on a dive job down there. I hurriedly consulted with the client, who approved the trip, and I was off to Grand Cayman the next day. Ah, the life of a PI.

I wasn't sure what job he was working on, except that it was some sort of underwater pipe construction. The job could have been on land as well as in the ocean. The water table there is pretty high; you can dig a hole 6 feet deep and hit water, so a diver might be needed even if the pipeline was on land. After settling in, I stowed my camera equipment in the rental car and went looking. There was construction along Seven Mile Road, and it looked like they were laying some type of pipe in a ditch alongside the road before repaving. It didn't take long to spot the subject, dressed in his dive gear, dropping into a hole filled with water. I guessed he was probably securing the pipe connections.

It was impossible to sit in the car anywhere close to the construction site and get good video. Construction vehicles blocked the view from the other side of the road, and any attempt at setting up surveillance from the rental car would certainly have resulted in my getting burned. In a situation like this, when surveillance seems impossible, you have to think outside the box. You have to step back, look around, and search for other alternatives.

I studied the surrounding area and noticed a two-story hotel directly across the street from the construction site. It looked promising, so I explored the inside of the hotel and figured out which room numbers would give me the view I needed. I rented the room, explaining that I wanted the roadside view instead of the ocean side because it was less expensive. In a few minutes, I had the camera set up on the tripod and was rolling video. Two days later, the pipeline had moved farther down the road, and so did I, into another hotel. After four days of watching our diver working 10-hour days, I consulted with the client, and we decided we had enough. I took the next day off to do some diving (after all, it was Grand Cayman) and headed home with the goodies.

The diver's attorney dropped the lawsuit as soon as he saw some of the video.

LEGAL TRAP

One caution on fixed-surveillance sites: if you're using a hotel room or other facility that has regular cleaning people, hide the surveillance equipment before the cleaning people enter. Cleaning folks are likely to report unusual equipment, like your long-range video lenses, to the management, who will report it to the local authorities. There is no better way to get burned than to have a squad of police cars come roaring into the parking lot and storming your room to see what you're up to.

If you can get a fixed-surveillance site, do it. Sitting in an air-conditioned room is so much better than sitting in a car, suffering from heat exhaustion in the summer and hypothermia in the winter. And room service is a lot better than trying to use your cell phone to persuade a pizza place to deliver to some guy under a bush behind a lamppost.

A fixed-surveillance site doesn't have to be a hotel room or rented apartment. In my firm, we've climbed trees and sat in them all day long to obtain video of subjects. I've hidden under bushes in the rain at 4 A.M. to document a newspaper delivery person unloading, folding, and bagging stacks of newspapers. My guys have hidden behind sea oats at the beach to catch surfers who could surf standing on their heads but couldn't work because of neck injuries. All of these—trees, bushes, and sea oats—constitute fixed-surveillance sites because, if the subject moves, you can't take the site with you.

Fixed-Mobile Surveillance

Private investigators universally use fixed-mobile surveillances for workmen's compensation, slips and falls, automobile accident claims, and other types of surveillances when obtaining video of the subject's physical abilities and range of motion is important. Not surprisingly, the most commonly used method is to use a surveillance van. However, pickup trucks with a cab over the bed work just as well if you're able to squeeze through the small window that separates the inside of the truck and the truck bed.

Surveillance vans come in all configurations. We always constructed our own from a bare, two-seated delivery van. Customizing your own surveillance van is fairly straightforward. Except for the windshield, the windows should be tinted. We always have this done professionally because, too often, the do-it-yourself tinting leaves bubbles in the window that tend to distort the video, which is hard to explain to the client.

I recommend that you carpet the van floor and also all the inside panels for sound control. Place blackout cloth over all the windows except the driver and passenger windows. Use Velcro so that you can pull one of the blackout cloths partway up for the video. Place a blackout cloth between the front seats and the cargo area of the van. This will keep the cargo area and you, the investigator, in near darkness and invisible if someone starts trying to peek through a window.

Paint the exterior of the van white or blue. There are more white and blue work vans on the streets than any other color. If you end up following the subject, your white van will look just like all the others in the subject's rearview mirror.

If the van is a little beat up, all the better. It shouldn't be a total junker, though, or you may find yourself being towed away after a call from an irate neighbor.

One more consideration with surveillance vans is the communication factor. You need to evaluate your needs based on the location of the operation. If all the surveillance is done in downtown or major metropolitan areas, perhaps a cell phone is the best bet. But at my agency we always carry a set of two-way radios so that if the surveillance turns into a two-man moving surveillance, we have instant communication with our partner.

Relying strictly on cell phones for communication between surveillance team members has its drawbacks. You can talk to only one person at a time. Frequently, fixed surveillances turn mobile and end up with two, three, or up to five persons on the street at the same time. The best solution is to have handheld walkie-talkies that share a common channel as backups to whatever primary communication device you use. Why? Things do go wrong. Your subject may lead you out of a coverage area for cell phones. I've worked a lot of surveillances in rural areas where there was no cell coverage. A backup is always a good idea.

When setting up the surveillance van, try to think like your subject for a minute. If he sees a van pull up nearby and park, yet no one gets out, he's likely to be suspicious. In fact, many subjects have been warned by their attorneys that insurance companies often use surveillance people.

So why set up surveillance at the subject's residence? For one thing, his residence might be the only place you can find him. Second, most good workers comp surveillance results are from around the subject's house, primarily from doing outside chores. How often are you going to find your subject cutting someone else's grass? This isn't always the case, of course. Your subject may be working construction or some other vigorous work, and then you can follow him to the work site when he leaves his residence.

To overcome your subject's paranoia, keep your video investigator safely out of sight in the back of the surveillance van while another investigator drives the van into the subject's neighborhood. The driver should park the van on the subject's street so that it gives a clear view of the subject's residence; then he should exit the van and walk away (to where he parked her car, a block away, out of the subject's line of site). If the subject is observing any of this from his house, you want him to assume that the van is now unoccupied. Another option is for the driver to raise the hood and fool around in the engine compartment, giving the impression that the vehicle has broken down.

After the driver walks away, don't be surprised if the subject comes out of his house and inspects the van to make sure that it's unoccupied. Of course it isn't, but if you've prepared the vehicle properly, he can't tell. Be sure to have the camera running, because your client will have a good chuckle when he sees the video of the subject walking, unaided, to check out the van—yet when you video him going to the doctor, he is limping heavily and using a cane, crutches, or even a wheelchair.

Setting Up the Cover

In a typical insurance claim, you want to park the surveillance van in a strategic location close to the subject's house, but not too close. Stay as far away as your video equipment will allow. If the subject starts mowing his yard, roofing his house, cutting down trees, or working on his car, you want to be able to capture his activities on video.

In some situations, you may want to use a surveillance van in conjunction with another chase vehicle. That way, if the subject leaves the house, the investigator in the van can radio to the chase vehicle that the subject is leaving and give a good description of what the subject is wearing, which vehicle he is leaving in, and in which direction he is headed. The chase car, which should have been parked with a clear view of where the subject would most likely leave the area, can pick up the surveillance. Leave the van in location until the subject is well out of sight. The investigator in the van can then follow as the second vehicle in a two-man surveillance team.

HIDDEN HINT

Purchase several sets of magnetic business signs to place on both sides of the van. Use a "safe" telephone number that you or someone else at your agency can answer using the business name. Two names that I used for a long time were South East Survey and Oasis Carpet Company.

Sometimes it may be necessary to park the van directly in front of the subject's residence, but try to avoid doing this. Look for alternatives. If there's a vacant lot across the street and the undergrowth is thick, perhaps you can hide in the bushes instead.

As a last resort, if the subject is outside the house and you must get the video, put survey signs on the sides of the van and park directly across the street. Instead of leaving the area, have the driver get out of the van, set up a surveyor's tripod, and go about the business of appearing to survey the street, or a ditch, or the vacant lot. Wear the typical orange safety vest, take strings and stakes, and spend a few hours tromping around.

LEGAL TRAP

Don't talk directly with the subject of an investigation, even if it's just casual conversation unrelated to the investigation. Most claimants in insurance investigations are represented by attorneys, and it's unethical for a PI to have direct contact with a claimant unless his attorney is present or unless the claimant himself initiates contact.

Another good cover is to do the other type of survey: take a clipboard and walk around the neighborhood, knocking on doors, filling out a questionnaire while the man in the back of the van is getting the video. Don't knock on the door of your subject, though: doing so can render your investigation inadmissible in a court of law (see the Legal Trap sidebar in this section for details).

Listening to What Empty Houses Have to Tell You

So you've set up your surveillance. You've sat for three hours, but nobody is home and no cars are in the driveway or on the street near the house. You make a pretext call to the residence, spoofing your phone number (see Chapter 7 for details), and no one answers.

You might consider walking around the property. (Don't walk on the property if it is posted with "No Trespassing" signs.) You might see some construction work or home improvement project underway, or a car being rebuilt in the backyard or in the carport, which you couldn't see from the street. Take a couple pictures of the projects—they just might come in handy for later use in court. If you see lumber or a pallet of bricks in the back and they have a company name on the delivery label, jot it down.

I recommend using your cell phone camera for this little adventure, in case someone is watching. Also be prepared with a large manila envelope with your subject's name on it. In case a neighbor approaches you, you can use the pretext that you have some papers for your subject. If he offers to deliver them for you, tell him. "No, thank you very much, but I have to hand-deliver them directly. Oh, by the way, do you know when Mr. Brown usually comes home?" The neighbor might tell you where your subject is working, what time he leaves the house, and when he returns.

I recently prevented a change in a child custody case. The father lived in our area, and the mother and two young daughters lived out of state. In that case, the father lived in a small mobile home with his current wife and two teenage boys. In the back of the house was a travel trailer, illegally hooked up to the power pole, with the air-conditioning running. I think he intended to put the two young daughters out back in this travel trailer. The electrical hookup for the trailer wasn't up to code, and the county code prohibited people from living on that lot in travel trailers, but the code enforcement bureau never would have known about the trailer because it wasn't visible from the street. I found it because I walked around the residence and then reported it to the code enforcement bureau.

Dealing with Pesky Neighbors

If you specialize in insurance fraud, workmen's compensation, and slip-and-fall defense cases, most of your surveillance will take place during daylight hours. Success here requires videotaping the claimants in some activity that they have previously sworn they can't perform. This type of activity usually takes place outdoors, and most people don't mow their lawn or do other outdoor chores at night. This is an advantage to the investigator because more than half of the neighbors will be at work and their houses will be unoccupied. That means fewer people to become suspicious.

If the man in the chase car has to park on a residential street, you can count on at least one neighbor to wonder what he's doing there. Wouldn't you, if you saw some stranger sitting in his parked car in front of your house for several hours?

You want to defuse the situation before it becomes a problem and without blowing the surveillance. If you notice a resident peeking out the window at you, leave the car and approach the neighbor in a nonthreatening manner. Walk up to the front door with your identification in your hand. Explain to the curious neighbor that you're a private investigator conducting a surveillance. Tell her that surveillance isn't on anybody in this block, but that you're waiting for the subject to drive by.

HIDDEN HINT

The best way to get nosy neighbors off your back is to tell them something. I suggest that, if you're female and working a potential insurance fraud case, you tell the nosy guy that you're working on a divorce matter. If you're working a divorce case, tell him you're working an insurance fraud case. Reverse the cases and the sexes. If the subject is a male, tell him you're watching some wayward wife. If the subject is female, tell him you're watching a cheating husband. Of course, that will make about 75 percent of the men in the neighborhood more paranoid about their own activities, but that's okay, too.

Many times, I've had women who are out for a late afternoon walk stop at my vehicle and ask me why I'm parked on their street. If it's a woman asking, I always tell them that I'm trying to catch a wayward husband. They almost always say, "I hope you nail the son of a bitch," and then go on with their power walk.

The inquisitive neighbor might ask you who you're watching. Obviously, you can't tell him that. Be careful here. You never know who knows whom in the subdivision. It is possible that this person and the subject are friends or even relatives.

Sometimes, despite all your precautions, somebody walking by the van realizes you're inside. They may have seen the van rock slightly as you changed positions. Or they may have heard you talking or your two-way radio screeching. Once they're sure you're inside, they will pound on the side of the van, knock on the door, or even call to you. This isn't good. You're busted big time. All you can hope is that your subject doesn't become aware of this commotion. If you're parked far enough away from the subject's house, chances are, he'll never know you were there.

The question then becomes, how do you get out of this situation? The easiest solution is to lay down the camera and cover it with a towel. Then open the side door, exit the van, and shut the door immediately so that nobody can peer in to see what's inside. Confront the people knocking on the van and tell them you had problems with some equipment "back there," and had to stop and make adjustments. It took a little longer than you thought it would, but it's fixed now, and you'll be on your way. Proceed to the driver's side door, get in, and leave.

PIs sometimes find themselves in confrontational situations. This can happen if you've been made by the subject and he's not happy about it, or if you're conducting an investigation in a high-crime neighborhood and the residents make you for a cop. Whatever the reason for the confrontation, don't let it escalate. Don't let your ego, your right to be there, or anything else exacerbate an already potentially dangerous conflict. Just leave. Don't get argumentative. Don't answer any questions. Just turn around and leave. Leaving the area always defuses any situation you might get yourself into. This technique will save you grief and might save you from being physically harmed.

Getting Rousted by the Cops

A time comes in every PI's life when he's sitting on a surveillance and a neighbor calls the police about a suspicious man parked in front of her house. Most of the time, you can take preemptive actions by approaching the neighbor, as I mentioned in the preceding section.

LEGAL TRAP

If you're not a licensed PI and you are rousted by the police, you have a problem. The best you can do is explain to the police why you're there, trying to catch your husband with his girlfriend or whatever, and hope you've found a sympathetic ear. Remember, no law says you can't be sitting in a parked car. However, if the police ask you to move, you must obey a lawful order. If you don't, you risk spending the night in the pokey, and it's really hard to do any surveillance from there.

Another method to keep the cops at bay is to advise the police that you will be doing a surveillance. As soon as you have your surveillance set up, call the police department and ask the dispatcher to alert the patrol units in the area that a licensed PI is working on a surveillance on the street. Give a description of your car. If you do this, you can count on at least one patrol car coming by just to see what is going on. Wave as they pass. Some of the less clever patrolmen will stop to chitchat, which does wonders for your cover.

I typically make it a policy not to notify the police. It's just too risky because, in many small towns, the police know the folks on the street where we're working and advise people that a surveillance team is there. I've also had neighbors or the subject himself call the police to ask about the van parked down the street, and the dispatcher replies, "Not to worry. It's just some PI doing a surveillance." Oh, yeah, that's a big help.

Only once in 20 years have I ever had a problem with a beat cop. In that case, the cop asked me to move on. I was sitting in the only place possible, several blocks from my subject's residence, where the subdivision exited onto a main thoroughfare. I told him I was on a public street, I was licensed by the state to be there doing what I was doing, and I had just as much right to be on that public street as the neighbor who complained had a right to park her car on that same street. He relented but said if he received any more complaints, he'd make me move. I told him that was fine, I would move then, but before he asked me to move again, he should check with his sergeant. I didn't see him the rest of the day.

If the police do show up, you have a problem on your hands. More than likely, the cop will turn on his flashing lights and bleat the siren once. All the residents in the vicinity will come out to watch. The cop will ask you to put your hands on the steering wheel or out the window, where she can see them. In the midst of all that, the PI must keep two important points in mind:

- **Be polite, and don't panic.** Make this a conversation between two professionals. Remember, the state has given you, the PI, a license to do what you are doing and to be where you are. Explain that calmly to the police. Don't fall into the TV cliché of the PI hustling the cop.

- **Keep your business private.** Despite the cop's repeated questioning, you're not required to reveal the identity of your subject or your client. In many states that license PIs, it's a violation of state law for a PI to reveal anything about the case he's working on, even to law enforcement, unless there are exigent circumstances. But check your own state's law, to be sure. Also, if you're working for an attorney, your video and your reports may be considered work product from the attorney's office and so fall under certain protections (see Chapter 20 for a discussion of work product).

Eternal Vigilance

Working a stationary surveillance leaves little time for reading, daydreaming, or taking care of bodily functions. As soon as you pick up that book because nothing is happening, the subject will come out of the house carrying a load of bricks, and you'll miss it. You can't read and do an effective job at the same time. You may think you can, but you can't. Nobody can. And that includes reading this book on surveillance. Put me down now and focus on the surveillance.

It's not unusual to have only one chance of obtaining video on some crucial activity. The activity may last only 15 or 20 seconds. By the time you put down the book and get the camera rolling, the important stuff will be over. It might be the one time all day that the claimant comes out of his house, and you just missed it.

Plan the surveillance. Know in advance how long you're going to be in the back of that van, or in front of the window at the hotel, or under the bushes, or in the tree. Take food and drink with you. Have a large-mouthed cup to pee into, and don't forget the lid. And for heaven's sake, don't spill it in the van. This is the advice I give both my male and female investigators. If you're going to be a successful surveillance PI, you have to do it. So think twice before slurping that 64-ounce iced tea.

Stationary surveillance may not be quite as much of an art as moving surveillance, which I address in the next chapter, but to be successful, you need patience, planning, fortitude, determination, and good luck.

> **THE SCOOP**
>
> Using a fixed-surveillance van is much more physically demanding than doing moving surveillance. Give me an air-conditioned car traveling 70 mph down the highway anytime over the sweltering heat inside a stationary van during a summer surveillance.

The Least You Need to Know

- Two types of stationary surveillances exist: fixed and fixed-mobile. With fixed surveillance, you watch the subject from a hotel room, tree, or some other site that can't be moved. With fixed-mobile surveillance, your vantage point is a van or car, but you usually don't leave the site to watch the subject. Both types of surveillance are designed to obtain information from one specific point.

- One method for setting up a surveillance in a residential neighborhood is to have the driver pretend the van is broken down and walk away, leaving a second PI in the back to get the video.

- Pesky neighbors are best dealt with directly. Introducing yourself and showing them your PI license will avoid a run-in with the police.

- If you are busted, make an excuse and leave the area immediately. Being rousted by the cops requires that you maintain your demeanor and speak as a professional. You must maintain your statutory obligations and not reveal, even to the police, the identity of your subject or the nature of the surveillance.

- Success in a stationary surveillance requires a constant alert status. The surveillance investigator cannot read a book, watch television, or leave the site. Have appropriate food and drink available, and use a wide-mouth jar or cup with a lid to pee into.

Moving Surveillance

In This Chapter

- Mastering five tricks to one-man surveillance
- Getting a leg up on foot surveillance
- Preparing for success
- Using additional manpower to maximum advantage
- The ins and outs of GPS
- Winning and losing with traffic lights

Coordinating and running a successful mobile surveillance requires experience, luck, and a sense—almost a mental gift—of knowing what your subject will do. FBI criminal profilers talk about putting themselves in the criminal's head. Likewise, a good surveillance man has the gift of putting himself in the subject's head. Unfortunately, no book can teach someone how to do this; instead, my intention in this chapter is to describe the esoteric sense of surveillance that good PIs develop with time and practice.

Not all private investigators are good at surveillance. Just as some people have a talent for playing the piano by ear, others have a natural talent for sensing whether people are going to stop at yellow lights or run the red ones. Moving surveillance is an art, but every art—be it painting, musical composition, or novel writing—has its craft that you can learn and perfect through practice.

Going It Alone

Unfortunately for private investigators, most clients won't foot the bill for more than one man on a surveillance, but a few will. I remember one case in which my agency was looking for a runaway teenager. We had six men on surveillance in multiple locations around the city, staking out this spoiled kid's haunts. The father had the checking account to cover the heavy expense. Usually, you're lucky if you get a client who will pay for a two-man surveillance team, not to mention six men.

So how do you run a one-man moving surveillance? Well, it's not easy. The sections that follow describe five tricks you can use that will make it go a little more smoothly.

Know in Advance Where the Subject Is Going

So now you're supposed to be clairvoyant? Not really. If this is a domestic case, your client may know where and when his spouse is meeting with her lover. Maybe she peeked at his texts while he was taking out the garbage. Or perhaps he listened to her voicemail while she was taking a shower.

LEGAL TRAP

I never suggest to a client that he tap his wife's phone calls. But if the subject happens to come up in the course of a conversation, I tell the client that it's probably illegal (laws vary from state to state) and then inform him that Radio Shack sells tapping equipment for around $85. Never suggest to a client that he break the law. If you do, your client may like the suggestion, tap his own phone, and later tell his wife what he's done. She'll go to her attorney and tell him you suggested it. The next thing you know, the state will be prosecuting you or taking away your license.

If you're following an insurance claimant, talk to the claim adjuster and find out when the claimant's next doctor's visit is scheduled. Scout the location of the doctor's office before the day of the visit. If you lose your subject on the way to the doctor's visit, no sweat. It's not good to lose him, but at least you know where to find him again and at what time. Claimants frequently run other errands en route to and from the doctor's office. It always makes for good theater in the courtroom when the claimant can climb ladders, cut the grass, or pump the gas without help. Then when he arrives at the doctor's office, he can't even walk without assistance. And what an amazing cure rate these doctors have! The poor fellow limps on his crutches to his truck as he leaves, but at his next stop on his way home, he seems just fine again.

Follow the Other Person

If you're hired by a spouse to find out if her husband is cheating on her, you can follow the other woman. Usually, the client knows who the other woman is. She's been told by friends, or the husband has said flattering things about this woman at work or has tipped his hand somehow. If you've tried to follow the husband and he has a lead foot, runs yellow lights, pushes the red ones, and makes lots of U-turns, he might not be a good candidate for a one-man surveillance. So don't follow him. Follow the other woman instead. She won't be suspicious. She won't be looking over her shoulder, and nothing is going to happen until the two of them get together anyway.

I worked a domestic case recently in which the husband was a doctor. He was difficult to follow, so we followed the girlfriend. It wasn't long before he showed up at her place. She had him out in her yard doing chores, taking down shutters after a hurricane scare, and raking the yard. I had a good laugh at that. He could have done chores at home, and it wouldn't have cost him his marriage.

Plan Your Exit

Working alone means working smarter because you don't have the luxury of being able to cover an entire residential subdivision or company parking lot. If you're working a domestic matter, talk to your client. She'll know which exit her husband usually takes. She can advise on which way out of the neighborhood from his house he always travels. The easiest time to lose the subject is when he's leaving a location. If the husband is at home, have the wife call you on your cell phone the minute he leaves the house.

If you've followed your subject and he stops at a business location and leaves his car, use the time to survey your situation. How many exits are there? Which way is he likely to go? Is there a median in the street so he can exit only one way, or could he come out and turn right or left? Plan your exit. You don't want to be right on his bumper when he leaves; that's the best way to get made. You don't want to be too far behind him, either; that's the best way to lose him.

You have to anticipate his exit strategy and put yourself in the best possible position to see him coming out (without him seeing you) and to be able to resume the surveillance. If there's only one way out and he can turn only one direction, go down the block and wait for him.

Don't Play Follow the Leader

Your subject has just made a left turn into a service station or a fast-food restaurant. What do you do?

Don't follow him into the restaurant parking lot. Instead, continue traveling past the restaurant he turned into. Keep your eyes on the rearview mirror, in the event he's making a U-turn. When you're sure he's parking and going to enter the establishment, reposition yourself and figure out his most likely exit and direction of travel.

Take into account the traffic flow. When the subject exits, can he make a left across the traffic or does he have to make a right and continue in your direction?

This is the nuts and bolts of one-man surveillance: watching the traffic and anticipating the subject's next move, based on traffic flow, concrete medians, stopped buses, and one-way streets. Be prepared for any harebrained moves he might make. Don't lull yourself into thinking he's going to do what you would do. Count on his actions being something entirely different from what any reasonable person might attempt. When he exits the drive-thru with his hamburger in one hand and a chocolate shake in the other, he's concentrating on not spilling his lunch all over his pants before he gets to his honey. Be ready for sudden illogical driving patterns. After all, he's on his way to see his mistress; do you really think he's got his mind on traffic?

Do Play Follow the Leader

Now you're two cars behind your subject (good, you've put some cover between him and you) and he's signaling a right turn into a large regional shopping mall. What action do you take?

You follow him in. I know, I just told you not to follow him into a business lot. That's true. But with a large mall lot, there are several reasons you want to follow him right on in:

- It's easy to lose the subject in a large mall lot. Don't be fooled into thinking you can cruise the lot later and find his car. It probably won't happen.

- He may just be cutting through the lot to get to the highway exit on the other side.

- The subject may be meeting his girlfriend in the lot and could leave in her car. If she's on time, he'd be gone before you ever found him. If you do find his car and they left in hers, you will have missed the big show. Or they may meet in the lot and leave in separate cars headed toward the motel. She didn't want to be sitting in front of a motel waiting for him, and since he's going to pay for the room, they arranged to meet in the mall lot first.

- He may be meeting his girlfriend inside, where she works at one of the stores. You may find his car, but you probably won't find him in the mall.

- She may park her car and walk into the mall and out the other side where the boyfriend is waiting in his car. I've seen this dozens of times.

Watch which aisle he takes in the parking lot. Once he's pulled into a space, park in a different aisle where you can see his car. You have to hurry here; don't lose him now.

Follow him into the mall and continue the surveillance inside, on foot. Make note of his purchases and anyone he meets with.

Effective Foot Surveillance

Following a subject on foot is fraught with difficulties. You must stay close enough to see whom he comes in contact with, but remain discreet and unobtrusive so the subject is unaware of your presence. Easier said than done. Holding a newspaper up to your face when the subject looks your way is overdone in the movies. How many people do you see walking through a mall reading the paper? Okay, no newspaper—so how do you do it?

Here are four basic principles of conducting moving surveillances that apply to all forms, whether you're operating on foot, driving in a car, or directing multiple people working the surveillance with you:

- **Always keep something between you and the subject.** In a mall, that means staying behind other people who are walking in the same direction. I harp on the importance of having cover throughout this chapter. It's a very important principle, but don't overdo it. No lurking behind pillars and tiptoeing between kiosks type of stuff. Most malls have pretty good surveillance security cameras hidden throughout, and if you make a spectacle of yourself, the next thing you know, two security guys will be hauling you down to their office to ask you a few questions.

- **Change your appearance.** A good surveillance person always has a couple of extra hats and jackets in the car with him. When you follow your man into the mall, grab a hat and coat, even if it's during the summertime in Florida. By varying those two articles of clothing, you can look like four different people. If you're a female, keep a scarf in the coat pocket, and now you can add five additional appearances, for a total of nine. And don't forget the sunglasses or regular glasses. Use anything you can to change the way you appear to the subject. (Anything except streaking—it might call too much attention to yourself.)

- **Don't get in front of the subject.** This third principle is particularly important if you're working by yourself. If you're with a partner, it's still a good idea to adhere to this, but you can make an exception if the situation demands it. If you're driving and he's behind you, he's looking at your tag, any bumper stickers you have, and how you part your hair. If you accidentally get in front of him again, he'll remember all of those things and will become suspicious. If you're on foot and you're in front of him, he'll notice how you're dressed and how you walk. If he sees you again, you're dead meat.

- **Carry an iPad or other tablet computer.** If you have to sit somewhere in public, you can appear to be reading a book, but really you're watching your subject. As he comes out hand in hand with his girlfriend, you can snap some good photos. Tablet computers work better than cell phone cameras for this sort of thing.

Putting the preceding principles of moving surveillance into practice goes a long way toward making your surveillance successful and keeping you from getting burned.

Two's Company

Say your client's a big spender, not some adjuster working for a tightwad insurance company, and he wants you to catch his philandering wife. If it takes two men to follow her, no problem—use whatever resources you need. He doesn't care what it costs; just get the job done. Hmm, he doesn't care what it costs ... that's music to any private investigator's ears.

Running a two-man surveillance requires skill and practice to know how to use the extra resource wisely. Remember, if you mess up the surveillance now and lose your client's wife with two men on her, you're going to have one unhappy client. With a multiple-person surveillance team, you want to focus on three things: communication, positioning, and information. I discuss each of these surveillance must-dos in the sections that follow.

Communication

Obviously, if more than one person is working the surveillance, you need good communication among all members of the team. The equipment you have depends greatly upon what is available in your geographic area. Keep in mind that a surveillance sometimes takes you to areas not covered by cell sites, so you need other communication equipment besides your trusty cell phone.

At my agency, we've given up our 25-watt VHF radios because they require an exterior antenna, and we want to be as discreet as possible. With two or more men on a moving surveillance, 5-watt handheld walkie-talkies such as the Motorola 350 are the way to go. I also recommend that you buy a cigarette lighter DC/AC converter that changes your 12-volt DC vehicle electrical system into 110/120 AC so that you can plug your 110/120 charging unit right into the converter.

I also recommend having an iPad or other brand of tablet computer. They're great for watching the subject's route if you've installed a GPS device on the car. The screen is large, and you can use your cell phone and still visibly track your subject.

Having the means to communicate and actually doing it are two different things. All the investigators on the surveillance must first be taught to talk. Seems simple, right? It's not. Talking means the *point man* must give a detailed running commentary on the subject's actions if he is on the move.

DEFINITION

A **point man** on a surveillance is the investigator who actually has "the eyeball," or has physical sight of the subject.

The running commentary means that the point man must alert the rest of the surveillance team when the subject moves, changes directions, turns a corner, stops at a red light, or runs a yellow light. It doesn't mean that he keeps his microphone keyed the entire time. He must make his comments brief and clear. As the point man indicates a change in direction or speed, the other surveillance units should acknowledge it so that the man on point knows he's been heard. Don't use the radios for idle chatter; the only communication during a moving surveillance should be pertinent to the surveillance itself.

Even with the best equipment and excellent organization, there will come a time during a moving surveillance when the lead vehicle will be separated from the rest of the surveillance team. The team might be stopped or slowed by traffic lights, crawling freight trains, automobile accidents, raised drawbridges, or the highway patrol. It doesn't take long for that distance to grow to half a dozen miles going down an interstate at 75 mph.

When this occurs, the point man should continue the surveillance and should broadcast his position *in the blind* even though he can't hear the rest of the team. Just because he can't hear their radio traffic doesn't mean they can't hear him. Radio transmission and reception depend on a number of variable factors, such as height of antennae, inclement weather, and even sun spots. As the lead car climbs a hill or bridge, he should report his position to the other cars. The increased height in his location of broadcast may be sufficient enough to allow the other units to hear what he says, even though he cannot hear them respond.

> **DEFINITION**
>
> Broadcasting **in the blind**—when the members of a surveillance team have been cut off from one another—is something that must be taught. It means that the broadcaster may not receive acknowledgment that his message was heard, but he's putting it out there anyway because his surveillance team members might hear it. It's a valuable technique used by those in law enforcement. Add it to your tool bag. Many a surveillance has been saved by an investigator smart enough to broadcast her position in the blind, thereby allowing the balance of the surveillance team to catch up to her and the subject.

Positioning

There are two reasons for having more than one man on a surveillance. First is the ability to cover more than one possible point of egress by the subject. A subdivision or apartment complex frequently has more than one exit, and the subject may some days use one and other days use another. Having two cars available helps eliminate the possibility of losing the subject before he's even left the immediate area.

The second main purpose for a surveillance team composed of two or more people is to confuse the enemy. A good set of surveillance investigators alternates the lead so that the subject is not seeing the same car in the rearview mirror for hours at a time. Likewise, if the subject makes a turn into a business, shopping mall, or another residential area, the lead car, which has been behind the subject for a while, can drive on past as the subject turns, and the next car becomes the lead car and makes the turn behind the subject. The former lead car makes a quick U-turn as soon as the subject is out of sight and plays catch-up.

> **THE SCOOP**
>
> If your subject lives in a subdivision with multiple entrances and exits and you can't get a clear view of the place from a fixed location, you may be tempted to drive by the residence periodically. Resist the urge. The same car passing by the subject's house multiple times may alert him and make him suspicious. If it is after dark and the house is not in a cul-de-sac, indulge yourself all you want. If you have two cars available, you have a little more flexibility, but you still shouldn't drive by more than once per hour.

I always recommend performing a little recon on the subject's house and general area a day or two before beginning the surveillance. Last month we worked a case, and I asked the client, who was from a northern state, how she happened to call us. I always like to know where our work comes from. She'd previously hired another PI—a definite clue that this was going to be a difficult case—from South Florida to drive up to

North Florida and follow her former son-in-law to work. She needed to know where he worked.

So this South Florida PI was paid $1,000 to drive to North Florida and follow the man to work. The PI parked in front of the subject's residence early in the morning. At about 6:45 A.M. the subject came out of the residence, got into his truck, and headed south away from his house. As soon as she said that, I knew what the problem was. South out of his residence, the street dead-ended in about a mile. When they hit the dead end, the subject turned around and blocked the PI's only direction of escape. He got out of the truck and confronted the PI. The PI denied everything (at least he did one thing right) and left the area.

The subject called the local sheriff's office. The dispatcher said, "Oh, yeah. We had a PI call us earlier and tell us he in was in your area doing some surveillance." She went on to give the subject the name of the PI's firm.

I asked her how she'd decided to use us, and she said she had a friend in the sheriff's office ask around. After a few days, the friend called her back and told her that our agency came well recommended by the sheriff.

This led to a two-man surveillance. There was no way it could have been done with one vehicle. The subject could have come out of his subdivision and then turned right and headed east on the four-lane divided highway, traveled half a block, made a U-turn, and headed west. One man sat farther down the road to catch him if he went east, and the other sat in the Dunkin' Donuts parking lot, in case he went west. You can guess where I sat. He went west, and we successfully followed him to work.

Information

My client, the wife, was handing her 3-year-old over to her soon-to-be ex-husband. The husband was supposed to bring the child back to the mother later that same night. The father had been taking the child to the new girlfriend's house and sleeping over. The mother didn't approve, thinking it set a bad example for her older children as well. She wanted proof, somebody who could testify to the judge that yes, the husband was indeed cohabiting and had the child with him when he did it.

The handoff was to take place after dark. This was a fairly busy residential area with major hotels and shopping areas. My client was supposed to call me from her cell phone as the husband approached so that I could creep out of my parking space and follow him.

She didn't call until after he'd left (lack of communication) and informed me he'd taken a turn through one of the shopping areas instead of driving past where I had parked. I scrambled to where he turned and saw his vehicle making the turn onto the main thoroughfare a quarter-mile down the road. I broke more traffic laws than I care to enumerate, but I eventually caught up and followed him the rest of the evening.

The key objective in this case was to follow the husband to the new girlfriend's apartment and identify her. Once we had her name, we would run basic background checks to include criminal and civil records. As it turned out, he did not go to the girlfriend's, but instead returned to his own apartment after picking up pizza. He parked his car in the garage assigned to his apartment but left the garage door open. Since it was dark, I waited about 30 minutes and drove by the apartment again. Another car was now parked directly behind his.

I wrote down the tag on this other car and ran it on my iPad. In a few minutes, I had our mysterious girlfriend identified. With just a few more minutes of database searching, I had her full name, her date of marriage, her Social Security number, her date of birth, her maiden name, her current address, five or six previous addresses, the address of her soon-to-be ex-husband, and the fact that she held a professional license in the health care field.

The father returned the child to my client on time and went back to his apartment, where the girlfriend waited. Now that I knew who she was, I didn't have to stay there late into the evening to attempt to follow her home. She probably stayed all night anyway. I saved my client the cost of five or six more hours of surveillance, and I could hightail it on home because I had information available to me when I needed it.

If you're a professional investigator and you're doing surveillance, you need to be able to run license tags and other online database searches while you're in the field. Either make sure somebody is at the office while you're out so you can call it in, or be able to run searches from your car.

You can run tags and data searches from your vehicle by using any of the following methods:

- **Smartphones with broadband connections:** These allow you to run database records and DMV info if you have an account.

- **Laptop computer or tablet with a cellular modem:** This gives you the same access as if you were in your office. Also, as you've probably figured out, wireless cards with significant download speeds have finally arrived. If you can get cell coverage on your cell phone, your wireless card can probably access your provider's broadband mobile signal. The best option is a tablet with a 4G connection.

The importance of having the necessary information at your fingertips is magnified if more than one person is conducting the surveillance. Had the preceding surveillance been a two-man gig, my client would have been paying twice the rate. Having the ability to run that tag and secure the database information saved her 10 man-hours.

> **THE SCOOP**
>
> Billing clients is also something of an art. Broadband wireless service runs about $50 a month. An investigator has to recoup those costs. The only way to do that is to pass it along to his clients. If he doesn't, he'll be closing his doors quickly. When the PI bills the client, he should bill the database charges at between two and three times what the database services charge him. For the wireless access, a smart PI adds a charge to the invoice. At our firm, we just call it the wireless data-base access charge. I've had clients question me about it but never complain. Do you think the mother we discussed in this chapter is going to complain about a $25 access charge when it saved her $420 in investigative time?

Getting into Gated Communities

A PI has to make his own luck. Getting into gated communities requires luck, talent, or somebody who lives in the area who will give you a gate pass or the gate code. You can tailgate another car through the gate. Cars do it all the time, and if there's no security guard, it's nothing to worry about. The only problem is, you can't always get in when you want to because a car might not be entering when you need to enter. If the exit is separate from the entrance, I don't recommend entering through the exit as a car leaves, because that's a dead giveaway that you don't belong there. But it may be your only way in late at night.

I was on a case once in which the subject lived in a gated community. I was waiting for a car to enter so I could tailgate my way in, when I noticed a visitor trying to punch in the code at the visitors' gate. I drove right up behind her, got out of the car in the rain, and in my friendliest voice, said, "This damn electronic pad always does that when it rains. What combination did they give to you?" "Pound, one, two, three, four," she said, giving me the combination. I hit the star key a couple times to clear the pad and put in the combination. The gate opened. Now it opens on command for me whenever I want it to—no more waiting to tailgate through. The lady thought I was doing her a favor, but really she did one for me. A good PI is always on the lookout to improve his luck.

Another method of getting into gated communities is to walk in. A guard may be at the front gate, but often there's no guard at the exit gate. I've walked in many times, carrying my camera and lens covered by a sweater. You can't loiter too long, but you can walk by, get the photo of the boyfriend's car, and snap another one or two photos on the way out. This works really well if you have a dog that you can take as cover. The dog likes it, too.

The Effective Use of Cover and Traffic Lights

You must follow two rules to successfully follow someone without being made. This applies whether you're a professional PI or you simply want to follow your own spouse to see what he's been up to on Thursday evenings when he says he's working late (but you know that he isn't).

Keep Cover Between the Subject and Yourself

Try your best to use two to four cars as a cover screen. If the subject keeps seeing the same car in his rearview mirror, you will get burned sooner or later—and probably sooner. If your cover turns off or passes the subject, leaving you naked, slow down until the guy behind passes you. If your subject changes lanes, don't change lanes with him unless you're sure he's going to make a turn. Even then, it's better not to make the turn with him. Let the rear surveillance unit make the turn, and you come back from the other direction.

If the subject pulls into a grocery store parking lot, don't park out in the open where you have a clear view of him, because he'll have a clear view of you, too. It's best to put a light pole and a whole bunch of cars between you and his car. Also, don't back into a parking space in order to see better out the windshield and make a fast getaway. This is a common mistake inexperienced surveillance investigators make. Don't do anything that will draw attention to the fact that you're sitting in your car. If you smoke, don't stand around in the middle of the parking lot next to your car and smoke. If you have to smoke, stay in your car, but it's best to wait until you're moving. Why? Because if you're holding a cigarette, you're not holding the camera ready to pounce on that unexpected meeting or quick kiss. You don't know who he's going to walk out with or who he's buying groceries for.

Play the Lights

This is absolutely a must. If you don't learn this trick, you'll lose your subject every time. "Play the lights" means to evaluate not when the next light is going to turn from green to red—you should already know that—but to figure out what the one ahead of that is going to do. Why?

You have two cars as cover. You're approaching a traffic light that's been green for awhile. It turns yellow, and your subject guns it, racing through the intersection. The two cars you're using for cover stop for the red light. You can pull around them and try to run the red light (not advisable), but if you know that the next light up is going to turn red before your guy gets there, no rush. Save your own life by sitting through the light and then moseying up to where your subject is patiently waiting for his light to turn green. If you don't know what the next light is going to do and when, you're up a creek. Always, always be aware of what the traffic light situation is two or three blocks ahead, if you can see that far. If the first light is going to turn yellow and the next one up is red now, you know it's going to be green when your guy arrives at that intersection. You'd better ditch the cover cars and hustle through with your subject, then lay back and get some more cover.

Playing the lights and keeping good cover are the two most important aspects of succeeding in moving surveillances.

Avoiding the Confrontation

Your friend Sally is convinced that her husband is cheating on her, and she enlists your aid to follow him one evening. Think carefully before accepting this invitation to danger. If he is unfaithful and the two of you catch him going into a motel, what are you going to do?

Sally's emotions will be redlined to the maximum. Her husband, headed into the motel room, will be very goal oriented, and if he's interrupted by his wife, he may turn his frustration at being deprived of his goal into anger toward Sally. We learned this lesson the hard way.

Carolyn asked us to follow her husband to what she believed would be a daytime rendezvous. With domestic cases, we usually maintain fairly close contact with the client. Frequently, they can advise us on whether the behavior we are watching is normal for the spouse. This case was no exception.

When we saw Carolyn's husband having lunch with another female, we advised her of that. When the husband left the restaurant and gave the female a hug and a kiss, we photographed it. The two of them drove off in separate cars, but in the same direction. Not long afterward, both vehicles entered the same motel parking lot. We photographed Carolyn's husband and the other woman going into the same room.

Our mistake was to call Carolyn and tell her what we were witnessing and which motel her husband was in. Twenty minutes later, Carolyn entered the parking lot of the motel with tires squealing. She raced up to the door of the motel room and began banging on the door. Seconds later, her husband appeared at the door with his shirt off, his pants unbuttoned, and his belt hanging loose.

An argument followed. The husband whipped off his belt and began beating our client. Shoot, what do we do now? As we all know, domestic disturbances may be the most volatile and dangerous situations for a responding officer. Carolyn had told us that her husband had beaten her in the past.

We called the sheriff's office and then proceeded up the stairs. As is typical in domestic violence cases, as soon as we approached the couple, they both turned their aggression on us. We backed off, and the two of them took their fight inside the room. The other woman came running out and hid behind us. In a minute, the police arrived, and they needed no directions to the room. The noise from inside was clearly heard through the walls. Both our client and her husband got a free ride in the backseat of the police car.

We made it a policy from then on never to tell a client the exact location of the cheating spouse until the following day. We keep them advised of what's happening, but we don't tell them where the action is at the moment. Many clients aren't happy with that policy because they want the confrontation. We don't.

HIDDEN HINT

If the relationship has a history of violence, consider all the factors before becoming involved in a similar situation. In this business, though, confrontations will happen, even when you do your best to avoid them.

Jacob was a bookie. He was a heavyset man who drove a large gray Mercedes and paid in cash. He and Martha were separated. A few months previously, Jacob had hired us to follow Martha for almost two weeks straight. I'd reported to Jacob about a man I saw entering Martha's house without knocking. I knew the man. His name was John, and he was an attorney who lived across the street from Martha. Still, entering without knocking or ringing the bell seemed a little strange to me.

Jacob pooh-poohed the idea that John could be Martha's lover. He was just a friendly neighbor. Yeah—real, real friendly, as it turned out. I'm sure she was getting good legal advice from John, and at a very good exchange rate as well.

Now, Jacob wanted Martha followed some more because Martha had admitted she'd had a fling with John but that it was over. I've heard that more times than I can count. So had Jacob. We were back on the case. Unfortunately, Jacob had told Martha that he'd had her followed before, so now she was paranoid and watching for us. Just because you're paranoid doesn't mean that somebody's not following you. We were certainly on Martha's tail, figuratively speaking.

One day, about 10 days into the surveillance, another investigator and I were conducting a two-man surveillance on Martha. We followed her down a busy four-lane road. A car similar to mine was riding her bumper all the way down to an interstate on-ramp. When Martha roared onto the interstate, this car still stayed right behind her. This unknown car was the same color and make as mine.

I was staying way, way back, keeping as many cars between my vehicle and hers as I could while still keeping her in sight. She exited the interstate, and this other car didn't. Finally, the other car was off her bumper. My other investigator was farther back than I was, so I sped up to follow her off the interstate. Once off the freeway, she could have gone any of four different directions, and we didn't want to lose her.

Well, unknown to me, she'd pulled off and stopped and was just sitting there. As I drove past her, she got on my tail. I tried to pull into a nearby gas station, but she whipped around in front of me and blocked my path. She hopped out of her car and jumped right into my face.

"Why are you following me?"

"Lady," I said, thinking as fast as I could, "I'm not following you. I just pulled into here to get some gas, and you're blocking my way. Are you okay?"

"I'm fine, damn it. And you are, too, following me. You've been following me for the last 15 minutes. I'll tell you why you're following me: you're following me because Jacob paid you to follow me. And you're not very good at it, either. How much did he pay you to follow me?"

I just shrugged my shoulders and motioned toward the gas pumps. "Lady, I'm just trying to get some gas."

"Well, I'm going to tell Jacob what a lousy PI he hired. He's wasting his money." With that, she jumped back into her car and took off.

What a blow to my ego. Of course, I wanted to tell her that I'd been following her for 10 days straight and she never knew it. And that I'd followed her for more than two weeks the month before and she never knew that, either. And the only reason she'd made me today was because of a case of mistaken identity. Of course, she was gone, and I couldn't have said those things anyway, but boy, did I want to. I did tell Jacob. He just chuckled about it and paid me in hundred-dollar bills. Of course, what she didn't know was that my partner had picked up the surveillance when she took off, and we held on to her for a few more days.

Here's a short checklist of what to do if you're confronted by a subject (don't use this list if you're made by the police; I deal with that in Chapter 10):

- Deny that you're following the person who confronts you.

- Don't identify yourself as a private investigator.

- Never reveal the identity of your client or your subject.

- Leave the area as quickly as possible, but not so quickly that you give the impression you are fleeing.

- Stop the surveillance for the day and give it time to cool off.

- If surveillance is reinstituted on another day, utilize different vehicles and, if possible, different personnel.

Why leave the area? I was with another investigator in St. Croix, U.S. Virgin Islands, working a surveillance. We'd followed our subject for most of the day when he pulled into a very small strip mall. My other investigator, Mike, pulled in right after him. (Wrong move.) The subject exited his vehicle, walked over to Mike, and asked why he was following him. Via our radios, I told Mike to leave the area. Did he? No. He got out of his car and engaged the subject in a heated discussion. Soon the subject's friends surrounded them. Shoot, I really didn't want to get into rumble. It was about 12 of them to 1 of Mike. I pulled in, got out of my car, physically pushed Mike into his car to make him leave, and then left myself. I went around the block and watched the strip mall. Within a couple minutes, the crowed had dispersed. We swapped our rental cars and got back on our man the next day. What was to be gained by having a confrontation? Nothing. Don't do it. Don't let your ego, manhood, or whatever over-rule the "no confrontation" rule.

Using GPS for Surveillance

Following a subject got a lot easier thanks to advances in GPS technology. Maybe. Check your state law on the use of tracking devices before investing. If it's allowable in your state, buy the equipment and rent it to your client. About two rentals will pay the cost of the equipment.

You can use *GPS* technology to track your subject in at least three ways. They all involve attaching a device to the subject's vehicle that reports the vehicle's location.

> **DEFINITION**
>
> **GPS** stands for Global Positioning System. It is a system of about 24 satellites that orbit Earth and send out closely timed signals. The GPS receivers on Earth receive the timed signals from multiple satellites and can calculate the receiver's latitude, longitude, and altitude.

- **A GPS receiver that records the travels of the vehicle.** You can remove the receiver and download and view your subject's itinerary. This is useful if you don't need real-time reporting but want to show that your subject travels a certain route or stops at a certain hotel for a specified period of time.

- **A GPS receiver that reports real-time data.** These devices use what is known as code division multiple access (CDMA) wireless cellular technology. This requires that the vehicle be in an area where CDMA is available. Likewise, some devices use the GSM network. Normally, you have to subscribe to the CDMA account for 12 months, whether or not you plan to use it for that long. These devices can be either hardwired to an electrical unit or battery powered. Some devices claim a battery life as long as 20 days. The larger the battery, the longer it broadcasts. Larger batteries mean it is more likely to be discovered.

  The unit itself is about the size of a pack of playing cards. You can view the vehicle as it moves about the streets of your city. Pretty nifty. Cost for the hardware? Less than $750.

- **A GPS-enabled telephone.** Again, you need an account with the provider. You can even duct-tape the phone discreetly to some part of the vehicle and retrieve it when the surveillance is over. Some providers allow you to view in almost real time where the phone is located at any given moment. Check your cell providers; they will be coming online with this feature if they're not there already.

Previously, the antennae of the device needed a clear view of the sky. No longer is this true. The GPS device still needs to be able to receive the satellite signal, but the devices are far more sensitive than they used to be. I usually try to mount the devices inside the fiberglass bumper, which provides plenty of access to both the GPS signals and the cell phone signal that these devices use to broadcast their location to the monitoring station. A good rule is to always try the installation on a similar make and model of car before actually mounting it to your subject's vehicle.

Tracking someone using a hidden GPS device might not be legal in your state. Many states have flat-out legislated against the civilian use of vehicle-tracking devices without the driver's permission. Other states, such as Tennessee, allow if for tracking minors but not for tracking spouses. Notice the word *driver*; ownership of the vehicle might not make any difference. It depends on your state law. Don't lose your license—or go to jail—because you installed a tracking device where it's not legal to do so.

Where do you buy these devices, and which ones are best? I use the devices supplied by www.GlobalTrackingGroup.com. I also recommend the devices sold by Jimmie Mesis at www.pigear.com. Jimmie is excellent to work with and stands behind his products. Do your homework. Ask other investigators which one worked best for them. To get you started, here's a link to a blog entry by PI Oleg Flaksman in which she reviews some of the devices on the market: www.oinvestigations.com/Private-Investigator-Blog/2012/10/gps-tracking-device-reviews/

In January 2012, the U.S. Supreme Court ruled that law enforcement personnel need a warrant to place a tracking device on a suspect's vehicle. Take note, though, that the recent Supreme Court ruling applies only to law enforcement, *not* private investigators. (The Fourth Amendment right to unreasonable search and rights to privacy apply only to the government, not to civilians.) Nonetheless, this is an area where you need to be cautious. Some states, such as Virginia, are in the process of making GPS tracking illegal, with some exceptions. Other states such as Georgia, Mississippi, and Arizona have no such statutes yet.

If a client wants to hire you to place a device on a spouse's vehicle, I recommend that you get the tag on the vehicle and run the registration. If the client is on the registration or title, you're probably okay to install it. However, if just the spouse is on the registration, well, now you're getting into a gray area. One argument for installing the device when your client isn't on the title is that, if your state is a community property state and the two are married, then whether or not your client is on the title, the vehicle is still half hers and she can give permission. At least, that's my line of defense if I get sued. I haven't seen any civil cases in Florida that have given any ruling in this area. Keep abreast of your state laws.

LEGAL TRAP

Do not rent the device to your client and let him install and monitor it. You don't know what vehicle it is tracking. Both you and your client could fall victim to the stalking laws.

The Least You Need to Know

- Know in advance where your subject is going by talking to the client or finding out from the insurance adjuster when the subject will be visiting the doctor.
- If a husband is impossible to follow, follow the other woman. She won't be looking for surveillance.
- Plan how your subject is going to exit from wherever he is, whether it's a subdivision or a grocery store parking lot.
- To conduct an effective foot surveillance, always keep some cover between you and the subject. Alter your appearance by adding and removing clothing and glasses. Don't get in front of your subject.
- Multiple-person surveillance requires good communication, the ability to position the rest of the team to maximum advantage, and the ability to obtain license tag information during the surveillance.
- The most important aspects of a moving surveillance are keeping cover between yourself and the subject and evaluating the traffic lights ahead of the surveillance so that you can make proper decisions when the subject runs red lights.
- GPS is an effective means to track a vehicle but you must make sure it is legal in your state.

Tricks of the Trade

In This Chapter

- Picking through the garbage to find buried treasure
- Pretexting to get the information you need
- Tricking your subject out of the house
- Obtaining the elusive hotel statement

Every profession has its tricks of the trade—shortcuts to help the professional achieve successful results more rapidly than traditional methods might allow. Although I refer to the techniques I present in this chapter as "tricks," they're actually advanced and sophisticated methods for obtaining information necessary for successfully resolving a case.

Getting Down and Dirty: Trash Covers

If you really want to get to know a person up close and personal, collect his garbage. Collecting another person's trash is called a *trash cover*, and it's a perfectly legal method of digging up information about a person. The law is pretty well established in most states that once a person has set his garbage at the front of his property for collection, it's considered abandoned property and fair game for anybody who wants it. The trash cover is a very good tool if you have the time and the stomach for it.

LEGAL TRAP

Before conducting a trash cover, check your state's statutes. State laws on picking up garbage that belongs to a third party vary from state to state. Most state laws agree that it is abandoned property and, as long as you don't trespass, there's no problem in conducting a trash cover. In the past, a few states have argued in court that until the trash is commingled with other trash, it is still the property of the original owner.

If your spouse is nagging you to take out your own garbage, why would you want to go digging through someone else's? Because it's ripe—not just with smells, but with very detailed information, such as bank account information, bills, credit-card statements, and new and expired credit cards themselves. You'll know what kind of liquor the person drinks and how much. You'll know what kind of snacks he likes to eat. You can find in the garbage rough drafts of letters written to friends, cards from lovers that he doesn't want his wife to see (and that he should have shredded), payroll stubs, and empty prescription bottles. You name it, and you can find it by performing a trash cover.

PIs use several techniques when doing trash covers. Evaluate your particular situation and decide for yourself which method works best. No matter what technique you use, you should first call the local sanitation company (or the city, if the city handles the trash) and find out what days of the week the garbage is collected at the particular address in question. Here are some common tactics you can use:

- **The switcheroo.** Scout your subject's house and look at his or her garbage cans. Most people set out their garbage the night before the collection. The most professional technique is to purchase garbage cans identical to your subject's cans. At about 3 in the morning, drive to the subject's house in a van and swap cans. Be sure that there's garbage in the cans that you leave behind so nobody gets suspicious.

- **The grab and run.** The next easiest method is to drive to the residence in the early morning, take the garbage out of the cans, and place it in the back of a pickup truck or a van. Put some plastic sheets on the floor of the van or truck, or repackage the garbage into clean plastic bags as you collect it. In addition to the paper products you're looking for, expect to encounter a lot of rotten food, dead animals, dirty diapers, and messy stuff of undeterminable origin.

Wear latex gloves when handling and sorting through the trash. Donning a mask to breathe through isn't a bad idea, either. Murphy's Law applies to trash covers: the papers with the information of most value will be the soggiest. Be sure to have a large, well-ventilated room to lay out the trash and examine it. You'll also need a drying rack or some way to spread out mushy paper so it will dry.

I'm not going to sugarcoat it: trash covers are disgusting, but I've always found them to reliably produce important information. You might not get what you're looking for the first time out, though. For a trash cover to be productive, you should plan on grabbing the garbage regularly for several weeks. Follow the rules of evidence that I discuss in Chapter 20. You never know what you might have to produce in court. Hopefully you won't need the dirty diapers—you're probably safe to just toss them.

THE SCOOP

Speaking of diapers, when Khrushchev was the Soviet premier of Russia during the era of the Cold War, one of the Central Intelligence Agency's greatest coups was snagging one of Khrushchev's bowel movements. By analyzing the premier's excrement, the government had an inside view into his health. And you thought it was just government waste.

Trash covers work with smaller commercial establishments as well—especially those that have their own dumpster. We've conducted trash covers on companies supposedly ready to file for bankruptcy and found shipping documents and notes on wire transfers out of the country.

Pretexting: Using Lies to Get the 411

A *pretext* is a subterfuge or ploy used by private investigators to encourage an individual to reveal information about himself or another party without being aware of the true reason for the conversation. In the course of responding to what appears to be a normal, everyday query, the individual unsuspectingly releases the information the investigator is seeking. A pretext isn't a mean-spirited lie designed to injure anyone. Instead, it's a clever lie designed to scam a person into providing crucial information about a case.

Before using a pretext to obtain information, make sure you're not violating any laws. You shouldn't run into trouble with the law if you use pretexts to obtain information that is generally available, such as a subject's employment. After all, his fellow employees know where he works. You could follow him to work. His employment isn't private. However, if you use pretexting to obtain private information, such as his financial data or phone records, you may be crossing the line into illegal territory. Stay on top of the current laws on this topic, and stay on the right side of ethical.

> **LEGAL TRAP**
>
> The Gramm-Leach-Bliley Act made it illegal to use pretexts to obtain another person's financial information by making false, fictitious, or fraudulent statements to a financial institution or to the financial institution's customer. The Federal Trade Commission regularly conducts sting operations on private investigators who advertise asset or bank account searches. Typically, those types of searches involve pretext calls to the banks and also the subjects. If you need financial information on a subject, try using a trash cover at his residence and office.

Surprisingly, the hardest skill for many private investigators to develop is the formulation of good pretexts. Being deceitful seems to come naturally to some people. But for those who never lie, developing good pretext skills may be difficult, but not impossible.

Identifying the Subject

Suppose that you're trying to locate Steve Brown. You think you've found him, but you're not sure whether you have the right Steve Brown. Whatever you do, you don't want him to know a private investigator is on his tail. Why? Because if he's the right one, you're going to begin surveillance, and you don't want him to be watching for you.

You call him from a safe telephone or spoof your number (see Chapter 7) and ask if Steve Brown is there. Be sure to use both first and last names. If you just ask for Steve, you could get any old Steve. More than one Steve might be at that phone number, or you might have dialed the wrong number. The person answering will say either yes or no. If he's there, ask to speak to him.

When he comes to the phone, employ your pretext. Assuming that you know the background on the right Steve Brown, ask if this is the Steve Brown whose date of birth is such and such. Give him the right Steve Brown's date of birth. Normally, he'll answer yes or no. If he answers no, you have the wrong Steve Brown, so keep searching. If the answer is yes, you must now give him a reason for the call that he will believe. A good pretext to use in this case is to say that you are looking for the Steve Brown, born such and such, for a high school reunion. The Steve Brown you're looking for graduated from Coral Gables High School in 1965. He'll say no, you've got the wrong Steve Brown, and hang up.

Now you know that you do have the right Steve Brown, and you also know where he is at this very moment. You can begin your surveillance whenever you please and be assured that you're on the right man. I know investigators who've spent days following the wrong person with the same name as their subject because they didn't do a simple pretext telephone call to verify that they had the right guy.

Finding Employment Information

Here's a pretext to use if you want to find out a person's employer. Telephone the subject, or his spouse, from a safe phone, or spoof your caller ID (I describe spoofing caller ID in Chapter 7). Tell him you are [make up a name] from [make up a bank name] and that he has been preapproved for a credit card with an introductory rate of 0 percent guaranteed for 12 months, with no annual fee and a preapproved credit limit of $9,500. Not everybody wants or needs a new credit card, but most of the people a PI deals with would kill for a card with a credit line of more than $500.

Explain that you need to have him verify only a few items, and you'll send him his new card within two weeks. If he's gone with you this far, he'll go the rest of the way. Here's the important part of this pretext. Start giving him details about himself to make him feel comfortable that you are legitimate. Say, "Let's see, you were born on October 10, 1972, correct? You reside at [state his address] and your telephone number is [state his telephone number]."

Now you have to get him to start giving you information. You say, "I'm going to give you the first part of your Social Security number, to verify that I'm actually talking to Steve Brown; then I need for you to verify the last digit for me." You give him the first eight digits of his Social Security number (so he knows you already know it), and he verifies the last one. Now he is starting to give you information. Next, ask him for his mother's maiden name to use as a code word for his account. Nobody ever balks at that question, and he's still spitting out information you didn't have.

Next, ask him how many cards he'll need, and does he want his wife's name on one of them? He is giving you even more information. It's not important information. It's not information you care one whit about, but he is growing accustomed to giving you information. Now you say to him, "The only thing left to verify is your employment. We're not interested in your salary, but we need to have in our records your current employer." He has time and emotion involved in the relationship with you, and he wants that card. If he has an employer and he's come this far, he'll give it to you. Get the employer's name, telephone number, and address. Bingo! You got what you wanted.

If you've developed a friendly rapport with this subject on the phone, you can push this pretext a little further. If you're going to do surveillance on him, it might be helpful to know what his work hours are. Say something to him like, "Oh, that sounds like an interesting job. Do you like that?" Chat with him for a minute about his job and then slide in a question about his hours. Does he have to be to work very early, or does he work a night shift? Ask whatever seems reasonable. If you're friendly with him and chatty, he'll volunteer his entire life story.

Getting Travel Details

A client wanted us to follow his soon-to-be ex-wife to Bermuda. I told him to twist my arm a little, and maybe I'd take the case. He thought she would drive from Florida to Atlanta and leave from there. The client was flying into our local airport to pick up his 8-year-old and spend two weeks at the beach. We had to follow the wife from the moment she turned over the boy because nobody really knew for sure where she was going. Bermuda was the client's best guess, and I was rooting for it, too.

He informed us that his wife had just undergone several different plastic surgeries, including a tummy tuck, liposuction on her thighs, and breast implants. He thought she probably had a lover. In Georgia, at that time, adultery not only was grounds for divorce, but it also figured big-time into alimony settlements, or lack thereof, according to the proof that was given.

I told the client we would need a two-man surveillance team for the job. He said fine; he didn't care what it cost. Got to love the sound of that. I chose one of my investigators to go with me. We had our carry-on luggage crammed with surveillance gear, radios, binoculars, and cameras.

The wife met our client at the airport and turned over the child. He left, and she got into her car, left the airport grounds, made a U-turn, and pulled back up to the curb of the terminal. She took two suitcases out of the trunk and gave them to a skycap. She then took her car to long-term parking.

I gave the skycap $10 and asked him where the lady with the bags was going. He took my $10 and then said he couldn't remember. Thanks a lot, bud. He did add that she was flying out on Continental, but he wasn't sure which flight because she didn't have her ticket yet. He had set her bags down near the Continental ticket counter.

Continental had two flights that left within 20 minutes of each other. One went to Los Angeles, the other to Houston. Nothing to Bermuda. Bummer. We needed to know where she was going so we could get on the same flight. Our only chance was to arrive with her and follow her from the airport. If we lost her here, or at the other end, we'd be out of luck and we'd never find her. The pressure was on.

When she came back into the terminal, I've got to admit, she looked like a million bucks. She was wearing a flimsy silk dress and, it appeared, nothing else. As she got into the ticket line, I stepped in right behind her. I didn't want to talk to her because if she saw me in L.A. or Houston, I didn't want her to recognize me.

The line moved slowly, but eventually it was her turn to approach the counter. My only chance was to get to the same ticket agent she was talking to. Other agents became available, but I pretended I was looking for my ticket in my carry-on luggage and let several people behind me go ahead. Eventually, she bought her ticket. As she left the counter, I hustled right up to the same agent, who happened to be a man. As my subject was walking away in her nearly see-through dress, I said to the ticket agent, "Man, what a fine-looking woman. Where is she going?"

He responded, "Houston."

"Well then," I said, "Give me two tickets to Houston."

He couldn't believe it. "Really, you want two tickets to Houston?"

"Yeah, really. I've got time. Maybe I'll get lucky," I said.

As he was printing the tickets, I inquired about seat assignments.

"Not to worry," he said. "I've put you right next to her."

What a nice guy.

I had him change the seats so that I was two rows behind her and my other investigator was a row in front of her.

What's the point to this story? Do you think that nice guy would've been as nice if I'd rushed up to him, pulled out my state-issued private investigator's license, and demanded to know where that woman was going? Not on your life. He would've started spouting company regulations about the privacy of records and the need for a court order or a subpoena, and a supervisor would have appeared out of nowhere. I would've drawn attention to myself and been made. Instead, I got exactly what I wanted and had the agent on my team, giving me more help than I needed.

You can get information from almost anybody. You just have to find a reason for that person to give it to you. You cannot coerce it from people. You usually can't pry it out. And I've never had any luck buying it from anyone, either. It has to slide out easily so they don't even know they gave you what you wanted. This trick can be used at any airport. Just adjust the facts to the particular case you're working on.

Getting Your Subject to Leave the House

Your client is a workmen's compensation insurance company. Your assignment is to get some productive video of the subject who is currently not working due to an alleged injury on the job. The problem is that the subject never seems to come out of his house when you have him under surveillance. How do you get him out of the house?

LEGAL TRAP

If you're working for an attorney and your subject is represented by an attorney, don't initiate any contact with the subject. The subject must initiate the contact. It's unethical for an attorney to have direct contact with another attorney's client. Although you're not the attorney, you're most probably acting as an agent for the attorney of the insurance company. Do not initiate the contact.

This little trick takes two people. One surveillance investigator is already set up, with the video camera on and ready. The other, who needs to be a female, is walking her dog or jogging. She approaches the subject's front yard, gets down on her hands and knees on the lawn, and begins searching carefully through the grass. This continues for as long as necessary until the subject can't stand it any longer and comes out of the house to see what is going on. The camera should be rolling.

The female explains that she was walking her dog, and her $6,500 engagement ring, which her boyfriend just gave her last night, slipped off her finger and is somewhere on your subject's front lawn. She tells your subject she was going to get it resized today but hadn't gone to the jewelry store yet (it helps to mention a local, high-priced store) to have it done. What is she going to do? Her fiancé will kill her if she can't find the ring. By now, if she's a good actress, she'll be in tears.

One of two things will happen. Your subject may get down on his hands and knees and begin combing through the grass to help her. This makes excellent video for a workmen's compensation case. Or he won't. She can look all she wants by herself. If the subject retreats to the house again, she should look for a while longer and then approach the door, ring the bell, and give the subject a name and phone number, asking him to call her if he finds the ring.

After she's been gone for a while, the subject will come out of the house and begin combing through the grass by himself, with no intention of telling her he found the ring.

If the subject doesn't come out of the house at the beginning of the pretext, he might not be able to see your female investigator from where he is in the house. After a few minutes, she should ring the bell and tell him what has happened to her ring, to get the plot moving along.

This little maneuver usually works really well. At worst, you'll get a little video of the subject and know what he looks like. It's not unusual to get a lot of video of your subject and his wife and everybody else in the house, out on the front lawn looking for that $6,500 ring after the girl and the dog have left.

Although you can't use this pretext on every case, it works for many situations. Adapt the facts to the neighborhood where your subject lives, and go for it.

LEGAL TRAP

There are some things you cannot do to your subject under surveillance. Some investigators flatten a subject's tire to record the subject changing the tire. Not only is this not fair, but it's malicious mischief and is against the law. The worst part is that you, the professional PI, will have to respond when the subject's attorney asks you in court whether you have any knowledge of how the tire became flattened. Are you going to lie and thereby be guilty of perjury?

Suppose that you lie. Then the attorney produces the subject's neighbor, who saw you let the air out of the tire. Now you've ruined your client's case and run afoul with the court, all at the same time. Good move, huh? That story will spread so fast, you'll never get another case from an insurance company or any local attorney. Play smart, play fair, and don't break the law.

Proving the Hotel Stay

Working domestic cases has lots of entertainment value. Some PIs turn up their noses at domestic cases. I've made them one of my specialties, for several reasons. For one thing, I collect a retainer up front and put the money in the bank before I start the case. I don't have to wait for some insurance company to pay me in three or four months, or whenever they get around to it. The other reason is that these cases can be a lot of fun.

PIs often get asked to prove that a client's spouse stayed in a particular hotel during a certain time frame. If the PI asks the hotel directly for a copy of a bill, the hotel will steadfastly refuse. Before I worked out this little trick, I even tried to bribe a hotel clerk, offering her $1,000 for a duplicate bill. She refused. I developed this trick I'm about to reveal to you here and got the invoice anyway. The next day, she was kicking herself for not taking the $1,000. She told me herself how stupid it was for her not to take the money, since I "tricked" the front office out of the bill. This trick works even if you're on the case several months after the hotel rendezvous.

Let's make up two names, Gary Fielding and Sheila Smith. Smith is the wife of my client and had a fling with Fielding at a certain hotel on May 5. My client wants the bill for two purposes. He's hoping that the invoice will show there were two occupants in the room. He also wants any long-distance calls charged to the room, as additional proof that his wife was there. Here's how you can get it.

Call the toll-free number for the hotel chain and make a reservation for the next day. Tell the operator there will be two of you in the room. Give the reservation clerk the name of Gary Fielding as the primary name and include your own name as accompanying Fielding; use your credit card to guarantee the room.

The next day, check into the hotel. Use your own name to check in, and tell them Fielding hasn't arrived yet. This is important: make sure the registration has Fielding on it.

An hour or so after you've checked in, ring down to accounting and identify yourself as Gary Fielding. You're in room such and such. You stayed here last month on May 5, but you seem to have lost your copy of the statement and you need it to attach to your expense report. Ask them to drop another copy by your room. They can just slip it under the door sometime today, if that's not inconvenient. In a few hours, you'll have delivered into your hot little hands exactly what your client wants, and it'll cost you (or your client) only the price of the room—plus your fee, of course.

If your client really wants to nail Mrs. Smith, there's more you can do while you're there. Once you get the statement, you'll know she and Fielding occupied, say, room 502. Call the front desk and tell them you'd like to move to room 502 if possible—if not today, then tomorrow, when it becomes free. In your spare time, snap some pictures of the door to room 502. Make sure the room number shows in the photos. When you get the room reassigned to you, unmake the bed. Toss some bathroom towels around on the floor and make the room look recently used. Take lots of pictures of the unmade bed and the room and bathroom. Forward the pictures, with your report and generous invoice, to your client.

At a pretrial hearing, your client can toss a copy of the room bill across the table to his wife's attorney. Then he can flip copies of the photos, one by one (very dramatic moment here), to the attorney, saying the pictures were taken of the room Mrs. Smith and Mr. Fielding shared after they checked out of the hotel. That's a true statement. It just so happens that they were taken *way* after they checked out ... a couple weeks afterward.

Sounds sneaky, you say? Not as sneaky as committing adultery and then trying to wring your spouse's wallet for all it's worth.

That combination works well and has saved my clients hundreds of thousands of dollars in alimony payments.

The Least You Need to Know

- You can use pretext telephone calls to confirm a subject's identity or other personal information.
- A good method for encouraging a subject under surveillance to leave his residence is to make him believe that something valuable has been lost on his front lawn.
- You can prove an overnight stay in a hotel by registering at the hotel, on a later date, under the name of the subject and then requesting a copy of the previous bill. Accounting will provide it with no questions asked.

In the Field

Okay, you've done your homework and you're ready to hit the street. What's your first case? In this part, I take you to the places where PIs work and teach you how to get the job done.

You learn professional tricks here, including how to locate telephone taps and install hidden video cameras. I describe, in fascinating detail, how to track down a runaway teenager, explain why you should never put "hands on" the runaway yourself, and emphasize the importance of listing every runaway with the local police. Sifting for clues of an unfaithful spouse and conducting electronic surveillance are also part of a PI's caseload. After studying these chapters, you'll be up for all the challenges PIs typically encounter, including working criminal defense cases.

Clues to Infidelity

In This Chapter

- Diagnosing infidelity
- Identifying the most common symptoms
- Gathering the evidence
- Presenting the facts

You have a runny nose and a cough, your sinuses are congested, and you feel feverish all over. What do you have? Probably the flu, right? Almost every human condition has signs or symptoms associated with it, whether it's illness, well-being, depression, or joy.

Likewise, the unfaithfulness of a spouse or partner is manifested by a number of symptoms or clues. A good private investigator is aware of these signs. In this chapter, I spell out clues that point toward cheating in a relationship.

Just as a runny nose by itself might not signal the onset of the flu, any of these clues, with the exception of the last one I tell you about in this chapter, might have another explanation. But add enough of them together, and you should be able to make a diagnosis.

Trusting Your Gut

Two weeks before Halloween, a new client, Becky, came into my office. She'd called because she "had a feeling" something was wrong in her marriage. Perhaps her husband was having an affair. She couldn't put her finger on why she felt that way; she just knew something was out of line.

It'd be impossible for me to count how many Becky stories I've heard. Some were longer, some shorter. Some involved lots of money; other times, money never came up. Some included children. Others focused on drugs, alcohol, and physical abuse. Each one is different, but if you cut to the core, they all have the same basic genetic makeup.

Some call it instinct—others might say it's intuition—that brought Becky to the realization that something was wrong. But it really wasn't instinct or intuition. It wasn't magic, either. She hadn't had her palms read or her fortune told. Becky came to see me because her subconscious recognized the symptoms of a foundering relationship, even though she couldn't consciously identify them herself.

Just like a doctor, it's a private investigator's job to be knowledgeable of these symptoms and make a correct diagnosis. If you screen out the paranoid schizophrenics that frequent my office, only twice in 20 years and hundreds upon hundreds of cases has a client's gut feeling been wrong.

If you think about it, if you've lived with another partner for 1 year, 5 years, or maybe 20 years, you know that person and his or her habits, quirks, and agendas. Your clients may not know how they're aware that their partner is cheating, but they can feel it in their gut. It's your job to analyze the situation and point out the clues. If they "feel" their spouse is cheating, 99 percent of the time, they're right.

Next, you have to prove it to them, their family members, their spouse (who will deny it to the end), and perhaps an attorney and a judge.

Behavioral Changes

Your client has lived with the same man for 15 years. All of a sudden, the husband joins a gym and starts lifting weights. He stops eating ice cream and French fries. His biceps are getting some definition. His abs aren't washboards yet, but his waistline is trimming down. He's going to live longer, and his cholesterol, triglycerides, and blood sugar levels are into a steep decline. Great. She should be pleased, right? But she still feels something's amiss. He's not paying much attention to her, so who is getting the benefit of all that exercise?

Almost all women and most men make an effort to improve their body image when a new love interest enters their life. They start—and this time stick to—a diet. The pounds melt away, and new clothes appear in the closet.

A man's behavior changes in more obvious ways than a woman's. Besides getting more fit, he works later and wears cologne every day, when before he hadn't worn it since being single. He's more aloof and less affectionate with his partner.

A woman is frequently happier because now someone is paying attention to her, telling her how attractive she is, and making her feel desirable again. She is more pleased with herself because she is trimming up and has a better self-image of her body.

Both men and women involved in extramarital affairs have blank spots in their days or evenings, periods when they don't answer the cell phone. If they do communicate during those times, they are short and curt with their speech and evasive as to their current whereabouts.

These behavioral changes don't necessarily signal a cheating partner. But keep a scorecard. Let's see what other clues we can look for.

Hang-Up Telephone Calls

Everybody receives hang-up calls. Some are rude misdialers who just hang up when they realize their mistake, without apologizing to the person on the other end. But there's also a technological reason. Telemarketing and collection firms use computers to dial your home. When you answer the telephone, the computer connects your call to the next salesperson in line. If no salesperson is available at that moment, the computer hangs up on you. Presto, a hang-up call.

> **HIDDEN HINT**
>
> In most telephone areas, it's easy for the caller to block the number from appearing on your caller ID. The person at the originating phone simply dials *67 and then the number. Your caller ID then shows up as a private call (see Chapter 7 for details). Many telemarketing and collection companies use T1 lines instead of standard phone lines. T1 lines don't have to transmit the caller identification information as landline phone companies do.

Naturally, hang-up calls or numerous out-of-area calls are not necessarily indicative of any nefarious doings on the part of your client or your client's spouse. However, as with every other symptom, they might be.

Kathy's husband taught history at the local university. When the calls first started, a female always asked for the professor. It seemed to Kathy that it was always the same student, the same voice. After she mentioned it to her husband, the student calls stopped, but the hang-up calls began.

Kathy rarely received hang-ups during the day when her husband was at the university. Usually she received them only in the evenings or on the weekends, when he might have reasonably been expected to be home. Sometimes, immediately after a hang-up, her husband went into his study or ran down to the corner store on some errand. That brings us to our next symptom: the need for privacy.

Need a Little Privacy?

Everybody needs a little alone time, but the desire for privacy may indicate a problem. The key here is the change in the behavior, not necessarily the behavior itself.

A few years ago, Samantha awoke at 2 A.M. and realized her husband wasn't by her side. They had two phone lines in their home, and she noticed that one line was being used. She assumed her son had failed to disconnect the upstairs computer from their Internet service. As she climbed the steps, she heard her husband talking in the spare bedroom. When she got to the top of the stairs, he hung up the phone.

Brian went shopping with his live-in girlfriend at the mall. They separated, each searching for something in different stores. He needed some advice from her and went back to the store where he'd left her. She was talking on her cell phone. As soon as she spotted him walking toward her, she ducked behind a rack of clothes, quickly finished her conversation, disconnected, and stuffed the phone into her coat pocket. You can bet she wasn't getting advice from her mother on choosing between the pink or the blue dress.

Sarah's husband began to take long walks alone. He'd be gone for two or three hours at a time. "I just need to be alone—time to think some things through," he'd tell her. Actually, he was hoofing it over to a girlfriend's apartment.

If your spouse hangs up the phone when you walk into the room, or goes to another room or outside where "the reception is better" to take a call, or waits until you've hung up the extension before she starts talking, or wants more time alone, you may want to see if she exhibits any of the other indicators in this chapter.

Or if your partner receives text messages while the two of you are together, reads them, and then puts the phone away with no explanation, you might chalk up one for a bit of suspicion.

Reviewing the Bills

Two major sources of bills provide dead-giveaway clues to infidelity: credit-card charges and cell phone statements.

Credit-Card Charges

Gretchen had a nagging feeling that just wouldn't go away. Her husband, Rod, a physician, attended a medical convention in Denver for a few days and then came home. Following her suspicions, Gretchen wanted to check the credit-card charges but didn't want to wait until the bill's usual arrival near the first of the next month.

She called me while her husband tended to patients at his office. After some discussion, I suggested that she boot up his computer at home and bring up his credit-card statement online. Rod used Internet Explorer as his web browser and had the AutoComplete feature turned on.

HIDDEN HINT

To find the AutoComplete option on Internet Explorer, click Tools > Internet Options > Content. The third listing under Content is Personal Information. There you'll see the AutoComplete button. Click AutoComplete and make sure User Names and Passwords on Forms is checked. Google Chrome has the same setting under Preferences > Advanced Preferences > Forms and Passwords. Safari also has it, under Preferences > Autofill.

Gretchen had an idea what his user name might be and typed in the first letter at the prompt. The rest of the name popped up, and the password, which she wasn't certain about at all, automatically inserted itself at the appropriate blank.

A few more clicks of the mouse, and there on the computer screen lay all of her husband's charges for the previous week at the Colorado medical convention. There were several charges in the $60 and $80 range from the hotel gift shop, and another from a national lingerie chain. The only gifts she had received when he had come home were some free pens bearing pharmaceutical company logos and two refrigerator magnets. There was no $80 item from the gift shop and certainly no lingerie.

In searching through credit-card charges, look for lingerie shops, sport shops, jewelry store charges, and the hotel gift shop. Large, unexplained dinner invoices or bar tabs are clues as well.

Cell Phone Calls

Most cell phone bill printouts reveal the phone numbers of dialed, completed calls and the duration of each call. These bills previously reported the phone number of incoming calls as well, but I don't know of any that do that currently, although the records are in the cell phone company's system and are retrievable. How long they keep them is anybody's guess, but you'll need a subpoena to get them.

If the spouse suspected of cheating has his own cell phone, I guarantee that he's used the phone to make calls to the alleged girlfriend (or boyfriend), if there is one.

Vicki's husband was always on the cell phone. He never turned it off, and it was always at his side. I suggested that she bring in his bill, which she had access to because he kept it at home. We went over it together. The last month's bill showed calls of 30, 40, and up to 90 minutes in length, at all times of the day and night, to a number Vicki didn't know. The bill also included a mix of shorter calls to other numbers.

We ran a reverse search on the telephone number of the lengthy calls and discovered that the number went to the residence of an office assistant he'd hired six months earlier.

You can run a reverse search on phone numbers yourself using one of the free white pages reverse searches we detailed in Chapter 5, but remember that this data is old. You might end up knocking on the wrong person's door.

If you try the telephone break methods outlined in Chapter 7 and can't come up with subscriber information, the number is probably not a listed home telephone number; it's likely another cellular number, a pager, or a nonpublished number. Check at www. phonevalidator.com and find out. It's a free search.

At the time of this printing, the wholesale price of cellular subscriber information (cell phone number break) runs about $55. This price includes only the name of the subscriber to a particular cell phone and the billing address; it does not include the phone calls made from that number. Most professional investigators double that price and charge the client $110 to $125. That is a reasonable, common practice.

LEGAL TRAP

Many clients ask you to retrieve their spouse's or partner's cell phone detailed call data. Even if you have a source for it, don't do it. You'll be in violation of the Federal Telephone Records and Privacy Protection Act of 2006.

Do not, under any circumstances, offer to obtain copies of the cell phone bills or the calling history for your client unless you have a subpoena. If you do, you may find yourself with a long-term roommate you'd rather not have.

Missing in Action

It's not unusual for persons engaged in the romance of an affair to have unaccounted time or to not be where they've told their spouse they were going to be.

Philandering doctors, male or female, frequently use the excuse of being called out on an emergency or making rounds at the hospital. They might be making the rounds, but not the kind their spouse expects. Nearly every profession has emergencies or provides its own brand of excused absences. Even private investigators are out late working surveillance or doing a *drive-by*.

DEFINITION

A **drive-by** is performed by private investigators to make a casual check of a subject's residence to see if he is home or to observe what activities are taking place at a particular location during a specific time.

Amy fulfilled her obligation to her country one weekend a month in the Naval Reserves. This required her to fly from Florida to a Midwest location. Her normal flight left on a Friday evening. Amy, being enamored with her old boyfriend, told her husband the flight left on Thursday so she could spend the night with the boyfriend before she left town.

One Thursday evening, a couple of punks broke into her van, which she'd parked on the street, and stole the stereo out of it. A passerby noticed the break-in, and the police responded. They checked the vehicle's ownership and called her home.

Imagine her husband's surprise when the police told him that their van, instead of being parked in long-term parking at the airport, had been broken into on the other side of town in front of Amy's "old" boyfriend's home. Busted.

Listen Up

An anonymous caller rings you and informs you that your spouse is having an affair with his wife. Do you believe him?

You ask your spouse directly, and he says, "No, of course not." Which one do you believe? Here are some other examples:

- Your friend tells you that your husband is cheating. Then someone from your church says she thought you had the right to know that your spouse was seen coming out of another woman's house.

- You're at your husband's office, and his secretary pulls you aside and says, "We need to talk sometime."

- Your best friend or sister says your husband came on to her or kissed her.

- You have a party at your house, and your 3-year-old asks why Daddy was kissing that lady in the hallway.

Do you believe them even though your spouse denies it? You'd better. Without exception, every one of my clients who'd been told something like that had an unfaithful spouse.

Nine out of 10 times, family, friends, or co-workers will know about it before you do. Unfortunately, most of the time they "don't want to get in the middle," "don't want to see you hurt," "don't want to be responsible for breaking up your family," and on and on and on.

If they finally gather the courage to tell you about your spouse's illicit behavior, check it against the other indicators in this chapter. What they've told you is probably true. Listen. Sooner or later, you'll have to.

THE SCOOP

Most clients still require proof, even after friends and family inform them of spousal infidelity. Their spouse will frequently deny it until the bitter end. This is the opportunity for the professional investigator to suggest surveillance on the spouse. Satisfactory photographic evidence puts your client in an emotionally superior position. Depending on the state where the divorce proceeding is filed, it could make a substantial difference in any monetary settlement.

Right to Privacy on the Spouse's Computer

I've talked about the "reasonable right to expectation of privacy" in other chapters. I have good legal opinion that, in a marital relationship, because it's so close, there's no "expectation of privacy" between spouses. One spouse is free to open the other spouse's mail, cruise through his computer, or listen in on the extension from the kitchen. Several state courts and appellate courts have ruled concerning access to a spouse's computer. If it's password protected, the line becomes slightly fuzzier. One court ruled as follows:

> And, using a Fourth Amendment analysis for purposes of analogy, one's expectation of privacy must be objectively reasonable; a person's expectation of privacy to a room used for storage and to which others have keys and access is not reasonable, and a subjective belief that the room was private is irrelevant.

> One who intentionally intrudes, physically or otherwise, upon the solitude or seclusion of another or his private affairs or concerns, is subject to liability to the other for the invasion of his privacy, if the intrusion would be highly offensive to a reasonable person.

> That turns on one's reasonable expectation of privacy. A "reasonable person" cannot conclude that an intrusion is "highly offensive" when the actor intrudes into an area in which one has either a limited or no expectation of privacy.

> The Appellate Division overruled the trial court's suppression of this evidence. Is rummaging through files in a computer hard drive any different than rummaging through files in an unlocked file cabinet? Not really.

A good PI site that has a number of different court rulings on this matter is www. dalmaninvestigations.com/id7.html. The law has many fine points, so you might want to have your attorney give his legal advice before encouraging a client to search a spouse's computer. But if it's legal in your state, doing a computer search can be a very good tool.

HIDDEN HINT

As a private investigator, your clients will tell you the most intimate parts of their lives. The tales will sometimes be bizarre and wild. Treat your clients with respect and empathy, and they will refer you to their friends and associates and help you build your business. And try not to snicker.

Diseases of the Body and the Heart

Infidelity in a relationship breaks the heart. Your client may know intellectually that her partner is unfaithful, but she finds it difficult to accept in the heart.

One sure sign of an unfaithful partner is a sexually transmitted disease (STD). Even when confronted with having acquired an STD, some clients attempt to make excuses for their spouses.

LEGAL TRAP

Medical records are considered confidential, and it is not advisable to call the doctor, pretending to be the patient, to obtain the spouse's records. Having those confidential records might backfire in court at a later time. After a divorce action has been filed, your client's attorney can subpoena the records, if necessary.

Joe had a casual affair without his wife knowing. After the affair ended, Joe began to experience symptoms of gonorrhea. He visited a urologist for treatment, and the disease left—or so he thought.

Ten days later, the symptoms reappeared. The urologist informed Joe he'd caught it again. Although he'd been treated and cured, he'd apparently infected his wife, and then she'd reinfected him. Serves him right, huh?

He dragged his wife down to the doctor's office with a story of an infected prostate. The doctor treated them both, and the symptoms were gone for good—that time.

Did she believe his story? She wanted to believe, so she did. Believing Joe was easier than facing his unfaithfulness and its consequences.

Her refusal to see all the symptoms didn't change the facts. Joe and his wife are still together. Joe still cheats on her.

THE SCOOP

The divorce laws of the United States vary from state to state. Many states are no-fault divorce states. In these states, fault isn't assigned to the divorcing parties, and the rules for property settlements and child support are set by statute. In other states, blame is laid to the party committing adultery, and generally, property settlements and alimony can be greatly affected if proof of adultery is submitted in court. Even in no-fault divorce states, some judges are more generous with alimony if adultery was shown to occur before a marital separation.

If your client has developed an STD and has been monogamous in a long-term relationship, then the client's spouse is unfaithful. And it's probably not the first time. Ask your client whether she has been suspicious on earlier occasions; the answer is almost always yes.

Counseling Your Client

With domestic relation cases of the type I talk about in this chapter, you have an obligation to your clients (or to yourself, if you're the client) to help them put together a plan of action.

THE SCOOP

A professional investigator gives a full accounting to his client of the work performed. This accounting should be in a written report prepared in a professional manner. Clients who perhaps originally don't want to pursue legal remedies may change their minds down the road. If you prepare your documents promptly and properly every time, you'll be prepared if you are called to testify in court or are subpoenaed for a deposition (see Chapter 21 for details on testifying and giving depositions).

The diagnosis of an illness has no value if you can't help with a cure. Likewise, in relationships, as a professional, once you point out the symptoms and identify the illness, you must solve the problem.

Ask clients direct questions. If you ask something general, such as what they want to accomplish, they won't have a clue. You have to guide them. Be specific: if you prove that their spouse is involved in an affair, will they divorce him? Some will say yes. Others will say no. Some will say they don't know.

Children, and the upheaval of their lives, must be taken into account. The financial repercussions of a divorce or separation are usually monumental. I counsel clients not to make a decision either way until they have all the available facts at their command.

Not to be forgotten are health considerations. I touched on those lightly in the previous section, but as we all know, life-threatening and life-altering diseases are spread through promiscuous behavior. Your client has to know and has a right to know the facts of the partner's secret life, if there is one.

At this point, explain that your client needs to know what the real facts are before she can make a decision. This is a momentous occasion in most relationships.

Most partners will not admit their infidelity. The next step is to gather enough irrefutable proof that the partner can no longer deny his action—and gather it in such a way that it is admissible in a court of law, even if, at this time your client does not intend to pursue any legal remedies.

Follow the techniques in Chapter 14, and you should get the proof your client needs.

The Least You Need to Know

- Infidelity has certain identifiable symptoms. These symptoms include changes in personal behavior.
- Two major sources of bills provide dead giveaway clues to infidelity: credit-card charges and cell phone statements.
- You can obtain tangible evidence of infidelity by examining credit-card charges, cell phone bills, emails, and surveillance photography.
- After you've identified the symptoms and gathered the supporting evidence for infidelity, help your client formulate a plan for resolving the problem.

Family Law Cases: The PI's Bread and Butter

In This Chapter

- Obtaining photographic evidence
- Dealing with child custody issues
- Walking the line between the gray and black areas
- Using GPS to track your subjects
- Revisiting the legal concept of the expectation of privacy

Some private investigators turn up their noses at family law or domestic relations cases. That's okay. Not everybody has talents in every area. Throughout this book, I recommend that you find the niche market you like best and then market the heck out of that niche. But if you do find yourself working a domestic relations case, I think you'll find some hints and tips in this chapter that can help.

How a PI Can Help

Why do we even need private investigators in family law cases? The first reason most people would think of is to catch the spouse having an affair, which can facilitate the divorce and have an impact on alimony settlements. But many states in the United States are no-fault divorce states, and adultery doesn't play a big role in alimony settlements anymore. Here are the three main ways a PI's talents and special skills can be useful in domestic cases:

- **Need to know.** If your client's spouse is having an affair, she has a right and a need to know. She cannot make decisions that will affect the rest of her life based on faulty information. She needs the facts, even if her spouse is unwilling to give them to her.

- **Child custody.** If there are custodial children from the union, your client needs to know whom the ex is associating with. Are they drug users? Would you want the alcoholic boyfriend of your ex-wife driving your children home from school?

- **Money.** In states where adultery reduces the likelihood of the adulterous party receiving any alimony, proving adultery can save your client thousands and even millions of dollars.

A Bird in the Hand

All clients want photographs. The wife who wants to catch her husband cheating can read your report. She already knows in her heart that her husband is unfaithful to her. None of that makes any difference. Remember, her husband will come up with some logical explanation of why he went to the mall, bought that watch, gave it to some lady, and followed her to a hotel.

The explanation? The lady was a client, the watch was a gift for her because she can get him a big account, and the two of them had a business lunch at the hotel. If the PI she hired says they went into a hotel room, he must be mistaken or he's lying to justify his bill. PIs are a sleazy lot anyway, and … now he gets mad at his wife for having doubts about him and wasting the mortgage money on a keyhole peeper. That's what he'll say to his wife.

Get the photograph of him and the other woman kissing, holding hands, and walking through the mall arm in arm. Your client needs to be able to throw it down on the coffee table in front of her husband when he comes up with excuses and gets defensive. "There, buster," she'll say, tossing the photograph at him. "Let me see you explain that."

The problem here for most investigators is that they're not properly prepared for that unexpected moment. When the good stuff happens—a kiss between lovers, or an insurance claimant's handstand to impress his 4-year-old child—you must be ready, camera in hand, to grab that shot. Sometimes it's the only shot you'll get, and you'll miss it if you're not ready. The lovers won't kiss again until they're behind closed doors, and the claimant's wife will remind him that he's out on disability and he'd better stop with the gymnastics. You've got to get the first piece of incriminating evidence because that might be all you ever see.

Recently, I placed a GPS on the vehicle of a client's husband. Our client, the wife, was on the title to the car and had signed our GPS contract, giving us permission for the install. (I discuss the legalities of using GPS to track subjects later in this chapter.) He was a supervisor at a county facility, and he'd admitted to previously having an affair with a co-worker whom he'd supervised, but he swore he'd broken it off. She knew better. We had the GPS set to report at five-minute intervals. Our mistake there. We should have had it set to report in every minute.

We saw him exit the employee parking garage downtown. As luck is always against us, he made it through a light and was across the bridge before we could get a green light. By the time we got across the bridge, the vehicle had stopped moving. The GPS showed it parked right in the middle of the river. We pinged the device time after time, and it still reported it in the middle of the river. That couldn't be, so my partner and I began driving the area around the riverfront. After an hour of driving through every parking garage within a half-mile, we found his car backed into a space in a hotel parking garage with four stories of concrete over it. The poor signal transmission caused it to give us the middle of the river as its location.

HIDDEN HINT

I typically recommend setting your GPS device to report in every five minutes. The longer reporting time saves battery life. A five-minute reporting time allows you to swap out the batteries once a week or every 10 days, if you want to push it. A one-minute or 10-second reporting time burns through the batteries very quickly. In some cases, though, you may need to up the reporting interval.

So we knew he was in this hotel where two conventions were taking place. I talked to the front desk, and they confirmed that someone with his name had a room booked there. We'd missed the opportunity to get the photos of them arriving and meeting in the lobby, but we still had the exit to work with. I sat in the lobby with a clear view of the elevators, cell phone camera turned and ready. I didn't want to miss this. I needed some good shots of the good-bye kiss to give to my client. I couldn't even leave my spot for a bathroom break. Eventually, they came out arm in arm. I got my first set of incriminating photos. As soon as they turned the corner, I radioed my second man and alerted him that they were on the way out.

We'd found her car in the parking garage also, and my partner was set up for the photo opportunity for the good-bye kiss. The husband walked with her halfway to her car, and they stopped in the middle of the garage and kissed for several minutes. By that time, I was back in my vehicle and shooting them with my 35mm SLR. Then they went their separate ways, back to work.

That case could have gone badly due to the glitch with the GPS, but because there were two of us, with cell phone cameras, SLR cameras, walkie-talkies, and very good bladder control, we saved the case.

This was sort of a two-fer. Not only was he in trouble with his wife, but if she were really mean-spirited, she had the proof of his liaison with a subordinate that he had direct supervisory authority over, and he probably would have been severely reprimanded by his employer. They are divorced now, and she got what she considered a very good settlement. He didn't want to haggle with her because of the possible work-related fallout. Of course, no amount of money fixed her broken heart.

THE SCOOP

I can't tell you how important it is that your firm accepts credit cards. I get at least one call a week from out of state in which a client needs something done in my area. I quote them our rate, fax or email our contract to them, and then ask how they would like to pay the retainer. They're always anxious to start, usually because the subject is traveling and they want to catch him when he's not suspicious. I tell them, fine, we'll get started as soon as we receive the retainer. My firm accepts MasterCard, Visa, American Express, and Discover. We take the necessary info over the phone, and we're off and running. Sure, I'd rather have a check or cash and not lose the processing fees. But I'd rather lose the processing fees than lose the case.

Who's Watching the Kids?

At least half of the domestic relations cases at my agency revolve around child custody issues. These issues can appear during the divorce process or maybe years later. We accept these cases, but each one makes my heart bleed. Unfortunately, they often seem to be more about control than they are about what's best for the kids.

If you're not a private investigator and want to investigate your own child custody case, you can do several things yourself. However, in the end, your attorney most likely will need to hire a PI to testify in court. The reason is that, yes, you can stake out your ex-wife's residence and get the tags on the guys who are coming over, but then what? Well, maybe you don't need the tags run. Maybe you already know who this person is. Okay, then what? So you go down to your local courthouse and run his name through the criminal records section and see that he has four arrests in the last five years for possession of narcotic equipment, burglary, and domestic violence. That's all good stuff, and you've done well.

But you need to show that he's regularly spending time at the home while your children are there. Even better, you need to show that he picks them up from school. And you also want to know the kind of work he does. So as a concerned mother or father, are you going to sit out there all night for five nights in a row to document what you need? Probably not, and you don't want to do that anyway. Why? Because when you go to court and testify to what you've seen, the judge will recognize that you have a bias in this case.

> **LEGAL TRAP**
>
> I'm amazed by how many people lie in court under oath. It happens all the time, especially in custody matters, where the plaintiff and the defendant will say whatever they need to say to gain custody of their children.

The judge recognizes a good private investigator as reporting the facts without any bias. Plus, he'll have photographs of the guy coming out of the house—maybe even some photos of him going into a bar and then going to the school to pick up the kids. A private investigator's testimony will carry far more weight in front of a judge than yours. You can get the facts, get the basics of what your attorney is going to need, and then turn it over to a PI. The more information you can obtain up front, the less work the PI will have to do, and it will save you some money.

Just a few months ago, I was retained to "get the dirt" on the ex-husband of a client I'll call Lori. The ex, Mark, had custody of their daughter and son. I don't know the details of how he had obtained custody of both children, but I expect there were reasons for that. Both Mark and Lori had a history of drug use. In doing my investigation I found that Mark, who was 25, was living with a 17-year-old girl named Charity. (Lori was 15 when she became pregnant with their first child. Mark obviously preferred his girlfriends young.) Because Mark was represented by counsel, I couldn't talk to him directly—nor did I really want to. But I did want to talk to the 17-year-old girl, Charity. Why?

> **LEGAL TRAP**
>
> It is unethical by most state law bar rules for one attorney to approach the client of the other attorney without going though the client's attorney first. As a private investigator working for an attorney, you're bound by the same ethical rules as the attorney. As tempting as it may be to approach the subject directly, don't do it if he is represented by another attorney.

Charity was now living with Mark and the two kids. Who better could tell me how he behaved with the children? Who better to tell me if he abused the kids—or her? Who better to tell me what kind of father he actually was at this time?

But I couldn't very well go up and knock on the door because Mark might answer. I can't emphasize too much how you have to think outside the box. The direct approach sometimes works, but slipping in the side door usually works better.

I had plenty of anecdotal evidence of Mark using drugs, driving drunk, and being physically aggressive. He would sometimes trim trees as a side job, and I had statements from several of his customers that he'd come over to see if they needed their trees trimmed and was so high that, after he was told no, he'd come back a half-hour later and ask them again.

Here's the side door I entered: I befriended Charity's family. I figured they must be concerned about their daughter, who had begun dating this older guy when she was 16 and now had moved in with him. Sure, Charity's entire family was dysfunctional, but that wasn't my problem. I told Charity's family that I wanted to get to Charity when Mark wasn't around. Charity's brother called me one day and told me that his sister and Mark had had a fight, and she had moved back in with her parents.

I hustled over there, and Charity, who was upset with Mark, began spilling everything about their relationship. Although those details were interesting, I wanted to know about Mark's drug usage and his interaction with the children.

She told me everything and gave me a signed statement. It was short but sweet. She said she knew "Mark shoots Roxy and morphine. The morphine he gets from his grandmother. The Roxy he gets from someone else. He shoots the drugs into his tattoos to hide the marks. He does this almost every day. I have seen Mark hit both children. He hit his son in the face and made him bleed. He'd spank the boy so hard that he had bruises on his butt."

With that statement in hand, I went to Lori and her mother, and they confirmed that, on the weekends they had visitation, the son often had bruises on his behind, but they didn't know where they were coming from.

Shortly after that, Mark was arrested for sale of prescription drugs. My attorney client called for an emergency hearing. Children and Family Services entered a motion to leave the two kids with the grandmother. I testified and presented the signed statement to the judge. As far as I know, that statement was the only negative testimony about the grandmother (remember, she provided Mark with some of his drugs). The judge awarded custody back to Lori, with some restrictions concerning regular drug testing.

HIDDEN HINT

If you can get someone to make a signed statement, do it. Ideally, you want the statement to be handwritten by the person you're interviewing. In this case, Charity wasn't available to appear in court, so I read the statement and then presented the original to the judge, who placed it in the file. I knew this was going to be an important interview and took one of my female investigators with me who was also a notary. She notarized the statement. There was no question in anyone's mind that the statement had been written by Charity and witnessed by me and the notary. For more on signed statements, see Chapter 21.

Working the Gray Areas

Family law cases are particularly prone to gray areas. Gray areas are those areas of investigative behavior that might be frowned upon by the state division of licensing but aren't actually illegal or unethical. Here's an example of a gray area: You climb a tree to look over a fence. Are you violating someone's "reasonable expectation of privacy"?

I often go into gray areas if I'm convinced in my own mind or could make a good argument in court that my behavior is legal. Private investigators are often asked to venture into black areas, like tapping someone's phone or installing spy software or keystroke logger software on a computer for a client. Don't go into the black areas. As for the gray areas? That's up to you. Be careful, though, or you might find yourself on the losing end of a civil suit or, worse, a criminal case against you. The bottom line is, if you have any doubt, don't do it.

As a professional investigator working family law cases, you will have to regularly address the types of situations I describe in the following sections.

Using GPS Trackers

Normally, I won't install a GPS tracking device on a vehicle unless my client is on the title or the registration and signs a contract with my firm. Florida is a community property state, so even if only one spouse is on the title of a vehicle, theoretically, the other spouse could give you permission to install the device. If you're working in a community property state and no statute on the books specifically governs civilian use of tracking devices, that's a gray area. I always run the tag to confirm the name on the title; sometimes my client is on the title and she didn't know it. Some states have clear-cut legislation that defines the rules of tracking device attachments; others have no statutes, and you're free to install a device.

Here's the California statute that governs use of tracking devices:

California Penal Code 637.7

(a) No person or entity in this state shall use an electronic tracking device to determine the location or movement of a person.

(b) This section shall not apply when the registered owner, lessor, or lessee of a vehicle has consented to the use of the electronic tracking device with respect to that vehicle.

(c) This section shall not apply to the lawful use of an electronic tracking device by a law enforcement agency.

(d) As used in this section, "electronic tracking device" means any device attached to a vehicle or other movable thing that reveals its location or movement by the transmission of electronic signals.

(e) A violation of this section is a misdemeanor.

(f) A violation of this section by a person, business, firm, company, association, partnership, or corporation licensed under Division 3 (commencing with Section 5000) of the Business and Professions Code shall constitute grounds for revocation of the license issued to that person, business, firm, company, association, partnership, or corporation, pursuant to the provisions that provide for the revocation of the license as set forth in Division 3 (commencing with Section 5000) of the Business and Professions Code.

The California statute is pretty clear that if your client's name is on the title, you can install the device. Florida has no statute that governs the civilian use of tracking devices at the time of this writing. That may change. Stay abreast of the laws in your state.

I recently had a client who was in the middle of a divorce. Her soon-to-be ex-husband was a contractor and refused to pay the child support he had agreed to in an arbitration hearing, saying he wasn't making any money and couldn't afford it. The divorce wasn't final, so even though the truck he drove was in his name only, paid for by his brother, my opinion was that the client still owned 50 percent of the truck because Florida is a community property state. I installed the device to locate his job sites. Then, after he moved from one job site to the next, I interviewed the homeowners on a pretext to determine the dollar value of the job. Normally, I would have just pulled the building permits, but this guy was sleazy and wasn't pulling permits.

In short order, I had a good spreadsheet with hundreds of thousands of dollars' worth of jobs on it. I also had photographs of the job sites, many of which had his yard sign in the front yard. When the case went to court, the judge reviewed my firm's work and then ordered the client's soon-to-be ex to come back one week from that date and to bring a check with him for the past-due support. He told the subject that if he didn't have a check with him the following week, "Don't leave a dog in your truck. Don't bring a friend who needs a ride home, because you will be going straight to jail."

Now, I think I did the right thing, even though that was sort of a gray area, since our client wasn't on the title. Because it was gray, I was careful to prep my client, and her attorney, not to discuss or disclose anything about the use of a tracking device.

Hidden Cameras and Expectation of Privacy

Information obtained from hidden surveillance cameras can be used in a variety of places, including the courtroom, as long as you follow ethical and legal standards when recording the subject.

The basic rule of thumb for the placing of covert or hidden cameras is this: Don't use them when a person has a reasonable expectation of privacy. My firm will not place cameras in bedrooms or bathrooms, where persons other than the client himself might be caught on tape. Obviously, if we're going to catch an underwear thief, the camera has to be in the bedroom. But we don't turn on the camera while that client is home. Again, in commercial buildings, we won't place cameras in restrooms. Somebody else might, but we won't, because most people would have an expectation of privacy there.

THE SCOOP

The U.S. postal inspectors used to have cameras and peepholes in the employee restrooms at the post offices. Postal employees would sometimes steal items from the mail and retreat to the employee restrooms, where they could close the door, open the package in secret (they thought), remove the valuables, and hide them on their own person before returning to work. At least, that was the alleged reason the postal inspectors said they needed to see what happened in the restrooms. Finally, the inspectors were forced to close the peepholes and remove the cameras to ensure privacy in the restrooms.

Suzanne was facing a divorce. Her husband was the son of a prominent businessman. The husband's family owned a professional sports franchise in the western United States, and her husband helped manage the business. The soon-to-be ex-husband smoked marijuana heavily. This habit wore on the marriage until, finally, Suzanne had enough of it. Obviously, his drug usage could prove embarrassing to the family because the team's management subjects the players to regular drug testing. It wouldn't look good for management to be hypocritical in the area of zero drug tolerance.

Proving her husband's drug usage would be difficult in court without some corroborating evidence. Otherwise, it would just be her testimony against his. Obviously, she expected him to deny the drug allegations. Who wouldn't? She didn't really want to create problems for him and the family, and she recognized that it was also in her best interest for the sports franchise to continue to thrive. After all, her future alimony payments would depend upon it. Basically, she wanted to extract a fair settlement from the husband without damaging his reputation and the business.

Suzanne showed me her husband's stash of marijuana. He really had quite a bit. Multiple mason jars of it were hidden in different places throughout the house and in the garage. He certainly had more than enough to be arrested for possession with intent to distribute (that usually takes a little more than 20 grams). She swore that he did not sell it, but only had it for his personal use.

This presented me with an ethical quandary, the gray area. Private investigators frequently find themselves in situations that make them privy to what might be illegal activity. To some, it may appear black and white, and they call the police immediately to report the illegal possession of marijuana.

On the other hand, the very key to the nature of private investigations is the fact that it is *private*. PIs are not officers of the court, nor are they sworn law enforcement personnel. Clients usually call on private investigators because the issues involved are civil in nature instead of criminal. Or if it is a borderline civil/criminal issue, the client doesn't want to involve law enforcement. Just as often, the local law enforcement officials refuse to become involved, even though they've been invited into the case (such as runaway teenagers, parental kidnappings, a partner in a business who's violating his noncompete agreement, an employee who's sleeping with a competitor and giving away company secrets, or members of a firm who are stealing company products). Banks, law firms, and high-profile local companies are particularly hesitant to involve law enforcement—and, hence, the media—in embezzlements or other high-ranking employee dishonesty matters in which the institution's reputation might be tarnished. They'd much rather prove to their own satisfaction that the transgression took place and quietly have the guilty party leave the company.

Each private investigator has to address this type of situation with his own conscience, subject to his own standards, and draw the line where he will. A good private investigator uses discretion, tact, and an experienced hand. In Suzanne's case, we agreed to help her without involving any law enforcement.

I placed a *pinhole-lens* camera in an air duct located in the study where her husband smoked his marijuana. He usually smoked when she was not in the house because he knew she disapproved. She had unfettered access to the study, so we reasoned that he could expect she might walk in on him, unannounced, at anytime; he really had no reasonable expectation of complete privacy. I transmitted the video signal to a DVR recorder concealed in an attic crawl space.

> **DEFINITION**
>
> A **pinhole-lens** is a lens on a closed circuit video camera that, when installed in a ceiling or behind an air duct grate, isn't seen by the casual observer. Typically, they're smaller than the holes in drop-down ceiling tiles.

Every two or three days, one of my investigator interns reviewed the video. At the end of a two-week period, I had a dozen instances of the husband rolling, lighting, and smoking joints while seated in his favorite chair. I made a composite copy with all the smoking sequences on it. My client received a generous alimony settlement shortly thereafter.

Some people might say that Suzanne blackmailed or extorted her soon-to-be ex-husband. This might sound cold, but I've worked this business too long to be bothered by such accusations. The reality of divorce is that it involves emotional blackmail, extortion, exposure of illicit acts, and the fostering of guilt on the part of both parties. In this case, I just documented the facts. That is our job as private investigators. How the documented truths of a person's actions are later used in negotiations is beyond the control of the private investigator.

You've read this before in this book, and you'll read it at least one more time before you turn the last page: the private investigator's job is to get the facts and reveal the truth to her client. Then she has to let the chips fall where they may.

The Ex, the Children, and the Boyfriend

Roger had an ex-wife, Shelly. He also had three children with Shelly: one son, 18, and two daughters, ages 13 and 16. Roger had moved out of state and remarried. As is often the case in family law cases, emotions run high and control becomes the paramount issue in the relationship instead of what is necessarily best for the children. Roger faithfully paid his child support and alimony obligations. But since he'd remarried, Shelly had lost some of that control that she used to exert over him.

Roger wanted more liberal visitation with his two daughters and wanted them to visit for the summer. Shelly's life had not stood still, either. She had an alcoholic boyfriend who lived with her and the kids. Roger wanted proof of the relationship to use, yep, you guessed it, to pressure her to allow the children to visit him. The fact that the boyfriend was living there might have been enough in some states to cancel Roger's alimony obligations. He wasn't interested in hurting Shelly financially; that would have also hurt the children. But the threat of the loss of alimony and the legal costs to Shelly would be enough to force her to agree to the visitation. Roger was also concerned about his two daughters living in that environment, but I'm not sure he wanted full custody of the children. But as long as we were working the case, he would like documentation that the boyfriend regularly, on his suspended license, drove the two girls to dance class on Wednesday afternoons and drove himself to and from work.

Shelly, the kids, and the boyfriend lived in what used to be the marital home, in a very exclusive gated community with no parking on the streets. Security guards patrolled the streets regularly. My firm was lucky to have several previous clients who lived in the same community, and they were glad to put me and the other PIs on the case on their visitor's list.

First to the alcoholism. The boyfriend, Greg, was 45 and had a bit of a checkered past. Yep, we checked his driving history, and his driver's license had been suspended for a DUI. That hadn't kept Greg from driving, though. He had a sales job in a large department store. He also had some disorderly intoxication charges, misdemeanors, which he had been charged with but were eventually dismissed.

To document that a boyfriend or girlfriend is living in the home with your client's ex and the children, you don't have to spend all night out in front of the residence watching for someone to enter at night and leave in the morning. What has worked for us every time we've presented this sort of evidence in court is to drive by the house while the lights are still on in the house and the boyfriend's car is parked in the driveway. Or follow him from work to the residence, and photograph him parking and entering the house. Then go back later and hang around until the lights are all off in the residence and the car is still there. Don't forget to set your camera so that it stamps your photographs with a time and date. (I recommend using a 35mm camera rather than a video camera for this.) You'll need a good low-light lens and camera. A reasonable person—and judges are reasonable—will assume that the man is in the house and has gone to bed. Then go to bed yourself.

The next morning, be at the residence by 5:30 A.M. Photographically document that the vehicle is still there and also document the time the lights come on in the house or you first see movement in the residence. If the ex-wife leaves first, that's okay. It's good to hang around at least one day, to show the subject exiting to his vehicle. About four nights and mornings of that, showing a regular routine, is all it takes.

For some reason, this subject had taken the license plate off our client's 16-year-old daughter's car and put it on his. Probably because his license was suspended, he couldn't get his tag renewed and he wanted the plates on his car so that he wouldn't get pulled over for having expired (or no) plates. We documented her tag on his car and followed him home from work one night. Yep, he stopped at a popular restaurant about 10:30 P.M. and sat at the bar for a few drinks before he drove himself the rest of the way home. I reported that to our client, who was totally incensed.

The subject had been a professional athlete at one time in his younger days and worked in a specialized portion of a sporting goods department that dealt with that sport. The next day, when I knew he wasn't at work, I went into the department and asked for him. Why? Did I really want to speak with him? Heck no. I didn't want him to know that I even existed. You can almost always get the information you need—you just have to be clever in devising a pretext that seems very reasonable to the person you present it to. What I wanted was his work schedule. The manager obliged and told me his schedule for the next two days so that I could come back and confer with him about my specialized sport needs when he was on the job.

I knew he would be off work at 9:30 that evening. At 8:30 that evening, I went to the parking lot and found his car with the wrong tag on it. Often a sheriff's substation is located in shopping malls, and in this case, a number of sheriff's deputies were parked together for their shift change instructions.

I approached the deputies and explained that I knew this fellow would be coming out that door, getting into that car, and driving off on a license that had been suspended for DUI. One of the deputies agreed to assist, and when the subject came out and drove off, a minute later, there was a flash of blue lights. Shortly afterward, the subject was arrested. He was hauled down to the county jail for the night.

> **HIDDEN HINT**
>
> When working domestic relations cases, ask for a retainer. Always, always, always get your money up front. Work the case until you're close to reaching the limit of the retainer, and then call the client and ask for more money. It's a lot easier to get money from the client in the beginning and middle of the case than it is at the conclusion—especially if the case goes badly.

Did I do the right thing? I knew that a violation of the law was about to occur, and I reported it to the authorities. I felt a little awkward doing that, but suppose he had driven to his favorite bar, as I'd seem him do the night before. What if he'd had a few drinks and then clobbered and killed someone in a DUI accident? Who would be to blame then?

Roger got his daughters for the summer, and Shelly is still living with this man.

The Least You Need to Know

- Family law cases are a mainstay for private investigators. You will testify in court more often in these cases than any others you work.

- You must have good photographic evidence. Your testimony is important and will be considered by the judge, but a photograph is better and is hard to rebut in court or in the client's living room.

- Know your state laws regarding community property and whether adultery is a direct bar to alimony in your state.

- Laws that govern use of GPS tracking devices vary by state. Typically, the law that applies to law enforcement doesn't apply in civil cases. Some states allow wide open use of tracking devices; some require the title holder's permission. Know your state law before you apply the device.

- Often family law cases might also involve criminal infractions. You may or may not decide to report the infractions to law enforcement.

Bringing Home Runaway Teenagers

In This Chapter

- Dealing with the police department
- Registering the runaway in the National Crime Information Center database
- Tracking down the teen
- Making other kids' parents your ally
- Using credit cards and cell phones to track the teen's moves

The wall clock reads 2 A.M., and your 15-year-old daughter, Lauren, isn't home. Acid churns in your stomach. One moment you're mad as hell at her for not being there; the next instant, you're close to tears worrying about your baby girl.

You're afraid to call the parents of any of her friends because you don't want to wake them up at such an awful time in the morning, plus you're feeling a little ashamed. As a parent, you should have better control over your teenager, shouldn't you? Boy, are you ever going to give it to her when she gets home. No dating until she's 21. No telephone for two years, and she can forget about ever, ever having a car.

You've dozed off in the chair for a little while. The first light of the day is creeping through the blinds. The clock reads 5 A.M. Now you know for certain that the reason she's not home is more than just a flat tire or an empty gas tank. In Lauren's room, you notice her makeup bag is gone. But she carries that in her purse, no big deal. You can't tell whether any clothes are missing, since she and her girlfriends trade clothes like they own a consignment clothing store. You don't know how they keep track of who bought what.

At 6 A.M., the phone rings. You lunge for it. It's Missy, a good friend of Lauren's. Missy is calling to relay a message. Lauren just called her and asked her to tell you that she's alright and not to worry. Don't call the police, though, because she's old enough to be on her own. Lauren doesn't want to live at home anymore. She's tired of you making her go to school. She doesn't like school, and school doesn't like her. She'll call you when she gets settled someplace. She has a few dollars, and she'll be okay. Not to worry.

Yeah, right.

Evaluating the Situation

If the evidence is clear that your client's teenager has run away and hasn't been abducted, the next step is to collect the facts at hand and make some hard decisions. Find out from your client why she ran away. Be probative in your questions and observant of your surroundings. You're not going to get the real answer at the beginning. Down the road, when you've located the missing girl and are ready to have her picked up, you have to be convinced that her home environment is better than whatever alternatives exist. Although your contractual obligation is to your client, your moral obligation is to the child.

Is this the first time she has run away? When I get calls from clients about a runaway teenager, almost invariably, it's not the first time the child has left for parts unknown. It's just the first time the parents haven't been able to find her.

Here are 10 things to do to get started and move the investigation along. For the questions, write the answers on a piece of paper. Gather the other materials. If you're the parent, you'll want to have this information handy when you go to the police or a private investigator. If you're the investigator, I tell you how you can use it later in the chapter:

- Find the most recent picture you have of her.

- What was she wearing when she left? Runaways don't change clothes very often, and she'll probably be wearing the same thing for several days.

- Does she have any tattoos, piercings, or other identifying marks?

- Where did she run to before?

- Is the same boy or friend involved? Get his or her address and phone number.

- How did she make her escape? Chances are, somebody drove a car and waited for her down the street. If you find the driver, you'll find the teenager.

- If she has a car and it is gone, write down a description of the car and the license plate number.

- Does she have a cell phone? What is the number? Did she take it with her? Get the last month's bill for her cell phone.

- Does she have credit cards or ATM cards with her? What banks do they draw on? Write down the account numbers.

- List all her friends, even if there are 50. Include their names, telephone numbers, and addresses. If you don't know their addresses and complete names, write down their first names and who else might know the rest of the name, and record how to contact them.

Next, make sure your client has caller ID on the phone lines. If not, call the telephone company and have it installed immediately. Usually, it takes only 30 minutes for the telephone company to add it to a service. Send somebody down to the store to buy a caller ID unit. When she calls home, she'll probably block the call, but if she knows that her parents don't have caller ID, she might not think to block it.

Handling the Police Department

I always recommend reporting the runaway to your local police or sheriff's office as a runaway/missing person. The reality is, thousands of teenagers run away from home every year. Unless there is some sign of physical abduction, your local police department has bigger fish to fry than to look for your wayward daughter, so don't expect much help from them until you've done the legwork and located her. However, it is still very important that you report her missing. I'm not talking about arresting your child—just having her picked up and transported home.

Reporting a child missing to the police accomplishes three things:

- When the kid is picked up someplace for loitering or is stopped for whatever reason and she is identified, the agency that stopped her will hold her, usually in a juvenile facility if it's in another city, until you can make arrangements to retrieve her.

- A timely reporting of the disappearance of the child shows that you are a caring and concerned parent. You'll have a lot less trouble with the police and the juvenile authorities if you've reported the child missing right away. If you wait three days before reporting it and she is finally picked up, you might have some explaining to do to the state family services department before they let her come home.

- Although your child will huff and puff and pretend to be incensed that you've involved the police, she will secretly be pleased that you wanted her back. Imagine how she will feel if she finds out she was gone for three whole days before you finally got around to reporting her missing. You think she'll want to stick around after that?

The police can give your child's name, date of birth, and description to the NCIC (National Crime Information Center) as a runaway or missing person—and you need to insist that they do this. Be sure to include any tattoos or other identifying marks. When kids are picked up by the police, they often deny their identity. A good description of a tattoo, especially one with a name or word on it, is very helpful to the patrolman on the street if he thinks he has a runaway.

If your child is placed into the NCIC system and she is picked up by police anywhere in the country, they will run her name through NCIC system. When they see that she's listed as a runaway/missing person, you'll get a phone call from the police department saying they have your daughter.

Unless you live in a small community, the police probably won't come to your residence to take a runaway child report. They may assign the case to an officer who handles juvenile offender cases. Find out who this person is, and write down name and contact numbers. If they don't have an officer who works juveniles, ask whom you can talk to in the future. You want to make additional contact with this person if the child is not found within 48 hours.

Police departments and juvenile workers will interview a runaway teenager before releasing her to the custody of her parents or guardian. They have a responsibility to make sure they are not returning the child to a harmful environment. If she makes allegations of physical or sexual abuse from her parents, stepparents, or another person in the home, even if it's totally false, a whole can of worms is opened. It's not unusual for a teenage girl to make false accusations against her parents. Be prepared for it. This is her defense mechanism and a way to hurt her parents. And it works very well.

Most runaway teenagers either return by their own choice or, if entered into the NCIC, are picked up and returned to their parents (or reach some sort of accommodation with their parents) within 48 hours.

The bottom line with police departments in midsize to large cities: don't expect any real investigation to happen based simply on the runaway report. If you know where the child is located at a given moment, you can call the police, and they will send a squad car to pick her up and return her to your home. Other than that, you're basically on your own in tracking her down. That's another good reason to keep this book handy—it'll help when the cops can't.

THE SCOOP

If your teenager is a good kid and a reasonable student, and gets involved in some illegal activity, don't call the police unless you absolutely have to. Having your child arrested and subjected to our criminal justice system is one of the worst things you can do to your teenager. I know that runs counter to what some say, but having been involved in this business for 30-some years, trust me: I'd do everything necessary to keep my child out of our jails and court system. The only time I'd consider having my child arrested would be if jail were a safer place than where he is now. If your child is endangering himself or others, give up your rights as a parent and have him arrested. Otherwise, handle the problem yourself. Some well-intentioned fathers say that a night in jail will be good for the kid. They're wrong. Once you put a child in that system, you lose control of the situation. You've abdicated your rights as parents and turned over those rights and responsibilities to society. Jails are nothing more than a school where delinquents can learn to be better delinquents.

Tracking 'Em Down

In the rest of this chapter, I go into the nuts and bolts of actually "running to ground" a missing teenager. I'm going to assume that you have unlimited financial resources. I know you don't, but I lay out here all the things you can do. Most of them don't require much in the way of money anyway. You can pick and choose what you can afford to do and decide for yourself where the action might fall on the cost-benefit curve.

People, even teenagers, are creatures of habit. If she's run away before, she might use the same support apparatus that she used last time. How did she make her escape last time? Contact whomever drove her away before or whomever she stayed with before. That's the first place to look. If she used a boy before and he is long out of the picture, don't discount him. Even if he hasn't had any contact with her for a while, if he's in the area, he'll know whom your daughter has the hots for and who has the hots for her. Maybe it's a boy she doesn't even like, but she'll use him as a vehicle to get away. The old boyfriend will likely know who that might be.

If she was missing overnight before, who put her up? She stayed somewhere with somebody, and she just might be there again. You have to be a little sneaky here. I wouldn't just call and ask for her—even teenagers have more street smarts than to fall for that. If you trust the parents, you might call them at work. Keep in mind that your daughter might be hiding in the house, and the adults might not even know it. Teenagers stick up for each other, so when those parents ask their children, they might lie to "protect" your daughter.

You have two options in this case: ask the parents to search their home after work and look for any signs that your daughter may have been there, or set up surveillance on the house or apartment and see if she shows up.

My client Ralph finally called me after his son, Jimmy, had been gone for three days. This was the second time I'd worked this runaway in two years. Jimmy was a big 14-year-old. He was bigger than his father and as tall as I was, and he'd kept me pretty busy.

I had his father make the list we talked about earlier in this chapter. In going over the list of friends, we evaluated the lifestyle in each kid's home. Remember, kids will hide each other and protect each other from their own parents. In a runaway situation, all adults are the enemy. One friend popped out. This friend had figured prominently in the previous escape. He lived in an apartment complex with his single mother. The mother worked during the day, so the kids were free to come and go as they pleased.

We thought this living arrangement might provide an opportunity for Jimmy to have a place to hide out during the day without any adult supervision. We had listed Jimmy as a runaway with the local sheriff's office, and we confirmed that his name had been placed into the NCIC.

I tried to make contact with the *courtesy officer* at the apartments, but he was working on duty at the moment. I didn't want to contact the management of the apartments and create any grief for the friend's mother. Single working mothers have it hard enough, and my intention is almost always to try to calm situations down, not inflame them.

DEFINITION

A **courtesy officer** is usually a local police patrol person or sheriff's deputy that is given some sort of discount in his rent at an apartment complex in exchange for parking a marked patrol unit on the grounds and handling disturbance complaints at the complex when he is present. This is usually considered a good deal for both the apartment management and the law enforcement department because it reduces crime and does not increase law enforcement costs.

In working surveillance at an apartment complex, it is normally a good idea to make contact with the courtesy officer, if there is one. Because apartment complexes have so many people coming and going, you can hide for several hours and usually the tenants won't be concerned over your presence when they do see you in the parking lot. However, employees of the apartment complex may notice you and will contact the courtesy officer to have you checked out. If you've already spoken with him, you can head off a confrontation and he'll tell management that you're okay.

We set up surveillance on the apartment where the friend lived. We saw a number of kids coming and going, and I felt it would be beneficial to have another investigator onsite so we could follow some of these other kids—they just might lead us to Jimmy. The client approved the second surveillance man. A few minutes after my second man arrived, a green Volvo showed up at the apartment. Jimmy hopped out of the back seat and ran into the building. In a few moments, he was back and into the Volvo. It left the complex, and we followed.

Jimmy's father had told me that Jimmy was using marijuana, and he hoped that when we had Jimmy picked up, we would find marijuana on him. He wanted Jimmy to spend a week or two in a juvenile detoxification center.

We followed the Volvo around the beach area until it finally returned to the apartment. The car left a few minutes later, but Jimmy remained in the apartment. At that point, since we had Jimmy located and he was not on the move, we contacted the local sheriff's office. About this same time, the friend's mother came home from work. In a while, the courtesy officer showed up and we explained what was happening.

We followed the courtesy officer to the apartment, where we found Jimmy hiding underneath a bed. The mother didn't know he was there. Jimmy didn't have any marijuana in his possession, so the sheriff's office would not transport him to the detox center. The clients arrived and, with them in the front seat and myself and my other investigator on either side of Jimmy in the back seat, we took him to the detox center, where he spent the next two weeks.

Checking Out the Ex

Some divorces are friendly, and some are not. With child custody thrown into the mix, divorces can get downright nasty. If your client has custody of the runaway and an ex-spouse is in the picture, take a good look at the relationship. If the ex is talking and being helpful with your client, the kid probably isn't there. But if there's animosity between the two parents, the ex-spouse may be hiding the child from the custodial parent.

Remember, all the ex is hearing is the nasty stuff coming from the teenager detailing the mistreatment and unfairness of living with the custodial parent. Perhaps the ex doesn't have the true picture, or if he does, he may be using this to cause some grief for your client. Childish, I know, but so is most of the bickering that goes on during and after divorces. Makes you wonder who the adults really are in this world.

In Jimmy's case, the third time he ran away, he was 16. That time he hid out at his mom's place for a while. The dad, meanwhile, was spending big bucks with my firm trying to find him. Making her ex (my client) spend money unnecessarily was part of her retribution plan.

We actually never found Jimmy at the ex's place, even though we did stake it out that time. We talked to the maid who worked there, and she told us the ex was expecting Jimmy to show up. She'd left instructions with the maid to let him use the guest bedroom when he arrived.

Be sure to consider that a runaway teenager might try to get to the ex's residence. If it is out of state or some distance away, that makes it even more attractive to the kid. In her mind, the more distance she can put between herself and "the problem," the better.

Likewise, if your client has a troubled relationship with any other of his own children, especially older siblings of the runaway who are already living independently, be sure to consider them as possible hosts for the teenager. The siblings might harbor the runaway and not tell their parents for a while; it all depends on the fundamentals involved in the relationships.

Rely on Other Parents

With all the missing and runaway teenage cases I've worked, I've almost always gotten good cooperation talking to parents of other children. Parents seem to stick together in this type of case. Parents of teenagers seem to have this "us against them" mentality, just like their offspring.

When Jimmy was 17, he ran off for the fourth time. This time we thought he'd taken off with a bunch of other kids his age for a skateboarding tournament on the west coast of Florida. The young men and women who worked at a local surf shop verified that he'd been in there earlier in the day, identified his picture, and told us that the boys were talking about who got the bed in the motel room and who had to sleep on the floor.

We tracked down the mother of a member of that group of boys. She worked as an early-morning waitress in a local breakfast eatery. I called on her at work the next morning, and she confirmed that her sons were headed to St. Petersburg, Florida, to participate in the tournament. She didn't know where they were staying but the kids had promised to call her when they found a room. She, in turn, promised to call us when she found out the motel and room number. That is just an example of the kind of cooperation you can expect from other parents.

As it happened, our client flew myself and another of my investigators to St. Petersburg that same day to try to intercept Jimmy at the skateboard rink. Again, we received good cooperation from the management at the arena after we promised them no trouble. Jimmy's friend, who was actually entered in the tournament, wasn't scheduled to skate until late afternoon.

When we arrived in St. Petersburg, I coordinated with the local sheriff's office, and they confirmed that Jimmy was listed in the NCIC as a runaway. They agreed to pick him up once we had him located and identified. See the value of making sure the child is listed in the NCIC? Wherever you go after he's in the NCIC, you will, to some degree at least, get local cooperation.

The waitress mom, true to her word, called me later that evening and told me which motel the kids were staying in. Parents of other teenagers are usually willing to help in runaway cases. Don't hesitate to be honest with them and inform them of the case you're working on; you might get unexpected assistance. And who knows? As a PI, you might end up getting a new customer when it's her turn to deal with a runaway child.

While we were waiting for Jimmy and his friends to make an appearance, the Daytona Beach Police Department called and said they'd picked him up in Daytona. Apparently, he wasn't in St. Petersburg at all. He'd had a change of heart, and instead of going to the skateboarding championship, he'd decided to catch a ride to Daytona with another friend.

My investigator and I hopped back on the plane and flew across the state to Daytona. Eventually, the Daytona authorities released him to us, and we returned him to his parents. How long do you think he stayed at home that time? Less than a week. I wasn't uncomfortable taking custody of him because there were two of us, a male and a female. It was unlikely he'd try to accuse us of anything in that situation.

LEGAL TRAP

Never pick up a runaway teenager if you're by yourself. Remember, PIs are not law enforcement and generally don't have the right to use force except as an ordinary citizen would in defense of himself or others. Also, unless you have a contract with the client/guardian that gives you temporary guardianship rights, you don't have parental rights, either. You don't want the client suing you later when the teenager, especially a female, alleges that you hurt or abused her. The runaway isn't going to be happy about being found, and she may lie about your actions as a form of revenge. It is best to ensure that she is listed as a runaway in the NCIC and then have the local police department pick her up.

If I were the parent of a runaway, I wouldn't pick up my own child, either. Suppose I go to a house where I know she is staying, and three 20-year-old males greet me at the front door holding baseball bats as they inform me that she's not coming home. What do I do? It's best to have the police make the actual pick-up and avoid any confrontations yourself.

Plaster the Country with Photographs

The fifth time Jimmy ran off, he was still 17 and not too far away from his 18th birthday. We didn't know for sure whether he had headed north or south. We did know that he was traveling with a guy who was about 22 years old, whom we were able to identify. He was from a town in New Jersey and had been involved in selling marijuana in the beach areas of northern Florida.

I prepared a one-page report on Jimmy, including his description, tattoos, the fact that he was a juvenile, and the name of the person we thought he was traveling with. I included five copies of Jimmy's picture plus a disc with his picture on it in *JPEG* and *GIF* formats. I first called the police department in the New Jersey town where the parents of Jimmy's friend lived. I asked for the name of the officer who worked juvenile and runaway matters. I then directed the letter and photographs to his attention. I did the same thing when we heard rumors that he was in Daytona and then again in West Palm Beach, Florida. It's amazing the different levels of cooperation I received.

DEFINITION

JPEG (pronounced J-peg) and **GIF** (pronounced the way it looks) are two common digital formats for graphic files such as photographs. If photographs are going to be transmitted to a police agency or another investigator electronically or via a compact disc, it is best to save them in either JPEG or GIF format because most computer photo programs can open and work with those formats. Other formats are not as common, and the police department might not be able to open and print the photograph.

In New Jersey, where I expected the least amount of cooperation, the police staked out the residence of the friend for a week and kept a close eye on the neighborhood for a long time after that. They called me every few days with an update.

In Daytona, they shrugged their shoulders and basically said, "So what?"

In West Palm Beach, we had a list of pay phones that his girlfriend was calling. Jimmy would call her from a pay phone and give her the number he was calling from, and she would turn around and call him right back at that pay phone, using her cell phone.

Since the girlfriend had the pay phone numbers Jimmy was calling from, it wasn't too difficult for us to get them.

We tracked down the location of the pay phones he was using and marked each one on a map. They were all within a three-block radius. (See Chapter 7 for a discussion of how to find the location of pay phones in this type of case.)

With the letter and photographs, I also sent to the West Palm Beach Police Department the list of pay phones he was using and their locations. They agreed to keep an eye on the phones for us. If our client had really wanted the boy back, we could have staked out the phones ourselves, and in a few days we would have found him and had him picked up.

I think our client was about ready to give up trying to force his son to stay in school or to lead a productive life. If the police found him, fine. Otherwise, he'd just let him turn 18, and then there was nothing he could do anyway. And that's exactly what happened. Interestingly, after he turned 18, Jimmy came home all by himself. Figures, huh? I was half expecting to get a call from Jimmy, saying that, the day after he'd come home, his dad had run away, and asking whether I could find him.

Checking the Credit

If the runaway teen has a credit card or an ATM card that belongs to the parents or for which the parents cosigned, the parents should be able to have nearly immediate access to the usage information.

HIDDEN HINT

A word of warning: some parents are tempted to cancel the credit cards immediately, but unless it's a serious money factor, you should advise your client against that. Credit-card charges can provide good leads to finding the runaway. If the child is under the influence of someone much older, he'll probably max out the card pretty fast—the person of influence will take the cash or goods. If the card has a high credit limit, you'll want to lower it ASAP. You have to balance the financial cost with the quality of the information you're receiving concerning your child's current whereabouts. There are no cut-and-dried answers on that one.

You can check the usage of most credit cards online. Most credit-card websites update daily. Depending on how a transaction occurs, however, it might not post until several days after the transaction. You can try talking to the credit-card company to see if they can tell you when authorizations on the card are received. Usually those are all done electronically, and the company itself might not know where the authorization comes from until the charge actually posts. In serious kidnapping matters, it's a different story. The information is there, but getting it out of the credit-card company depends on the stakes.

ATM transactions, even on an ATM machine that's not part of the bank network, usually put a hold on the account almost immediately for the sum withdrawn and post the same night that the transaction takes place. The client's bank should be able to tell which machine was used for the transaction as soon as the hold is placed. With that information in hand, you might be only hours away from the teen. Hours can transform into hundreds of miles, but then again, you might get a handle on the child's direction of travel. Many ATMs have video surveillance cameras. You should liaison with the bank security folks to get photos from the surveillance tapes. You might also get lucky and obtain a photograph of anyone the runaway is traveling with. That person might be easier to track than the runaway. I've had good luck getting the banks to make available photos from their surveillance cameras. If you don't ask, you won't get it.

Tracking the Cell Phone

In the previous edition of this book, I talked about obtaining cell phone records. The legality of this practice has come into question, so I no longer acquire those unless I have the subscriber's permission or a subpoena. There is an aspect to cellular usage that is more immediate than the monthly statements. Each cell phone has its own electronic serial number (ESN). When a cell phone is in the "on" position, it periodically broadcasts this ESN. This is how the cellular company knows where to route a call when one is received for any particular cell phone customer. The company computers keep track of where all the active cell phones are at any given minute.

THE SCOOP

When a cell or telephone bill has dropped, it means that the billing cycle has ended and the charges are en route to the consumer. Usually even the customer cannot access the list of phone charges until the bill has entered the billing system's computer. With enough pressure, in exigent circumstances such as a runaway situation, you might get the cellular company to give you the calls daily as they're made.

Under the right circumstances, a cellular company might be convinced to alert you when the teen's cell phone is turned on. Again, it will take some pressure—and perhaps even some law enforcement intervention—to get the cell company to do this, but it's worth it. Why? Because when the cell company picks up the ESN signal, its computers will know that it's coming from a specific cellular site. This pinpoints the location to an area of no more than a few square miles or, in a downtown area, within a few blocks. Today almost all teens have cell phones. With GPS-enabled phones, parental cooperation, and law enforcement involvement, you should be able to pin-point exactly where the teenager's phone is when it's turned on.

No other case likely carries with it so much emotion as a missing child or teenager. Some of us wish our teenagers were missing more often. (Just kidding.) More than one mother has said that she wouldn't sell her teenager for a million dollars, but some days she would flat out give her away.

Except for the mother in the preceding paragraph, usually the parent of the missing youth has emotions that run the gamut from worry, to fear, to anger, to hurt, to frustration, to desperation, and, finally, to resignation.

When dealing with these clients, be sensitive to their needs. Keep the welfare of the child uppermost. Don't make promises you can't keep. Be the calming influence, the face of reason, and the beacon of hope.

In one of my cases, a 15-year-old female had run off. She'd been living with her mother and stepfather. She'd had an argument with her mother, and a half hour later, she was gone. The next day, the mother seemed unconcerned, but the stepfather called us. He knew that the girl, Mary, had been dating a guy, Frank, who was 20 years old. She'd also dated one of Frank's friends, who was 19. Both Frank and his friend lived in their respective parents' homes.

The stepfather didn't know the boys' last names but had gotten their parents' home numbers off the caller ID on the phone. We suggested that he call her in to the local sheriff's office as a runaway to make sure she was in the NCIC system. He did that, and a deputy was dispatched to his residence to take the report. There was some question regarding why the mother wasn't reporting her missing and he was. But all he knew was that the mother and daughter had had some sort of argument.

I got to work right away and, in short order, spoke with the boyfriend's parents. Both sets of parents said they hadn't seen their sons in three days. But Frank's mother knew that her son was staying at a local low-rent motel and gave us the name and street corner. The motel clerk would not confirm that the boys were there but did confirm that there were two boys and a girl in one room.

I called the sheriff's office and waited. In about an hour, a deputy showed up and we went through what we had. He checked NCIC, and she was listed as a runaway. He spoke with the clerk, got the room number, and went up. In a few minutes, he had the girl loaded in the back seat of the car and drove her home.

The stepfather was home. Apparently, there was a long conversation between the girl and the deputy. Certainly, the deputy was assuring himself that there was no unacceptable behavior between the stepfather and the girl. There was not. He was just a concerned stepfather who knew it was not safe for a 15-year-old girl to be out, and especially for her to spending her time in a motel with two older boys.

The Least You Need to Know

- Runaways should always be listed in the NCIC by informing the local police departments. The police should be informed of the missing child as soon as possible, as a sign of good faith on the part of the parents.
- Consider surveillance of possible friends and ex-spouses' residences where the teen may be hiding.
- Parents of other teenagers usually will cooperate in a runway case. Use them.
- Send photographs of the teen to police departments in cities where the teen might be.
- Charges on credit cards, as well as ATM withdrawals, can provide timely information on where the teenager is located or direction of travel.
- Once the teenager is located, have the local PD pick up the kid. Don't put hands on the child yourself because you risk being accused by this teenager of inappropriate behavior.

The Ins and Outs of Electronic Surveillance

In This Chapter

- Distinguishing between bugs and taps
- Searching homes inside and out for phone taps
- Building your own butt set
- Exploring the legalities of tapping lines

The second-most-common request clients make at my PI agency is for a countermeasure sweep. Callers don't use those exact words, but that's what they want. Normally, a client says, "I think my phone is tapped" or "My husband and I are getting a divorce, and I want to make sure he's not recording my telephone calls." Another reason a client may want a countermeasure sweep is that he has told somebody private information on the telephone, and the news has leaked. He didn't tell anybody else, and he's sure that the other person didn't relate it to anybody, either; hence, he thinks that his phone must be tapped or his house bugged.

A *countermeasure sweep* is an active measure by an individual with the goal of finding or countering an aggressive action taken against him. Typically, the term is used in the sense of actively searching for and eliminating any electronic transmitters (bugs) or wiretaps that are directed toward locations or facilities where the target of the measure would likely be heard. A variation of the term is used with respect to surveillance. *Countersurveillance* is surveillance initiated by an individual to determine whether he is under surveillance by an outside group. If properly conducted, countersurveillance can identify the entity conducting the surveillance so that you'll know who at the diner counter is watching you.

Conducting a complete countermeasure sweep involves six aspects:

- Evaluating the threat level
- Intercepting wire communications (telephone sweeps)
- Locating compromised cell phones
- Discovering tracking devices
- Intercepting oral communications (transmitters)
- Locating hidden video equipment cameras

In this chapter, I examine the first two countermeasures. Sweeping for concealed transmitters (bugs) is beyond the scope of this book. If you have a situation that calls for this type of action, contact a reputable PI firm that specializes in countermeasure sweeps. I cover compromised cell phones in Chapter 7.

Before I go into details, though, you have to understand exactly what you're looking for.

Bugged or Tapped: It's Terminology

I frequently receive telephone calls from a new client who says, "I think somebody has bugged my phones." Is that possible? Sure. Is it likely? Not unless we're dealing with a bug instituted by law enforcement under a legal warrant.

Can somebody bug your house? Sure, it happens all the time. Can somebody other than law enforcement tap your phone line and record your conversations? Sure, I see it at least once a month. But bugging your phones is unlikely. Confused? That's because the general public doesn't make a distinction between a bug and a wiretap. It's a matter of terminology. To understand intercepts, you need to understand intercept technology and get the terms right:

- **Bugs:** These are combined microphone–transmitters that are used to capture conversations between two or more people within the same room. You're probably familiar with the bug disguised as an olive in a martini glass used in spy movies. In that case, the olive is the microphone–transmitter, and the toothpick is the antenna. The microphone picks up the conversation, and the transmitter sends it out using radio frequency (RF) energy. There are other ways to get a conversation transmitted out of the room without using RF.

A conversation can be picked up by a microphone and transmitted outside the residence by using the power wires. A recorder can be connected to your power line outside the house and can record the conversations overheard by the microphone. High-tech, sure, but it can be done. If you hire somebody to "debug" your office and all they do is search for RF transmissions, they've done only half the job.

- **Phone taps:** These are interceptions on your *landline telephone line* (if you still have one) that enable a third party to listen to and record your telephonic conversations.

> **DEFINITION**
>
> A **landline telephone line** refers to a normal telephone line that has a physical demarcation point at a residence, business, or pay telephone. The phone call at least begins and ends its transmission along a pair of wires, regardless of whether transmission of the call includes microwave or satellite in between both ends. This is in contrast to a cell phone, or any type of radio communication, which is considered wireless communication—literally, not connected to the ground at some point with wires.

Other forms of communication, such as cell phones and portable handsets, can be compromised as well. If any conversation travels through the air or through wires, it can be intercepted.

Evaluating the Threat

Paranoia runs rampant in our society. We like to say in our business that just because you're paranoid doesn't mean someone hasn't tapped your phone. (It's a variation of the old axiom "Just because you're paranoid doesn't mean that there is nobody following you.") The real question you have to ask yourself, or the client, is whether anything you're saying on the phone is so valuable to another person that someone would be willing to go to an awful lot of trouble and expense to listen to your conversations. The content of your conversation doesn't have to be illegal. For example, is the client involved in big-money deals? Then it might be worth the effort for the competition to listen in.

LEGAL TRAP

Generally, in most states, tapping your own home telephone to listen to your spouse's calls is illegal. Special circumstances in which you tap calls involving your minor children may be legal; check with your attorney for details.

If you're searching for a phone tap or a transmitter placed by your client's spouse, chances are you can find it with the instructions from this chapter. Even if the spouse has big bucks, it's unlikely that he'll spend the tens of thousands of dollars it would take, assuming that he knew the people who could do it, to tap the phone in such a way as to make detection impossible.

If you think the FBI or Homeland Security has tapped your phone and a PI offers to sweep the phone lines for $150, you have the wrong PI. When law enforcement executes a legal telephone tap, they basically have the phone company run an extension of your phone line into their offices. No physical connection is made at your house or business. Instead, an electronic connection is made at the telephone company's central switch to have your calls routed both to your phone at home and to the local FBI office. That puts a few chinks into some of those television shows and movies, doesn't it?

Some equipment manufacturers claim their test equipment can alert the technician performing a countermeasure sweep that a legal tap is on the line. How? In a legal tap, the length of the telephone circuit has basically been extended to include the local FBI office. The manufacturer is selling you on the ability of the equipment to test for a change in the length of the circuit. Don't waste your money. If you really think your phone is tapped by law enforcement, that means it's been done with a warrant by highly professional people, and this chapter won't help you find the tap. And if you're up against law enforcement, don't buy the fancy testing equipment. Instead, hire a good lawyer.

However, if you're thinking it's an illegal tap by a cowboy cop, there's a good chance you'll find it. If the telephone tap threat is from your spouse, your next-door neighbor, or the guy who lives two floors below you in the same building, then spending $250 per line to check your phone lines is reasonable because finding that sort of wiretap doesn't require a high-tech search. Still, the person doing the sweeping has to know what he is looking for. Before this chapter is over, you'll be able to do it yourself.

Tapping telephones without the consent of the parties involved, or without having a warrant for the tap, is illegal in every state. That means you have to consider in advance what action you'll take if you discover that your telephone is tapped or your house is bugged.

Do you call the phone company? Call your lawyer? Call the police? The natural reaction is to want to nail the person responsible, but you need to stop and think it through. Do you really want the person responsible to go to jail? If the guilty party is a soon-to-be ex-husband, just remember that he won't be able to pay child support or alimony if he's in prison. You might have to go to court to testify, and that risks making everything part of the public record for anyone to read. Are you sure you want to do that? Think this through very carefully before you involve law enforcement, because once you start the legal system in motion, there's no turning back.

Know what you're going to do before you start looking, and then be prepared to photograph the tap for later evidence.

Finding Taps in Your Home

The easiest way to access your phone lines is from within your residence or the property in question. If your spouse or partner or some other person who has regular, daily access to your home wants to tap your telephone line, it's probably being accomplished as an "inside" job.

More often than not, when a spouse taps your phone, he's probably using a telephone recording control device from Radio Shack. The product number is 43-421. That's what you're looking for. Search under every bed. Get a flashlight and look behind every piece of furniture. Using the light, search every wall in the house for a phone jack. If there are wires coming out of any phone jack, examine them to make sure they are going only to telephones, not to a control device or a tape recorder.

Physically run your hands along the wires from the phone jack and trace them back to the phones. Don't just eyeball it. A clever guy will splice the wires partway up the line and put the recorder and controls behind a piece of furniture. If you just look at the wall and at the phone, you'll say to yourself, "Okay, nothing there." So run your hand all the way down the line from the telephone to the wall jack.

Check under the beds and in your home office. Do you have a locked drawer or cabinet in your study? Do any wires lead to that drawer or cabinet? Check the spare bedroom, too. You have to check every room, every wall, and every phone jack.

Still didn't find it, but you're sure it's there? Hit the garage. He's going to be sneaky, so you have to be as thorough as he is clever. Look in every closet. If your spouse is the least bit technical, he can splice into the phone line in the attic and put the recorder up there. Or he can run a line from the splice in the attic to another location in or around the house.

Walk around the outside the house. Are there any phone lines coming out of the crawl space that you can't identify? Most people won't know which lines are supposed to be on the outside of the house and which aren't. That's okay. Just follow them visually to see where they go. No need to run your hands on these wires. You might accidentally be following an electrical wire that is not grounded and fry yourself, so don't touch any wires outside the house. It'll be pretty obvious if they go into a box that your spouse has made to hold the tape recorder.

Spouses frequently hide the recorder and controls in a box under the porch or under a wooden deck, so get a flashlight and look there. If you don't want to poke under the porch yourself, find a PI who advertises countermeasure sweeps and get him to do it. But you can save the $250 by spending an hour and doing it yourself, since you know what to look for.

The Outside Job

In most areas of the country, tapping a neighbor's telephone is fairly easy. I say *neighbor* because tapping the phone also requires that you be able to listen to or record the conversations. The farther away the listening post is, the more difficult the exercise becomes. A method to circumvent the distance problem is to tap the phone outside the house or at the *junction box* and hide a recorder in the bushes somewhere nearby.

> **DEFINITION**
>
> A **junction box** is a piece of telephone company equipment that houses several customers' telephone lines and is connected to a phone company cable. Typically, these junction boxes house from two to two dozen connections. There is normally one on every block, or one for every 10 to 12 subscribers.

Remember the old gangster movies of the 1940s? Neither do I, but I've seen a few remakes. In the old movies, when the guy wanted to tap a phone, he went down to the basement of the building and found the telephone junction box where all the phones in the building came together. Then he clipped on a couple of wires using alligator clips and ran those wires to another set of wires that went to an apartment in the same building, or maybe to a small room or closet in the basement. He could then sit in the room with a headset on and listen to the phone calls all day. The PI would bring him coffee periodically throughout the day and ask if there was anything new. Ah, the good old days.

Well, surprise. The good old days are basically still here. Things haven't changed that much. You can find most local telephone taps with three tools: your eyes, a screwdriver, and a *butt set*.

> **DEFINITION**
>
> A **butt set** is a handheld device that looks like a cordless phone, has a touchtone keypad, and is used by telephone and electronic service people to identify telephone lines. It has a set of wires with alligator clips at the end. You can buy butt sets for less than $100 over the internet or at Radio Shack.

Making Your Own Butt Set

Type "butt set" into any internet search engine, and you'll find lots of listings. You can spend more than $1,000 if you want, or you can make your own for less than $20. Here are full instructions for making your own:

1. Gather your supplies. You need a touchtone telephone (use an old one or buy one from a local phone store), a short phone extension cord (costs $3), and a couple alligator clips (costs $3). You don't need any special type of phone; the plainer, the better.

2. Plug one end of the extension cord into the telephone.

3. Cut off the other plug end from the cord. Strip the outside wire cover back about a foot. Strip the red and green inside wire covers back about 2 inches, baring the copper wire. Assuming that it's a two-pair extension cord, clip off the yellow and black wires—you won't need them. Attach the alligator clips to the red and green bare ends.

There you have it—a homemade butt set for the cost of a telephone and $5 in parts. I show you how to put that butt set to use a little later in this chapter. First, though, you need a basic understanding of how telephones work.

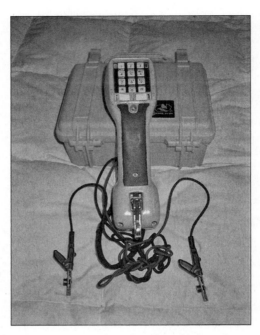

A butt set is a tool used to identify phone lines.

How Phones Work

Phones require two wires. These two wires are referred to as one pair, just as two shoes equals one pair. If you have two pairs of shoes and only one pair of feet, like most of us, then you have an extra pair of shoes. If you have two pairs of wires and only one phone line (one active phone number, not to be confused with extensions with the same phone number), then you have an extra pair. Almost every house in America that is wired for phone service has at least two pairs of phone wires in the house. Many newly constructed houses have three or four pairs of wires so that a single location can have three or four different telephone numbers.

All these pairs of wires run throughout your house and lead from your building to the telephone interface and then to the junction box. Typically, the active pair of wires are the red and green wires, known as tip and ring. The other pair is usually yellow and black, but these can be blue and blue/white, or orange and orange/white, or any other two colors.

A typical phone system junction box.

Your telephone wires from inside your house interface or connect with the phone company's wires. Do not confuse this telephone interface with the telephone junction box.

A telephone interface joins the lines you own with the lines the phone company owns.

The telephone interface attached to your garage or outside your house is usually a gray box divided into two sections. You can open your side with a flat-bladed screwdriver. The other side belongs to the telephone company and normally requires a special tool to open it. You don't really need access to the telephone company side of the interface anyway.

Locating the Junction Box

Now you need to locate the junction box. How will you recognize one when you see it? The junction box is usually a 2½-foot-tall cylindrical green metal post or cabinet. It is located on the ground, and you might find it in the middle or at the end of a block, or any logical place where phone lines come together.

One client, Heidi, asked us to check her lines for taps. She was suspicious of a neighbor who lived across the alley from her. He'd been insinuating that he was listening to her telephone calls after she'd ended their relationship. He wasn't stalking her, but he clearly pined for her. He also had occasional access to her apartment because he fed her dogs for her when she was out of town. Consequently, we did the inside checks, as described earlier in this chapter, and then went outside. The figure of a typical junction box on the preceding page is actually Heidi's junction box exactly the way we found it. It is not unusual to find them falling open or with the covers askew; that certainly makes getting into them easier.

Cable television junction boxes are similar and frequently are shorter and more round. However, just to mix you up, some cable boxes are larger and more square. Walk up and down the street or around your subdivision, and you'll see the phone junction box. It probably has a phone company logo or sticker on it, but sometimes it may be weathered off. The cable boxes usually say "cable TV" on them.

You can open a junction box using a flat-bladed screwdriver. Some phone companies have recently begun utilizing security screws, which require a special tool. Don't let that stop you. Most of those boxes are left unsecured by careless telephone serviceman anyway, as was Heidi's. Often they've been run over by cars or backed over by trucks, and that usually leaves them open as well.

On the older models, the front cover lifts up and then slides forward. You shouldn't need to completely remove the cover. Newer versions are totally round, and the cover lifts completely off.

Inside a telephone junction box.

Finding Your Phone Line

To tell whether your phone line has been compromised, you have to find your terminals inside that junction box. When you open the junction box, it may look daunting, but it's really not that difficult. Sometimes the telephone numbers are written on paper or plastic tags and attached to the wires. I hope you're one of the lucky ones, but don't count on it.

The inside of the junction box looks similar to the one in the previous figure. In this box, the serviceman wrote one of the phone numbers and the address inside the box for us. I like that guy.

Telephone wires carry about 52 volts of direct current. That's why your phones still work even if the electricity to your house is shut off, unless you have only cordless phones, which require the base station to be plugged into the AC current. There's not enough amperage to really hurt you, but you can get shocked, so no messing around in the junction box in the rain. The trick here is to find your lines and make sure that nobody has connected them to another pair of wires, as described earlier in this chapter.

So you open the junction box and none of the phone lines are tagged or labeled. How do you figure out which one is yours? Just use your butt set to dial either 1-800-444-4444 or 1-800-444-3333. You may have to navigate through a set of menus to get the number repeated back to you. An even easier option is to dial your cell phone and see what the caller ID on your cell phone reveals. If it reveals your own home landline number, you've found it.

If the 800 numbers I give you don't work, and you don't have a cell phone with caller ID or you're out of range of your cell tower, there's still another way to determine which pair of wires in the junction box belongs to you. Have a friend sit in your house and make a phone call to anybody. Have him continue talking while you're at the junction box, methodically plugging into one pair of wires and then the next, until you eventually hear your friends discussing your paranoia. Voilà.

Attach the alligator clips of the butt set to the first pair of terminals in the junction box. Make sure the clips don't touch each other while you do this. It's not dangerous, but you won't get a dial tone if the alligator clips are touching. You should hear a dial tone. If you don't, that pair is inactive.

Disconnect the clips and move down to the next pair of terminals. At each dial tone, use the touchtone keypad on the butt set to dial your cell number; it will tell you the telephone number for the phone line you are connected to. If you connect to a line and hear voices, you are listening in on your neighbor's conversation in progress. Simply disconnect and move to the next one, or else you will now be the one who is illegally tapping someone else's line. Even though it's accidental, it's not nice. Sure, it could be interesting, but don't be nosy—and certainly *don't talk*, because if you do, they will hear you, just as if you had picked up an extension in their home.

Eventually, you will find your phone line. Examine it closely. Does anything look out of the ordinary? Anything different from the other lines and terminals in the junction box? I recommend that you mark the terminals with a felt marker so you'll be able to identify your lines in the future. If you see a set of jumpers from your line to another, then yes, your telephone is tapped. Mark both sets, photograph the inside of the junction box, and replace the cover.

As I mentioned earlier, if your line is tapped, you have to decide what action to take.

In Heidi's case, I checked the junction box. The cover was half off the box, as you see in the photograph. I opened the junction box and easily found Heidi's phone lines. How? Because I could see that one set of terminals had a pair of wires running to another set of terminals farther down the box. I checked the phone number for the first set of suspicious terminals by using my butt set and dialing my cell phone. These were Heidi's lines, all right.

I then went over to the telephone interface, the gray box where the phone lines entered the subject's apartment, and checked there. Yep, he'd basically run an extension of Heidi's phone to his place.

Heidi didn't want to involve the police. After photographing it, I disconnected the tap and closed the box. One of the investigators who works for me is about 6 feet, 4 inches tall and 260 pounds. When I walk down dark alleys, he's the one I take with me. I usually let him lead the way. He and I went and had a little talk with the neighbor who'd tapped Heidi's phone. She hasn't had any trouble with him since.

Tapping a phone by jumpering wires has its dangers. It's possible that an alert phone company serviceman will discover the tap while he is in that junction box working on someone else's line. The phone company may then report it to the police.

I don't advocate tapping phones. I get asked to do it all the time but refuse to do so. It's illegal, and I won't do anything illegal because it's not worth losing my license for a few thousand dollars. However, let me emphasize that it is not illegal to find out if your own phone line has been tapped.

Legalities

The recording of telephone conversations is covered in most state statutes under the interception of wire communications. To record or intercept a telephone call without breaking the law, under federal statutes, one party to the conversation has to be aware of the fact that the telephonic conversation is being recorded. This means that under the federal law, I can record a telephone conversation I'm having with another person and not advise them that the call is being recorded. This is called the one-party rule.

Some states have a narrower view of recording telephonic conversations than the federal government. These states insist that all parties to the telephone conversation be aware that the call is being recorded. This is called the two-party rule, and states with these laws in place are called two-party states. Note that two-party actually means all parties in the conversation, so if you're on a conference call with multiple people, they all need to know about the recording. See Appendix B for a list of one-party and two-party states. The laws do change, so keep abreast of the relevant laws in your own state. Also, you should note that California (an all-party state), considers it illegal to record conversations as long as one party to the conversation is in California even if the recording is taking place in a one-party state.

THE SCOOP

Remember Linda Tripp and her recording of her telephone conversations with Monica Lewinsky? After the President Clinton-Lewinsky fiasco, the state of Maryland brought charges against Linda Tripp for the illegal recording of those telephone calls. Why? Because Tripp was in Maryland, which is an all-party state, meaning that all parties are supposed to be notified that the phone conversation is being recorded. Lewinsky was in Washington, D.C., which is a one-party jurisdiction. Tripp didn't tell Lewinsky she was recording the phone calls, so she was in violation of Maryland's interception of wire communication law, but not Washington's. Eventually, the charges were dropped against Tripp, but it took a while and probably some big-dollar attorney fees.

The Least You Need to Know

- The term *bug* refers to a microphone–transmitter combination that transmits room conversations to another location. *Tap* refers to an interception of wire communications.

- Assess the threat level before taking action. If the suspected source of the bugging or tapping is the FBI, you'll need more sophisticated equipment to determine whether both the room and the phone lines are secure. If the threat is a soon-to-be ex-spouse, other, less-sophisticated techniques are probably adequate.

- Tapping telephones without consent of the parties involved and without having a warrant for the tap is illegal in every state. Upon discovering an illegal tap, evaluate whether you want to involve law enforcement. If the guilty party will be paying your alimony, you may not want him in jail.

- Most illegal telephone taps can be located with your eyes, a screwdriver, and a butt set. You can make a butt set at home or buy one for less than $100.

- Thoroughly check every phone jack and every conceivable hiding place in the house for a tape recorder and a telephone remote control device. Also check the garage, the attic, and the bushes outside the house.

- To find an outside telephone tap, locate the junction box and examine the appropriate pair of wires.

Criminal Defense Cases

In This Chapter

- Reviewing the discovery material
- Walking the crime scene
- Setting a legal visit with a prisoner
- Dealing with prosecutorial misconduct
- Working with informants

Criminal defense cases provide private investigators a unique opportunity to work within the law enforcement community, interact with law enforcement (LE), and still maintain our own standards of professional conduct. Our criminal justice system is built upon the precept that a person is innocent until proven guilty. However, all too often, criminal suspects are arrested and overcharged with crimes. The principal criminal charge might be sale of drugs, but suspects are also often charged with possession of the drug, intent to distribute, manufacturing, possession of drug paraphernalia, and sale of drugs within 1,000 yards of a school or community center. Each carries a separate penalty, and if convicted on all counts, the suspect might serve a very, very long time in jail for basically one offense.

The forces are massed against anyone who is arrested for a crime. Law enforcement has all the resources it needs at its command. The police or sheriff can put 20 men on a case. They have the services of the state bureau of investigation and the FBI, if needed, plus all their forensic people and local, state, and federal laboratories to help them make their case. They have multiple prosecuting attorneys who each can be assigned one aspect of a criminal case, and the prosecuting attorney's office has its own investigators as well. They probably have already talked to the suspect and may have extracted some incriminating remarks from him, maybe even a confession, before you are ever assigned the case.

So before you ever get started working with a suspect in a criminal investigation, you're way behind. Perhaps you're working for a court-appointed attorney who has received permission from the court to hire an investigator at a rate that's significantly lower than your normal hourly rate, and the maximum you can bill is going to be less than what is necessary. With all these forces marshaled against you, why bother taking the case?

I would say take it for truth, justice, and the American way. But also do it because criminal cases make for interesting investigative work. My most satisfying cases have been criminal defense cases. Having a jury declare your client innocent after all the manpower and work the prosecution put into the case just plain feels good. To know that you kept an innocent person out of jail for a crime he didn't commit—there is no better feeling. Do innocent men go to jail? All of the time, often because of the factors I just mentioned. Criminal defense investigators are outmanned and outgunned. That means you have to be smarter than the police—and more thorough, more precise, more diligent, and more committed. That's what you learn in this chapter.

Guilt or Innocence: Does It Make a Difference?

Criminal defense cases usually come to you from attorneys who specialize in that field. Market to those attorneys if you want to work criminal defense cases.

When you begin a criminal defense case, the first thing you have to realize is that your client might be guilty. Nevertheless, he's entitled to the best defense that you can provide him. Most all of us are guilty of something. But is your client guilty of the crime with which he's being charged? And was his case handled properly, allowing your client full access to the justice system? Later in this chapter, I introduce you to Justin, who is on death row for a double homicide. I'm not convinced that Justin committed those murders. I do know that he shouldn't have been convicted of them because the State's Attorney's Office used what they knew was perjured testimony to convict him.

Where do you start? The case will most likely come to you through an attorney, but it may come directly from a family member who has the resources to pay your regular hourly rate. For the sake of this chapter, I assume that you've been contacted by a criminal defense attorney. You'll sit down with the attorney, who will explain the basic facts of the case and what he needs to defend his client. The attorney will most likely have some sort of direction for his defense planned out.

Work out a game plan with the attorney. Generally, the attorney will want to use the "some other dude did it" defense. If your client is innocent and a crime was committed, then somebody else had to do it. You'll spend some time trying to find this "other dude." But you don't have to find the "other dude" if you can prove that your client was someplace else or has a credible alibi, or that the police investigation was so faulty that any number of other persons might have committed the crime.

THE SCOOP

In criminal cases, the burden of proof is on the prosecution. They have to prove "beyond a reasonable doubt" to the judge or the jury that your client committed the crime. The same is not true for civil cases. In civil cases, a preponderance of the evidence is enough to win. The standard of guilt in criminal cases is much higher.

The Discovery Evidence

When you're on board with the case, the attorney will probably provide you with boxes of the discovery material that the prosecution is required by law to hand over to the attorney. In that box may be copies of DVDs of the interviews that the police conducted with the subject. Watch the DVDs closely. Listen to what the subject says and how he responds to the police questioning. Don't form your own opinion yet; you've still got a lot of work to do.

The police are often lazy in their approach to conducting investigations, and they just don't act like professional investigators. I know that sounds harsh, but let me give you an example.

I was investigating what I believe was a murder, or a case of Russian roulette gone bad. This young man had been in the passenger seat of a vehicle. He had just called his mother and told her to meet him and his new girlfriend at a local popular restaurant. His mother had said she would be there in 20 minutes. The girlfriend had been driving the car. Both the girlfriend and the victim had been using drugs. There was one cartridge in the revolver; the other five chambers were empty. It was about 8 P.M. and was getting dark. The victim, my client's son, was right-handed. Somehow he ended up with a bullet in the left side of his brain. We believe they were taking turns pointing the gun at each other, spinning the cylinder on the revolver, and pulling the trigger as they drove down the road.

When the gun went off, the girl pulled into a shopping parking lot, leapt from the car, and began screaming. A couple close by told me later that the girl had said, "My boyfriend has just been shot"—not "My boyfriend just shot himself." The police arrived, followed by the CSI techs, and they took the photos and collected the evidence. The witness couple was never interviewed in any depth by the police until I gave them copies of my report. I spent several hours with that couple going over everything they could remember, taking recorded and signed statements.

I obtained all the photos from the sheriff's office and even went into the office and had the CSI folks bring out the clothing so we could photograph it and send it to our own *blood spatter* expert. The coroner ruled the death as an "accident," and the sheriff's office stopped any further investigation. When we went over the crime scene photos very carefully, we discovered some very interesting facts that the police had missed.

> **DEFINITION**
>
> **Blood spatter** (not splatter) is the blood that is discarded during a violent crime. By the study of the blood spatter, the size of the drops, and the velocity and direction of the spatter, one might be able to determine how the crime took place.

The following photo is the left hand of the deceased. Notice the blood spatter on his palm. If he were holding the revolver and had shot himself in the left side of his head, there should have been a shadow or clean spot where the palm was covered by the revolver's handle. Yet the left palm is covered with blood spatter.

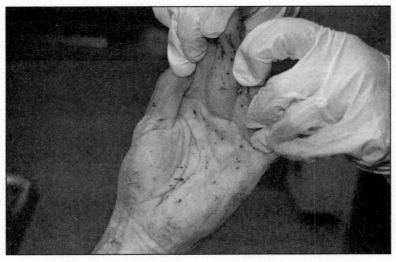

Autopsy photo of victims' left hand. Note blood spatter on left palm.

The weapon used was a six-shot revolver. For those unfamiliar with guns, let me explain how a revolver works. As you pull the trigger on the revolver, the cylinder that holds the cartridges (bullets) rotates so that, with each trigger pull, the firing pin hits a new cartridge. If it didn't revolve, you would get one shot and then the hammer would keep falling on the same, now empty, cartridge. Look at the next photo. You can see that the hammer is resting on an empty cylinder. The bullet that killed this boy is to the left of the hammer. This means that the trigger was pulled, the gun fired, the bullet entered the boy's head, and then the trigger was pulled a second time, leaving the hammer on the empty cylinder. We're convinced that his female companion was mad enough at him to pull the trigger twice.

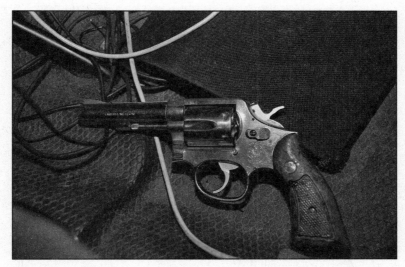

One spent shell in the cylinder to the left of the hammer indicates two trigger pulls.

Despite the gun evidence and some blood spatter evidence that indicated he didn't shoot himself, the case was not further pursued.

The Crime Scene

The next step is to go out to the crime scene. Go even if the crime occurred several years before and the house where it occurred has burned down. Do your best to walk through what the police say happened, and then walk through again keeping in mind what your client says. This is probably the area criminal defense investigators neglect the most, which is unfortunate because it's usually the most important part of the case. Sure, you can look at the photos of the crime scene. They will be in the discovery material. But often you can find important facts at the crime scene that aren't in the discovery material.

Matt was charged with selling a single $20 rock of crack cocaine. He had been approached in a sting operation by an undercover policeman. Undercover policemen in four cars had watched the transaction or were in the near vicinity. Matt denied that he sold the crack to the cop and claimed the police arrested the wrong man. Matt did have two previous convictions for selling crack, so this would have been his third strike.

According to the prosecution, the arrangement was for the buyer (the undercover cop) to leave a $20 bill under some bushes in a hedge. The drug dealer would go get the crack and swap it for the $20. The undercover cop would come by in a few minutes and take the crack. This all occurred near the front of a community center, which escalated the crime from a misdemeanor to a felony. Two cops were parked down the street observing. Another car was a block away and didn't have a clear view of the transaction; they were placed there to help with the arrest in case the drug dealer took off running in their direction.

Matt lived across the street from the community center. He claimed that he walked out his door and around the corner past the bushes where the alleged transaction was to take place and joined some of his friends hanging out in front yard of the community center. Once he was with his friends, the police came in and began asking for identification for all the people there. They ran their names through the police computers and, when they found Matt's name and saw that he had two previous convictions for drug sales, they arrested him for this one as well.

Of course, the question is, why did they have to run all those names before arresting Matt? Well, Matt's attorney had him plead not guilty and asked for a jury trial. The first trial ended in a hung jury. The state attorney did not want to let it go, so she pushed for a second trial. That one ended in a hung jury as well. That's when I got the call from the attorney. He needed some expert help.

The defense attorney explained the facts to me, and he and I both went down and walked through the crime scene together. The first obvious question I had was, why were there no photos of the transactions? Why no video? Did the police use binoculars to observe this? Any beginning PI would know enough to video or photograph the transaction, to avoid any case of mistaken identity. Did the police do this? No. Too lazy? Too unprepared? Why? Well, we'll never know the answer to that question.

Then I went to work. I measured the distance from the surveillance point where the police said they were parked watching the bush in question. It measured over 408 feet away, a third longer than a football field. It would be probably impossible to get any good facial identification of a subject from that the distance. I placed cones in the street at various distances and photographed people standing by the cones using a 35mm camera. In the film age, a 35mm photograph shot with a 50mm lens approximated what the naked eye would see. In the digital age, it depends on the camera, but a 35mm camera using a 31.4mm lens gives you the same view as the naked eye. So I used a 35mm lens, which was as close as I could get.

Not only would it have been impossible to tell two faces apart, but there was traffic on the street. I set up at the same location where the surveillance police were sitting and counted the number of cars and trucks that came up and down the street during the time that "the transaction" took place. Also, full-grown oak trees and other shrubs would have made getting a clear view of any transaction very difficult.

I made numerous copies of each photo.

Cones are, first to last, distances from Ionia & 2nd St.
1=332 ft, 2=385 ft, 3=408.6 ft

From this picture, you can clearly see that, with the naked eye, facial recognition from over 400 feet away would be impossible.

The third trial took place, and I testified as an expert on surveillance. This time the jury came back with a not guilty verdict. Since I was testifying, I couldn't sit in the courtroom and listen to what the police testified to, but according to the attorney, their testimony was way too rehearsed and became more consistent and rehearsed with each trial. Was Matt guilty? Was he the drug dealer? Maybe, maybe not, but the police didn't have their act together enough to convict him. I called my wife after the trial and told her it was a red-letter day; I'd just help put a drug dealer back on the street.

The part of Matt's case that really bothered me was that the State Attorney's Office spent thousands of dollars and used up three judges' days and the juries' time to try to prosecute one $20 crack case. But if I hadn't gone down and walked through the "crime scene" and observed firsthand the problem with the state's case, Matt might have his third strike against him and be doing life in prison for a crime on which he ultimately was found not guilty.

I can't emphasize enough the need to go over and over the crime scene. It is the bridge between your client being found guilty or not guilty, and the police often miss things when they process the crime scene. Remember, they are looking for evidence that proves your client guilty. You are looking for evidence that proves "some other dude did it."

I mentioned Justin earlier in this chapter. Justin was accused of a double homicide using an axe to kill a drug dealer and his pregnant girlfriend. Unfortunately, Justin's first attorney didn't come to me before the trial. But his father came to me after Justin had been convicted and retained me to go over the evidence and see what the defense attorney had missed. I spent many hours with Justin on death row going over the facts. Justin denies that he committed the murders, and had no real motive for doing them. When I first met with Justin, he admitted to me that he was a career criminal. He had been involved in home invasions with a gang of four or five other young men. Their home invasions typically targeted drug dealers in homes where they knew substantial sums of money or drugs would be present.

The victim in this case was a low-level drug dealer who was known for cheating his customers. The home invasion crew kept all their black clothes in a duffle bag together. When prepping for their next home invasion, they would meet, pull out the black masks and sweatshirts, and put them on. Sometimes each person wore the same mask, but most often, they just grabbed the first mask they came to. Justin was smart. One time he had to kick in a back door. To make sure the police couldn't trace the shoeprint back to him, he'd later burned the tennis shoes he'd been wearing.

What evidence did the police have against Justin in this double homicide? Four days after the incident, a gardener for a church behind the victim's house had found a black sweatshirt and a black mask dumped next to an air-conditioner unit. They'd found some blood and some of Justin's DNA on the clothing. Now, remember, the home invasion crew kept all their clothes together in a duffle bag, so anyone with access to that bag could have used those clothes, and Justin's DNA was probably on all the clothes in the bag. They also found other DNA on the clothes that they couldn't identify.

I find it incredibly difficult to believe that Justin, who had burned his tennis shoes, would just dump the clothes he'd used to commit these murders nearly on the property line, where they could be easily found. To show you what a lousy job the police did at the crime scene, they were called back three times as neighbors found other evidence on the property, including a glove caught on a barbwire fence and the murder weapon, the axe, in the backyard.

All the DNA on the sweatshirt proves is that, at one time, Justin wore that piece of clothing. The victim's blood on the shirt pretty well establishes that whoever committed the crime wore that shirt that night or took it with him to plant blood on it. It does not prove that Justin was wearing that shirt the night of the murders. So the police needed something else.

As for the "other dude did it" defense, I'd come up with a plethora of other dudes who had much stronger motives for such a crime than Justin.

Witnesses

Interviewing witnesses is usually a larger part of a criminal defense case than any other aspect. I discuss at length in Chapter 8 how to warm up a witness. Those techniques are universal. In criminal defense cases, many of your witnesses are going to be criminals themselves, so they may be a little hardened in their attitudes. But the techniques still work. Give them a reason they should help you, and many of them will.

In Justin's case, the only witness against Justin was Mike, a fairly successful cocaine dealer. He would travel to southern Florida to buy several kilos of cocaine and then sell them in northern Florida for double what he paid for them. Mike testified at Justin's trial that one evening Justin had come to Mike's house and, in a conversation, admitted that he had killed the two victims. The police told Mike that the sweatshirt put Justin at the scene, but Mike's testimony put the axe in Justin's hands. That was their case.

I asked Justin about Mike's testimony, and he said, "If you ever get the chance to talk to Mike, just ask him to tell you the truth." I thought that was an interesting statement for Justin to make. Sounded like an innocent man to me. As so often happens in criminal cases, while I was working Justin's case, Mike had been arrested in south Florida for killing a man in a drug deal. Mike was certainly a possible "other dude" in Justin's case. Another possible "other dude" was the son of the victim, who was currently in a federal prison for drug offenses. This son was very mad at his father for abandoning his mother and impregnating the new girlfriend, the second victim. I had a number of people tell me that the son had sworn the new child "would never see the light of day."

When Mike testified at Justin's trial, he stated that the prosecution had not promised him any sort of deal in another case he was being tried for. The prosecution makes these sorts of promises all the time, and really I think the courts should put a stop to it. No, Mike did not have a written deal with the prosecution for a reduction in sentence if he testified against Justin, but he had it verbally that they would reduce a potential sentence of 15 years to 6 years in exchange for his testimony. As soon as Mike testified and Justin was convicted, they reduced the charges against Mike.

I guess it's karma, or "what comes around, goes around," because now the axe victim's son wrote a letter to the state's attorney in south Florida and said he would testify against Mike, that Mike had told him he shot the dealer in south Florida but wanted a reduction in his federal time. A deal was worked out, and the son testified against Mike. I was in the courtroom for a week because I wanted to get a feel for Mike and how to approach him. I heard the prosecution ask the son if he had been promised any sort of deal for his testimony. Of course he said no, but that was a lie. How the prosecution, in good conscience, can allow that is beyond me. It is fairly common, unfortunately, even though the U.S. Supreme Court ruled in *Giglio* v. *United States* (U.S. 1972):

> Withheld promise of immunity to co-conspirator upon whose testimony the Government's case depended required reversal of conviction because "evidence of any understanding or agreement as to a future prosecution would be relevant to the co-conspirator's credibility and the jury was entitled to know of it."

The Northern California Innocence Project found more than 700 cases of prosecutorial misconduct between 1997 and 2009.

I also found an instance of what I believe was a *Brady violation* in Justin's case: the prosecution did not deliver in their discovery material to the defense a diary that the female victim had kept. I was told of this diary by a very close friend of the victim. The victim told my witness that she and her drug-dealing boyfriend were sometimes so screwed up on drugs that they couldn't remember who owed them money and who they'd sold drugs to, so she'd started keeping a diary of each transaction and everybody who visited the house. The next day when they were sober, they could go over the diary and know what transpired the night before. The diary was not listed in the materials the police claimed they had. Yet when I looked closely over the crime scene photos, the day-planner diary was quite clearly visible in some of the photographs. I took the photograph to my witness, and she identified it as the drug dealer's diary. I took a notarized signed statement from her to that effect.

> **DEFINITION**
>
> The term **Brady violation** comes from a U.S. Supreme Court case, *Brady v. Maryland* (U.S. 1963), that ruled that, under the Fifth and Fourteenth Amendments, a prosecutor has a duty to disclose favorable evidence to defendants upon request if the evidence is "material" to either guilt or punishment.

Well, Mike was convicted and now sits in a Florida state prison. A month after Mike's trial, I visited him in prison.

Prison and Jail Visits

If you're going to visit a prisoner in jail, it is best to take the following steps.

If it's a state or federal prison, call the prison and get the name of the assistant warden or the official who approves "legal" visits. Write that person a letter, stating that you're working a case and that the prisoner is a witness in your case and you would like a "legal" visit. You will need to write the prisoner's ID number after his name. Include all your personal information, a copy of your state PI license, a copy of your driver's license, and your contact information.

> **HIDDEN HINT**
>
> Schedule your legal visit to the prison for a time after lunch so that you don't conflict with the prison's meal schedule. The last thing you want is to be right in the middle of an important discussion, or getting a signed statement, and have the prisoner pulled out so he can eat his lunch.

Also state the date when you would like to visit. State that you will bring with you a pad and pen and a digital recorder. If you don't list the recorder, they won't let you take it inside. Be sure you bring your driver's license with you, since they usually take that from you and return it to you when you leave the prison.

If it's a county jail, you can usually just call in advance and tell them who you are and who you want to see for a legal visit, and then show up. Be on time. They will show you through the gates and lead you to an interview room, where the prisoner is most likely already there, secured with cuffs to a chair.

In a legal visit to a prisoner, you will be in a private room and are guaranteed the right to privacy. After the guard leaves and shuts the door, the two of you are alone. *Always, always,* repeat the following words before you begin. Announce your name and say, "This is a legal visit between (insert prisoner's name) and (insert your name). The matters we are to discuss are work product from an attorney's office and are not subject to being recorded, listened to, or monitored in any manner. If there are recording devices or any sort of monitoring devices being used, they should be turned off now."

Making such a statement puts the prisoner at ease because he will know that whatever he tells you is between you and him and nobody else, unless you choose to release it to someone. Next, start your interview. Find a common ground; make him your friend.

In Mike's interview, I began talking about another murder case that I thought he had some involvement in and for which no one yet has ever been charged. Mike actually went into great detail about how he was present when the other drug dealer was killed. Finally, we got around to Justin's case. I told him that Justin had asked me to ask Mike to tell me the truth.

Mike was actually contrite and said he felt bad about testifying against Justin. Justin had never gone to Mike's house or told Mike that he had committed the double homicide. Mike had made up that story because he'd been mad at Justin. Justin had been an informant for the local sheriff. The sheriff had obtained a wiretap order on Mike's phone, partly based on some of the things Justin had told them. Mike said he'd read the wiretap order, and there were 14 informants' statements used on the order. He could tell by what they said who each of the 14 were. He understood why the other 13 had said what they said. They'd been mad at Mike for one reason or another. But Mike felt that Justin was his friend, and Justin had betrayed that friendship by telling the sheriff about Mike. So to get even, Mike had lied on the stand and made up the story of Justin confessing to him.

Justin still sits on death row as his new attorney goes through the appeal process. Did Justin kill that man and his pregnant girlfriend? I don't know. I do know that he was convicted on perjured testimony and shouldn't have been found guilty. I also know of six other "dudes" who had a greater motive for killing them than Justin did.

Informants

Working with *informants* is similar to interviewing witnesses, but there are differences as well. You must first develop the same level of trust and rapport with an informant as I mentioned in the preceding section and go into detail about in Chapter 8.

Informants usually have some motivating factor, something that drives them to help you besides the bond you develop with them, such as a secret desire to be a private investigator themselves. It's good to kid with your informants about "putting them on the payroll." It feeds their need to live an exciting life vicariously through yours.

DEFINITION

An **informant** is an individual who cooperates, usually without the knowledge of others involved in the case, by providing information during an investigation. This person might or might not be a witness or participant in the particular case under investigation. Frequently, an informant receives compensation, or other benefit, for the information, whereas a witness never should.

Forget what you've seen on television about police and informants. The tough-cop routine, slamming the informant against the wall, threatening him, and then expecting him to work for you, is ridiculous and just pure fiction. You should never call an informant a "snitch." It's derogatory, and if you think about him in derogatory terms, your actions, mannerisms, and tone of voice when speaking will betray your true thoughts. He will sense your demeaning manner, and you can kiss that informant good-bye. Repeat after me: your informant is a friend first, an informant second.

When Does a Private Investigator Use an Informant?

An informant can simply be a neighbor of a subject in a domestic case under surveillance who will let you know when the subject arrives home. This informant may call you when your client's wife, who is supposed to be at the gym, just showed up for a different kind of workout. To motivate this informant, you must build a bond with him. Chances are, however, the two neighbors have some sort of ongoing dispute. It could be something as trivial as your subject's dog relieving himself on your informant's front lawn every morning. Regardless, whatever the reason, your informant is probably using you to get even with your subject.

Can You Pay Informants?

Money and informants seem to go hand in hand. You can perform favors for informants. You can pay informants. But you can never pay an informant if that person may be a potential witness in a civil case. A witness may hint to you that, for a little money, her memory might improve. After all, her testimony might save your client, an insurance company, millions of dollars or result in a not guilty verdict in your criminal defense case. Regardless, you can't pay her.

If you were to pay a witness in a civil case and then that witness was called to testify, her testimony would be thrown out. You might see witnesses paid on television shows. No matter. You can't do it. Now, with law enforcement and criminal cases, the story changes. Police can pay informants, but civil cases have different rules than criminal law. There's no quicker way to be embarrassed in open court in a civil matter, lose the case, and lose a very good client at the same time than by paying a potential civil witness. Don't do it. The exception to that rule is the "expert" witness, who can be paid.

In criminal cases, I have often paid informants—usually not more than $100, and more often $50. If I'm looking for a particular person and I don't know where they are, but a friend of that person can tell me exactly where they are working or living, then it's certainly worth the $50 to find the person I'm looking for rather than waste a day or two trying to hunt him down. I've also bailed informants out of jail on multiple occasions. I've never gone higher than $500 to bail a person out.

Now, be careful here. The informant in jail will try to strike a bargain with you. He'll say, "Bail me out and then I'll tell you everything I know." No, no, no. First get the information from him. Get the signed statement, the recorded statement, everything you can—and then bail him out. If you do it his way, he'll be out and impossible to find, and you'll be out the bail you put up, with nothing to show for it.

The Least You Need to Know

- Discuss in detail with the attorney the plans for the defense.
- Always be on the lookout for the "some other dude did it" defense.
- Walk through the crime scene, even if it's years later. Carefully go over every crime scene photo. The police miss lots of evidence.
- Interview in depth every possible witness.
- Don't hesitate to interview witnesses who are in jail or state prison.
- Obtain your information from your informant before you pay him or bail him out of jail.

Advanced Techniques

Now that you've learned the basics, it's time for the heavy-duty cases. You should be up to the challenge; you've learned the techniques.

These chapters teach you how to check backgrounds and even get tips on starting your own background-screening company. I provide you with skills and tips that enable you to triple your billing rate. I also give you pointers for properly handling the evidence and preparing your case for court. And when the big moment finally arrives, you'll be ready to present your case in a professional manner in front of a judge and jury.

Background Investigations: Uncovering the Dirt

In This Chapter

- Uncovering personal identifiers
- Finding criminal records
- Verifying applicants' educational backgrounds
- Adhering to the rules of the Fair Credit Reporting Act
- Using a web-based client interface

Every third inquiry for services a private investigator receives is a request for some type of a background investigation. Generally, the new caller has no idea what she's looking for—only that she needs somebody checked out, doesn't have a clue how to do it herself, and has no idea really of what a background investigation encompasses. As a professional investigator, you have to determine the actual needs of the client and then educate her about what is possible and what isn't.

Most people have a vague notion of what a "background check" might include but are not really clear on the specifics. In this chapter, I talk about two basic backgrounds: dig-up-the-dirt background and pre-employment background screening. These are two totally different backgrounds and are subject to different laws and requirements.

Knowledge is power. In this chapter, I show you how to get that knowledge and offer up some items to consider if you're thinking about setting up a pre-employment background-screening company.

Reasons for Doing Backgrounds

Let's look at some typical reasons someone might want to hire you to dig up some dirt on somebody:

- A father and former husband is concerned about the ex-wife's new boyfriend. The ex-wife has custody of the children, and the boyfriend appears to be a slimeball. If the father can prove that his ex-wife is letting some degenerate hang around his kids, perhaps the father can get custody.

- A woman has her wedding planned, and the date is soon, but some doubts linger in her mind about the soon-to-be husband. Some of the things he says just don't add up.

- A new boyfriend claims to be a secret agent, or an ex-Navy SEAL, but his beer belly has his girlfriend wondering. What else is he lying about?

And here are a few reasons for doing a pre-employment background check:

- A small business owner has a new employee and wants to make sure the person he just hired is honest, hardworking, and dependable.

- A mother and father are thinking about hiring a nanny full-time. They want to ensure that the new nanny isn't a child abuser or, worse, a molester.

- A couple has a new cleaning lady. They're going to be out of town on cleaning day. Do they give her a key to the house?

All these reasons are real problems from real people. Their lives are tied in knots until they can get answers to their questions and resolve the doubts in their minds.

The components that make up a good basic background or employment check are as follows:

- Conducting a criminal arrest and/or conviction search (general background and pre-employment)

- Conducting a civil records search (general background)

- Verifying and checking with previous employers (pre-employment)

- Interviewing personal references (pre-employment)

- Obtaining a driving history, if applicable to your needs (general background and pre-employment)

- Verifying credentials and education (general background and pre-employment)
- Running a credit check (pre-employment)

General Background Checks: Obtaining the Basic Goods

Before beginning any background check, you must assess the level of detail and depth of the check you desire. Regardless of what type of background investigation you intend to perform, you must have the name, date of birth, and Social Security number of the person you're checking out. Although a current address isn't necessary, it is highly desirable.

If your purpose for the background is employment, you'll have all this information on the candidate's application. If you're doing a search for other reasons, you probably don't have much information about the person—which is why you want to do a background check in the first place.

Finding the Name

You'd think that knowing the name of the person you want to check out would be a simple, commonsense matter, but you'd be surprised at how often that little detail is difficult to come by. I can't tell you how many times clients have come to my office because their ex-spouses are seeing new people, and my clients are concerned about the new love interest—they want to find out what they do for a living and whether they've had any run-ins with the law. The trouble is, they don't have a name to start the check.

A good father who doesn't have custody of his children should be concerned about another male who is living with his children or might have influence over them. The last thing you want is somebody who is abusive or with a history of child molestation living with your kids. If the client doesn't know the individual's name, how do you, the PI, find it? Here are four good methods that work:

- If the client is on good terms with the ex, have him ask her. Most of the time, however, our clients aren't on very good terms with the former spouses.
- If the kids are old enough, ask them. If they are young, they may know only a first name or the name by which the ex refers to him. If you can get a first name, that's a start.

- If your client is allowed regular access to the ex's house, perhaps when picking up the kids, have him check the caller ID on the telephone or the list of dialed and received calls on his ex's cell phone, if he can get his hands on it. Chances are, the new friend has called, and his telephone number and name might be right there. Even if his name isn't shown, his number might be recorded. (I tell you how to do reverse phone searches in Chapter 7.) Even if you have a list of 30 numbers, spend $23 at 555-1212.com to buy a hundred searches—the smallest package available—and run all 30 numbers.

- Jot down the license tag on the guy's car. This means you'll have to be there when he shows up. That might be easy, and it might not, depending on your situation. If you can't be there, perhaps you can get a friendly neighbor to do it for you. By running the license, you'll get the name, date of birth, and an address (a bases-loaded home run). As a professional, I always go right for the tag. With the tag info, you can then get the Social Security number, which you might need to further identify this person.

HIDDEN HINT

Keep in mind that the name a person goes by may not be his real name. We have spent many useless hours and incurred countless database charges because our client told us the person's name was Scott, for instance, only to find out later that Scott, which is the name he goes by, is actually his middle name.

Finding the Date of Birth

To run a criminal record check, you need two things: the name and date of birth. A Social Security number is nice but not necessary. Race and sex are also helpful as identifiers, and in running criminal records, you usually have to include both items in the request. Race and sex should be easy for you, although these days, with spiked hair and baggy clothes, a person's sex might not be obvious.

To get the date of birth, go down to your local voter's registration office and check the voter's records, which are usually considered public information and include the name and date of birth. Different states have different rules concerning taking notes while reviewing the voter's registration records, but often they won't let you write anything down. That's to keep people from coming in and making marketing lists. You'll just have to remember the date of birth until you can step around the corner and write it down.

If the new boyfriend isn't a registered voter, head for the clerk of the court's office and check for previous marriages and divorces. Many clerks of the court have their records online. There you will find all the identifiers you need.

Excuse me, you say, but I've spent half a day running around the courthouse only to discover that the new boyfriend isn't a registered voter and was divorced in another state. Now what? You can tap into one of the subscription databases I discuss in Chapter 6 and have it in a matter of minutes, or you can make a pretext call.

Before attempting this, check out Chapter 12 for detailed instructions on how to perform pretext calls. I've used the following pretext quite successfully in the past to uncover the date of birth. But take note: you can't use the pretext on the subject himself. It is best used on a close relative, like a parent or sister, or on a roommate. In any case, the subject cannot be present when you make the call.

Call the phone number you got off the caller ID when you're sure the subject is not home. If you know anything about the subject's parents, call them instead. Be sure to use one of the tricks I discuss in Chapter 12 to block your phone number before calling.

When Mom answers, tell her you found her son's wallet in the parking lot of a nearby shopping center, referring to the store by name. (If the mom lives out of state, better still.) Explain that you're not sure that you have the right family, but you'd like to get the wallet back to its owner. If Mom asks how you got her number, tell her it was in the wallet. If Mom will just confirm the date of birth you found in the wallet, you'll make arrangements to return the billfold. Tell her you'll need the person's current address to take the billfold to him. Now you've turned your base hit into a double (date of birth and address). I used to go for a triple, asking for the SSN, but now with identity theft such a hot item, I wouldn't push it. Be happy with the date of birth and the address if you can get it. I've never had this pretext fail.

The Local Sheriff's Office

If possible, you should always check the local police jurisdiction's files in addition to the court records when performing a criminal background check. They might have records of incidents that never went to court because nobody was ever charged. In some states, you can get the arrest records for a small search fee (typically about $5), right there while you wait.

Suppose the new boyfriend was beating up his live-in girlfriend. The next-door neighbor calls the police when she hears the girlfriend pleading for help. The police arrive, but there is no blood spread around, so they calm down the couple and leave.

Before they leave the scene, they write up a domestic disturbance incident report. Nobody was arrested; no charges were filed. There will be nothing in any court file. But still, you'd like to know about that incident, wouldn't you?

Frequently, patrol officers stop somebody who is acting suspiciously or loitering. When they do, they always ask for identification and usually run a computer check on the subject to see if there are any warrants on him or her. In most jurisdictions, the officers fill out what is known as a *Field Identification (FI)* card, or they might write an incident report if they were responding to a call. Those FI cards and incident reports contain a lot of information and should be reviewed.

> **DEFINITION**
>
> A **Field Identification (FI)** card is a card patrol officers use when questioning persons who might have been acting suspiciously. It contains the subject's identifying data, the date and location of the incident, and a short synopsis of why the subject was questioned.

When you check the local police department, they'll do the searching for you. Usually you write the name and other identifying information on a form and hand it to a records clerk, who searches for the information while you wait. There is almost always a nominal charge—anywhere from $3 to $15—for this search.

While you're at the police department, ask them to check for 911 calls from the residence address. Most private investigators don't even think to do this, but you'd be surprised how often I find that the ex-wife has called 911 because of the new boyfriend assaulting or threatening her.

The Driving History

If you're conducting a general background check, you're looking for dirt. Your ex-spouse is dating some guy who, from time to time, has your kids in his car. You don't like the guy, but you have no control over the situation. So run a driving history on him. If he has a DUI on his record or a bunch of points for speeding or reckless driving charges, you can probably get a court order to prohibit your ex from letting your kids be in the car with him when he's behind the wheel. There are two reasons to do this:

- You'll feel better having taken some action.

- You can hire a PI to catch the creep driving with the kids in the car and then go for permanent custody. These are your kids. You need to do all you can to ensure that they are in a safe environment.

Driver's license information is still one of the single best sources for identification purposes. But unfortunately, as John Q. Private Citizen, this information is probably not available to you. The Driver's Privacy Protection Act (DPPA) pretty well limits driver's license information to government agencies and licensed private investigators, which has posed a problem to some PIs in states that don't issue PI licenses. It's sort of a catch-22 for private investigators in those states. So if you need the driver's license information because you can't find your subject's identifying information anywhere else, hire a PI to get it for you.

THE SCOOP

In 1989, Robert John Bardo hired a private investigator to get the home address of actress Rebecca Schaeffer, who, at that time, played on the television sitcom *My Sister Sam*. The PI got the information from the California Department of Motor Vehicles (DMV) and sold it to Bardo. Schaeffer was expecting Francis Ford Coppola to come to her door to discuss an audition for his film *The Godfather Part III*. When the bell rang, Schaeffer opened the door and found Bardo there instead. She asked him to leave and closed the door. Bardo went away but returned very upset. He rang again but hid so that Schaeffer had to step out of the apartment to see who was there. Bardo shot her once in the chest and fled. As a result of this incident, the U.S. Congress passed the Driver's Privacy Protection Act. This act prohibits the release of information pertaining to driver's licenses but includes 14 specific exceptions. Licensed private investigators are listed as exception #8, as long as the information is used for one of the other 13 reasons.

Locating the Address

A party in a civil case is identified by name and address, so you don't need his date of birth or Social Security number to research any civil cases he was involved in. You can usually get by with just the person's name. If it's a common name, you need the address to differentiate all those Bill Smiths or Steve Browns.

If you have the person's name and date of birth, getting the address is a cinch. Here are two quick ways to find it:

- **Get the vehicle tag.** This is by far the easiest and most direct approach. Sometimes, though, people change addresses and don't notify the DMV, so the vehicle registration might not always be current. The good news is, 8 times out of 10, it is.

- **Use the telephone records.** Reverse-search the number you got off the caller ID, and you'll have the address. If it's a cell phone, use the techniques I discuss in Chapter 7.

Sometimes clients really want the address, for reasons other than checking the civil records. Maybe the client needs to see for himself what's really going on at the new boyfriend's house, or maybe the client needs to prove that his ex-spouse has moved in with a man. This can figure into alimony adjustments in a big way, as we discussed in Chapter 5.

Here are two surefire ways to locate the address:

- **Check local property records (real property tax rolls).** If you have reason to believe that the person dating the ex owns his home, go to your local property appraiser's office and check the records. If the person rents his house or apartment, that won't work.

- **Follow the subject home.** This almost always works. Be sure to read Chapter 11 before you attempt this. A lot of tricks go into a successful surveillance, so study up. The last thing you want is for your ex to find out that you've tailed her new boyfriend to his apartment. And—this is very important—you certainly don't want a confrontation.

The Criminal in Our Background

In Chapter 5, I walk you through the process of getting records from both the clerk of the court and the state criminal record system. Now's your chance to put that knowledge to work. Yeah, it means you've got to spend a couple hours driving to the courthouse and getting someone to help you. Actually, at most courthouses, you'll spend more time looking for a parking space than you will inside looking for records. Twenty minutes, in and out, is all you should need if you're checking only criminal cases. Be sure to check both the upper and lower courts. In the lower courts, you'll find the misdemeanors. Remember, a lot of misdemeanors began as felonies and were *pled down* to misdemeanors. So you want to review the file and examine the original charges.

DEFINITION

To **plead down** means that, to expedite the flow of cases, as well as lessen the load and burden on the court, the prosecuting attorney reduces charges from higher offenses to lesser offenses. He or she does this if the defendant agrees to plead guilty to the lesser offenses.

Before you go to the courthouse, see if your county posts its criminal records online. Call the clerk of the court and ask, or use a search engine and search for "clerk of the court [your county, your state]." For example, if you want to find out whether Clay County, Florida, has its criminal records online, type "clerk of the court Clay County Florida." If you happen to search Clay County, you'll see that its criminal records are online and that you can access them for free.

The Sometimes Not-So-Civil Cases

I always recommend checking civil-court files in prenuptial investigations. Divorce files, in particular, contain some of the most bizarre allegations you'll ever see. Husbands and wives in the midst of a bitter divorce spill all the dirty secrets about each other, including drugs, sex, adultery, violence, anger, and perverted behavior. And you can find it all right there in the divorce file, a public record in most (but not all) states, available for anybody who cares to read about it. Certainly, were I to remarry, presuming that my wife-to-be had been previously divorced, I would want to review her divorce file before popping the question.

A while back, a stockbroker called me, indicating that she was going to be married in 10 days. She had some lingering doubts about her fiancé, who was from another state, and thought that, before the big day came, she should check into his background. "A little late," I thought, but we took the case.

I had my man in the western state the gentleman was from start with the civil records and the local police department. Guess what? In the clerk of the courts office, he found a marriage record but no divorce on file. True, he could have gotten divorced someplace else, so we kept on digging.

Across the street at the police department, guess what we found? Nope, not an arrest record, but a missing person report filed by his still-legal wife, nearly a year before. Apparently, the man just left his family of 20 years and headed east, leaving behind his wife and three sons. They had no idea where he was or whether he was dead or alive, but they did know for sure that he hadn't been divorced. Well, what's a little bigamy between friends?

The kicker is, my female client decided she was still in love with the guy, postponed the wedding, waited until the divorce was final from his first wife, and then married him anyway. At least she knew what she was getting into. After all that, do you still think doing a prenuptial background is silly?

Starting Your Own Background Company

You've been in the PI business for a long time and are tired of leaving home at 5 A.M. to follow some plaintiff with an early tee time to a golf course where he can swing a club but can't swing a paint brush. So you want to start an employment background-screening company and not worry about keeping your camera dry when it rains. Good for you. Here are some tips.

Starting a Brand New Company

First, you need to incorporate a new entity that has nothing to do with your PI-licensed firm. Remember back in Chapter 6 when I talked about the credit bureaus? The bottom line is, if your background company holds a PI license, the credit bureaus probably will not grant you access to their files. Many employers want a credit report run on their prospective employees. If you have no access or have to buy the credit report through a third party, your costs will go way up.

Whole books have been written on how to do background screenings, but I cover some of the basics in about six pages. This isn't meant to be all-inclusive, but it is intended to give you an idea of how to proceed. I wish I'd had this information when I began my background company. Just knowing about the client interface I tell you about would have saved me a year of wasted effort.

Obeying the Fair Credit Reporting Act (FCRA)

Provisions in the FCRA affect your new company. The FCRA is cursed by many private investigators who don't understand it, but it really opens several doors for background companies. As a background-screening company, you're considered a consumer-reporting agency, just like the big credit bureaus; it also means that you're bound by the same rules. As a small employer who performs your own backgrounds before hiring people, you're also bound by those rules. So let's have a look.

You can find the complete text of the FCRA at www.ftc.gov/os/statutes/031224fcra.pdf. It's 84 pages long; if you want to read it, knock yourself out. Meanwhile, I want to point out one important provision of the report that you absolutely must be aware of when using it for employment purposes:

Section 604 of the FCRA states that if "adverse action" is taken in whole or in part because of the consumer report, the prospective employer must communicate to the applicant within three days that adverse action was taken and should name your company as the consumer-reporting agency.

The prospective employee has a right to a copy of your report and, if he requests it, you must send him a copy. He may dispute anything in your report that he believes is inaccurate. Wow, sounds like a mess, huh? If you're a small business, you might want to reconsider performing your own backgrounds and hire my company, or some other background-screening company, to deal with all of this. But if you *are* the background company, you have to know the rules of the FCRA.

Creating Your Own Website

I haven't talked much about websites for private investigators. That's a whole book by itself. But I do need to spend a couple minutes on your background-screening company's website. Why? Because most of your background work will be conducted from your office, and it doesn't make any difference whether you're in Austin, Texas; Chicago, Illinois; or Boone, North Carolina. Your website should imply that your firm is national in scope. The big boys do most of their work from just one location, and you can, too. Your client doesn't need to know that the company is just you and one person running the data sources. You can have just as big a presence in Los Angeles as can some firm with 40 employees that is based in New York City.

In designing your website, pay attention to how your competition does theirs, and make yours better. You'll understand why this is so important in the next section.

The Client Interface

Most progressive background-screening companies have gone to a web-based client interface, in which established clients can log in and enter the applicant's data. This data is saved on a server that you access from your office. Creating an interface might sound like a lot of computer knowledge is needed, but that's not necessarily the case. You can hire a company to provide this interface. They charge for it, but it's a pretty slick product. When your client clicks on the login at your site (try mine if you like, www.hindsightinc.com) the URL address at the top of the screen changes from www. hindsightinc.com to a secure server with a different name. But did you also notice that the look of the server has the feel and look of my company's home page? Most of my clients never realize that they've been moved to another server.

After the client has input a new applicant's data, I'm notified immediately by email or, if I'm in the database, I see the new application come up in the work queue on the server. Either way, I can start working on the application right way.

To find companies that provide this service, I recommend using your favorite search engine and searching "employment screening software," but three websites of reputable companies are www.ssctech.com, www.tazworks.net, and www.frssoftware.com. Do your research and figure out what works best for you.

Working the Application

When you have a web-based client interface set up, much of the application process can be handled automatically. These servers interface with the credit bureaus, driving record suppliers, Social Security traces, and criminal record retrievers. You can configure your website so that when a client inputs the application data, a Social Security trace is automatically pulled. I talk about why you might want to do this in a minute. You can also configure the program to automatically pull a credit report, a driving history, and a criminal history. My staff can be drinking piña coladas by the pool and let the computer do the work. Of course, if I catch them, they're out of a job.

Pre-Employment Background Checks

A proper employment background check involves a lot of components, but the major components are as follows:

- Criminal record search

- Credit report

- Driving records

- Social Security trace

- Educational verification

I delve into each of these components in the following sections.

HIDDEN HINT

If you're going to specialize in certain niches, like airline pilots, for instance, you need to do your own homework to find out what other information to look into.

The Criminal Record Search

The general idea in searching for criminal records is to search the best available data. The norm is a county-level criminal search in the counties where the applicant has resided within the last 7 to 20 years. The records searched should be current to within 30 days. Some states allow consumer-reporting agencies to search back only seven years; others allow you to search back forever.

To find out, you need to know the laws of the states where your clients and the applicants are located. And keep in mind that laws and regulations change frequently, so use more than one resource when checking the laws.

So your client needs a criminal records search conducted in Bibb County, Georgia. How do you get it done? Several companies have put together nationwide networks of local county courthouse researchers. Here are four that I recommend:

> Phoenix Research (www.hrliability.com)
>
> National Background Data (www.nationalbackgrounddata.com)
>
> Omni Data Retrieval (www.omnidataretrieval.com)
>
> G.A. Public Record Services (www.gaprs.biz)

Other companies specialize in a particular geographic region or state. National Background Data doesn't compete with you; they sell only wholesale and do not sell directly to individual clients. But the others do a very good job, and you might want to take a look at them.

There is one, and only one, possible way to do a national criminal history search. That is by searching the FBI's Criminal Justice Information Services Division records. The records at the division can be searched by fingerprints, or you can initiate a search of the Computerized Criminal History section of the Bureau's NCIC computer, which can be searched by name and date of birth. Any honest person in the employment-screening or background-investigation business will admit that there is no other national criminal history check. Period. A search through the FBI's records and the NCIC computer is available only to law enforcement and a few other federally mandated organizations.

THE SCOOP

Some "search firms" sell what they call a "national criminal check." These searches usually include department of corrections and sex offender records and many county court records. But they don't search all records in all jurisdictions. If you decide to use one of these searches, make sure it covers the county you need.

The Credit Report

Fewer employers bother pulling credit reports on job applicants these days. Still, some clients want that service, so you'll need to provide it. Plus, you'll get requests for tenant screening, which usually involves a credit check. We talk about three major bureaus in other chapters, but in case you turned to this chapter first, here they are:

> Equifax (www.equifax.com)
>
> Transunion (www.transunion.com)
>
> Experian (www.experian.com)

Driving Records

Many employers couldn't care less about a person's driving history. Others, particularly those that provide company vehicles, insist that their employees have clear driving records. You have multiple choices for providers of driving records. One good company is American Driving Records (www.mvrs.com). First Advantage used to be the elephant in the room when it came to background companies, but they were recently bought out by CoreLogic, which owns a whole host of background-screening companies and other diverse companies in the background screening arena.

The Social Security Trace

A Social Security trace is a cheap tool for finding where your applicant has resided in the past. It also verifies that the applicant's Social Security number has been issued and is not made up. It is largely based on credit header information and lists addresses that your applicant reported in the past, usually with the dates that the applicant supposedly resided there. It is a good tool, but since it is derived from credit data, it's often inaccurate. National Background Data, a firm I mentioned earlier in this chapter, sells one called "AIM" that is better than some, and the cost to its affiliates is less than a dollar.

Educational Verification

Some universities verify dates of enrollment and/or degrees given to their students if you call the registrar's office at the school, but many universities now farm out this task to independent companies. National Student Clearing House has a number of universities enrolled in their systems, at www.studentclearinghouse.org.

Education verification is the one employment search where applicants lie the most. It's incredible. They'll claim to have degrees from universities when they don't. They'll indicate three years' attendance when they attended only one semester. It goes on and on.

Think about this. If applicants misrepresent facts or lie on their employment application, what does that make them? If you hire them anyway, don't be surprised when you catch them in a lie later.

Other checks that employers should consider include checks for previous employment (especially salary information), references, medical databases required for hospital personnel, credentials and special licenses, Patriot Act–compliance search, PACER, and some other specialized searches for special fields, such as the National Driver Register and the FAA Accident and Incident database for airline pilots.

HIDDEN HINT

If you are going to begin an employment-screening company, you might as well include tenant screening also. But that's another book.

The Least You Need to Know

- A basic background check usually includes a criminal history, civil records search, previous employers, and personal reference contacts.
- Before driving to the courthouse, check to see if these records are online.
- You must have at least the name and date of birth to conduct a background search, and preferably a Social Security number as well. Obtaining this information involves some tricks.
- There is no "national criminal" search other than the NCIC, which is run by the FBI. Don't be fooled.
- Civil suits, particularly divorce files, contain many allegations between suing parties and provide good leads for additional witnesses.
- Applicants routinely lie about their educational credits. Many universities use outside agencies to report enrollment and verify degrees.

The Diligent Search: Adoption and Estates

In This Chapter

- How diligent adoption and estate searches differ from other searches
- Getting to know the legal steps of a diligent search
- Extracting information from the post office
- Doing a complete investigation

A diligent adoption search is a search that's required by law in many states before parental rights can be terminated and a child can be adopted without the consent of one or both parents. A similar search, called a diligent estate search, is used in estate cases when there's a missing heir. In both types of cases, if a diligent search is performed and the parent or heir can't be found, an estate can be settled or a missing parent can be served by publication. (Service by publication is a method in which an individual is served with process without physically laying papers in his hands. If one party cannot be located, a notice can be published in a newspaper in the county where the court action is to take place over a period of several weeks. When this is accomplished, the individual is considered to be served.)

This chapter is for professional investigators who'd like to increase their billing rate. When conducting a diligent adoption or estate search you can earn $200 plus per hour instead of your usual $85 per hour. Normally, PIs bill these cases at a flat rate of between $500 and $750, but the actual time you spend on the case might be only three hours.

Aside from the money involved, another reason these are great cases is that you're not sneaking around trying to catch people doing things they don't want to be caught doing. You're not hiding under the bushes at 4 A.M. trying to video a guy folding newspapers before he goes on his route. They are straightforward searches in which you can be forthcoming about what you're doing and who you're looking for.

Your client in these types of cases is typically an attorney. Often, however, your fee is paid directly by the "to be" adoptive parents or the estate of the person involved.

Some attorneys are not happy when you locate the subject. That's because it's easier to serve someone by publication. But the really good attorneys recognize that if the subject is located and served, there's no way they're going to be sued for doing an inadequate diligent search.

What Is the Law?

State laws vary on the guidelines for a diligent search. Before offering your services, check your state law requirements. This is a highly specialized area. If you don't know the specifics of your state, the attorneys who specialize in this field will write you off as incompetent.

For this discussion, I use the Florida statute as the guideline, but many states have similar statutes. Some are less stringent than Florida. Some states, like South Carolina, specify that a search for the missing parent must be conducted but don't specify exactly what the steps must be.

The series of steps I walk you through in this chapter results in a very thorough search that should satisfy most state laws. You'll locate your subject about 70 percent of the time in these cases.

When I locate subjects in diligent adoption searches, I find that many of them are afraid they are being sued for child support and are delighted to be told they're actually being relieved of their parental obligations. Jerks. (Just my thoughts on deadbeat parents, in case you can't tell.)

A common statute reads something to the effect that if the location of the missing parent is unknown but the identity of that parent is known, and that the parent has not executed a consent to the adoption, the people in charge of the adoption process must conduct a diligent search for that parent, and the search must include the following steps.

Locate the Last-Known or Current Address

The first step in any diligent search, whether for an adoption or an estate, is to determine the last-known "current address."

The Law Requires ...

You must attempt to locate the person's current address, or any previous address, through an inquiry of the United States Postal Service through the Freedom of Information Act (FOIA).

The Reality

The law wants you, the investigator, to send a letter to the postal service and request the current address or any previous address of your subject. Right. That's really going to work. Try sending that letter, and the postal FOIA officer for your district will respond with, "Sorry, the post office has no information concerning the individual in question." Think about it. The post office doesn't have a master list of everybody in town by name. The post office data is *address* specific. You have to search by address to get information from the post office.

So how do you satisfy this requirement? Postal Regulation 39 CFR 265.6 (d)(5)(ii) provides for the post office to relinquish a forwarding address if you have a subpoena for that subject. The information can be disseminated as long as it is for the purpose of "service of legal process in connection with actual or prospective litigation."

In these cases, if you can locate the subject, he will be served, so your request clearly falls within the scope of the postal regulations.

The Form

Now, how do you get the information? Regulations state that you should deliver the appropriate form to the postmaster at the post office that covers the address in question.

The post office has a form for change of address and box holder information, which you can find at http://about.usps.com/handbooks/as353/as353c5_002.htm#ep797495. Copy it and print it on your letterhead.

But if you live in Phoenix and the address of your subject is in Oklahoma, go to www.usps.com and click the button on the left that reads "Find Locations." Input the last-known address, and you'll get the address and the fax number for the post office that covers your subject's address. Fax the form to the postmaster and mail him a hard copy as well.

Often the postmaster will fax the form back to you. Just as often, he or she will mail it. I always follow up with the postmaster every other day until I've bugged him enough to get it done. It may be rude, but it's effective.

THE SCOOP

The post office forwards first-class mail for 12 months. During months 13 through 18, the mail is returned to the sender with the new address. After 18 months, all address data is purged from the computers and first-class mail is returned to the sender endorsed "Forwarding Order Expired."

So far, your cost in requesting the information from the post office has been exactly zilch.

We professionals don't give up easily. Check off these four additional steps for locating the address, and you've graduated from a journeyman investigator to a true craftsman:

- Send a letter to the subject, but mark it "Return Service Requested."

- Address a letter to the subject and put on the envelope "Please Forward." Send it to his last-known address, asking him to call you. He might actually call you. If the letter is returned to sender, you can still document your efforts.

- I look up the owner of the property of my subject's last-known address (see Chapter 5). I address a letter to the property owner asking him or her to call me. If I don't get a call, I try to locate a phone number for the property owner and call them. Often landlords have some idea where the subject moved to.

- Look up your subject on Facebook. If you find him, send him a message asking him to contact you. I also look at his family members and message them. Sometimes they contact me; sometimes they don't.

Find the Last-Known Employer

You probably want to pick up the telephone and call the employer.

The Law Requires …

You need the last-known employment of the person, including the name and address of the person's employer.

The Reality

Talk to the relatives—the ex-wife, the grandparent who is going to adopt the child, and so on. If you can't find any information on the last-known employer, then in your affidavit, you just have to state that you checked all logical leads couldn't find any information about previous employment.

LEGAL TRAP

Trying to secure current employment information from the Social Security Administration or your state board of wages and employment is probably illegal. In the early 1990s, half a dozen private investigators paid a Social Security Administration employee to obtain employment-reported data. Then they resold it to other private investigators and their own clients. The PIs went to jail. Don't do it.

Check with the Regulatory Agencies

Regulatory agencies generally are considered government agencies within the state and local jurisdictions where your subject was last known to reside or in the area where you have an indication that she might have moved.

The Law Requires ...

You must contact any regulatory agencies your subject might be listed with, including those regulating licensing in the area where the person last resided.

The Reality

Your subject's line of work might require state licensing. For example, if your missing parent is a nurse, medical doctor, chiropractor, lawyer, massage therapist, surveyor, landscape architect, accountant, body wrapper, or nuclear medicine technologist (well, you get the idea), he or she must be licensed to work in that professional field. If this is the case, the regulatory agency might have information.

To complete this portion of your diligent search, you must also check for a business license. Most cities require a business license, even if your subject is just operating a hot dog stand. Oh, right, hot dogs—don't forget to check for food and beverage licenses and health certificates. Generally, the city will have the business license filed only under the business name, not by the name of the owner. Do the best you can.

HIDDEN HINT

Check the state's secretary of state to see if your subject is an officer, director, or registered agent for a corporation. The secretary of state's records might not strictly fall under the guise of a regulatory agency, but don't tell them that. Usually it's a free search and can be done online while you're watching the football game on Sunday afternoon.

Contact the Families and the Relatives

If family members are adopting the child, sometimes they don't want the subject located, for fear that the missing parent will object to the adoption. Nevertheless, the law requires that you address this issue.

The Law Requires ...

You need names and addresses of relatives to the extent that they can be reasonably obtained from the petitioner or other sources, contacts with those relatives, and inquiry into the person's last-known address. The petitioner must pursue any leads of any addresses to which the person might have moved.

The Reality

The single best source for locating a subject is the relatives. Your client is most likely some sort of relative to the subject and the child—a grandparent or an uncle or aunt. They'll tell you they don't know where your subject is. Note that in your file. But also ask for names of other relatives of your subject. Track down those relatives and question them.

When I was looking for Jack Reading, his parents told me he worked on offshore oil rigs. They thought he was in Louisiana or Texas, but they hadn't heard from him in more than three years. When I completed the searches, my affidavit read that his parents hadn't heard from him in over three years. It was good enough for me and the judge.

But when I was looking for Mary Chambers, I talked to her aunt. She gave me Mary's cell number. I left her a message. Mary called me back and gave me her address in Ohio. She asked for the phone number of the people who had custody of her 4-year-old son, whom she hadn't seen in three years. I'd have liked to accommodate her, but I thought better of it and gave her the phone number of the attorney. We had her served three days later.

Find Out Whether He's Dead or Alive

Your affidavit must include a statement as to whether you've checked sources to determine whether your subject has died. After all, you don't want to serve a dead person by publication.

The Law Requires ...

You need information on whether the person died and, if so, the date and location.

The Reality

In the matter of diligent adoption searches, this is probably your easiest step. In Chapter 4, I introduce you to the Social Security Death Master File, which the Social Security Administration maintains and which records the deaths of everyone who has a Social Security number. You can access the Death Master File from a number of different professional databases, but here are two free searches I recommend:

- www.genealogybank.com/gbnk/ssdi/
- www.stevemorse.org/ssdi/ssdi.html

I filed an affidavit in an estate matter for Roger Ball. Roger was from New Jersey. He'd disappeared 20 years ago in Oregon at the age of 23 and had never been heard from since. In 2006, both of his parents died and left a valuable estate. I completed all the steps I outline in this chapter. I even ran his New Jersey driver's license, which showed no activity for the last 20 years. He's either deceased as a John Doe or he's out of the country. I provided the affidavit, and the court decided that, for the purpose of the estate, he would be considered deceased. If the court had ruled otherwise, his share of the estate would have gone to the State's Unclaimed Monies Fund. With the court accepting our affidavit, the estate was split four ways instead of five—a considerable bonus to the remaining children.

Six years later, as of the time of this writing, a police detective from Arizona called me and told me that authorities there had found a dead body alongside a rural road. I had filed a missing person's report with the Oregon police, and they had entered the information into the National Crime Information Center (NCIC) database. The Arizona authorities had found the information in the NCIC and thought it was possible that this decomposed body might have been Roger Ball. Again, I can't emphasize enough how important it is to make sure missing persons and runaways are entered into the NCIC. (See Chapter 15 for details on the NCIC.)

LEGAL TRAP

The quickest method for an attorney to be sued for malpractice is to have an adoption "go bad." This usually happens when one of the child's parents cannot be located and the attorney serves the missing parent by publication. The child is adopted, and later the delinquent parent comes knocking, claiming that he would have been easy to locate if only somebody had taken the time to search for him. The missing father now wants custody of his child, who has brand-new parents. The attorney is sued by his clients. It's a big mess. Attorneys don't like big messes.

Look Up the Telephone Numbers

Directory information is easy to come by, but not all telephone directories are equal. See Chapter 7 for the scoop.

The Law Requires ...

You need to get the telephone listings in the area where the person last resided.

The Reality

This step in the diligent search process is easy. Search a number of different directory information resources. Each time you get a new lead on your subject's whereabouts, check one of your pay directory sites. Make a note in your file of each city that you check so that you can include them all in your affidavit.

HIDDEN HINT

If you want to save a nickel, this is the place to do it. Because the free White Pages listings have old data, you might find your subject listed even though your up-to-date pay site shows no listing. He's moved, but he used to live there. The old data might provide an address with the listing. Sometimes old data can provide good leads. If you find him in the old listings but not the current ones, use the pay sites to get the listing of whomever is living at that address now and call them. They might know where the previous occupant moved to.

Inquire at Local Law Enforcement Agencies

Generally, searches can be conducted at the local level of law enforcement.

The Law Requires ...

You need inquiries of law enforcement agencies where the person last resided.

The Reality

Local law enforcement agencies often respond to phone calls. Ask for the records section and see if they will check your subject's name and give you the results over the phone; if they won't, ask if you can fax or mail a request. They might charge a small fee (usually less than $15) for this search. If they won't do a search for you, be sure to document that you tried.

Search State Law Enforcement Records

Some state law enforcement records are easily searched, and others allow no access.

The Law Requires ...

You must search highway patrol records in the state where the person last resided.

The Reality

Whoever wrote the bill and included this requirement had no clue what records a state "highway patrol" would have. So what do you do? We put on our gypsy fortune teller robe, turn the lights down low, and figure out what the bill's author had in mind.

In some states, the highway patrol maintains the state's criminal record database. Most highway patrols investigate traffic accidents on the state's highways. You'll probably need accident report numbers to search for accidents, but you might find a state that allows searches by name or driver. The important item here is to make sure that this area is covered in your affidavit. If you can't search the highway patrol office records, search the state criminal record database.

Search the Prison System

The prison system in the United States is basically divided into three systems: the federal prisons, the state prisons, and the county and/or city jails. As a general rule, prisoners are held in county and city jails for six months or less or while awaiting trials. Federal prisoners are also held in county jails while awaiting trial.

THE SCOOP

Approximately 311,800,000 persons reside in the United States. According to the U.S. Department of Justice, Bureau of Justice Statistics, in the year 2011, about 7 million people, or more than 2 percent of the population of the United States, was either in prison, in jail, or under some type of active "correctional supervision." About 4.4 million adults moved to or off probation.

The Law Requires ...

You must search Department of Corrections records in the state where the person last resided.

The Reality

Most state correction facilities have websites where you can search. Use your favorite search engine and search by state name and "Department of Corrections."

As for the federal penitentiaries, you can search the entire federal system at www.bop.gov.

In a recent diligent search, I found that my subject had been released on parole. I noticed that the correctional website had provided current addresses for parolees. Guess where mine was? Yep, he was back in the county jail. I called the jail and verified he was there. This search was so easy that I felt compelled to return a large portion of the retainer I'd received. The subject couldn't really avoid service and was served within a couple of days. I now receive adoption diligent searches from this attorney on a regular basis.

Inquire at Local Hospitals

You'd think that with *HIPAA* and all the privacy surrounding medical care, getting information out of hospitals would be difficult. That's not the case.

> **DEFINITION**
>
> **HIPAA** is an acronym for Health Insurance Portability and Accountability Act. It was passed in Congress in 1996. A minor part of the act, but the part most quoted by medical providers so they don't have to release any information to you, is a section that deals with the security and privacy of health data.

The Law Requires ...

You must search hospitals in the area where the person last resided.

The Reality

The hardest part of this search is determining which hospitals are in the surrounding area of your subject's last known address. As strange as that sounds, it's true.

Use an internet mapping service like www.mapquest.com to locate the city where your subject last resided, and find the surrounding cities. Go to one of the free Yellow Pages searches, or use one of the pay White Pages searches and search using a keyword of "hospital." Print all the returns.

Now start calling. Ask to be transferred to patient information. The purpose of this search is to prove that your subject is not incapacitated by an accident and lying in a hospital bed.

Ask patient information if your subject is a patient in the hospital. They'll politely tell you no, and you go on to the next one, right? Wrong. They'll politely tell you no, and then you ask to be transferred to hospital records. You ask the person in records if she has any record of your subject having been there, ever. Eight times out of 10, they'll check and tell you yes or no. Amazing, but true. In fairness, they're not releasing any information that they shouldn't. It's basically the same information patient information gives you, only it's back-dated.

HIDDEN HINT

If you're searching a really large city, narrow your hospital search by zip code. Most telephone directory searches allow for searches within a certain zip code.

Your affidavit will be more complete if you can say that he has never been a patient in those hospitals.

Utility Company Records

Searching utility company records is sort of a crap shoot. Sometimes you make your point, sometimes you seven out.

The Law Requires ...

You need records of utility companies, including water, sewer, cable television, and electric companies, in the area where the person last resided.

The Reality

In some municipalities, the utility companies are open to the public. More often, the companies will not release the records.

Call the city hall and ask for the name of the major utility carrier in the area, both electric and water. Call the utilities' customer service numbers and ask if they have any subscriber by your subject's name. They'll want the Social Security number. Often you'll get a customer service rep who will decline to give you any information. But sometimes you'll get someone who will say, "Yes, but we can't give you the address or any information." Or they might indicate that they used to have service but no longer do. They might give you the date the service was terminated, but they usually won't give you the address.

I was searching for the mother of a child in Colorado. I called the publicly owned water company in a city where I thought she might be. The customer service rep referred me to her supervisor, where I left a voice mail. Three times I called him, and he never returned my call. The information should have been public, but he didn't want to divulge it, so he just ignored me. The customer service rep did say that they refer people to the city police department for background checks.

Right, I thought. I'm going to call the city police, and they're going to run a record search for me over the phone. Now in Colorado, you can run the entire state over the website www.cocourts.com for about $8. I'd done that and found a few old cases, but none of them helped.

Finally I thought, what the heck, and I called the records department of this small Denver suburb police department. The fellow checked his computer. They had my subject listed as a complainant on a malicious mischief case. Someone had keyed her car. This gave me a recent address.

Excited, I checked the address. No luck. My subject had moved out a few months earlier. I checked the free White Pages listings (remember free = old data) and found the name the phone at that address had been listed under. Then I did a search in the pay White Pages database (pay = current data) and found a listing for the same fellow in a nearby city. I called that number, and guess who answered the phone. Bingo! My subject, the mother of the child up for adoption. We had a nice chat, and she was served within a few days.

In this same case, I found the father of the child living in a tack shed on a horse ranch in Colorado. He came to the phone at the ranch house. He agreed he wished to do whatever was best for his son. He gave me the street address where the process server could find him. When you find the subject, you don't have to complete the affidavit (I talk about the affidavit in detail later in this chapter), but you've still earned your fee.

Ask the Military

Finding one particular military person can be challenging. And service of process to military people, especially in a war theater, requires a whole chapter by itself.

The Law Requires ...

You need to search records of the armed services of the United States to determine if there is any indication that the subject is currently serving in the armed services.

The Reality

Search the Defense Manpower Data Center site set up for compliance with the Servicemembers Civil Relief Act (www.dmdc.osd.mil/appj/scra/scraHome.do).

You input your subject's name, Social Security number, and date of birth, and it'll let you know whether your subject is on active duty. If he is, well, you just found him. Getting him served is a whole different problem, and in some venues, you can't serve an active duty military person. In some, you can.

Check with the Tax Man

Earlier in this chapter, I talked about checking for business licenses and state-required licenses. Here I deal with taxable obligations on the state and local levels.

The Law Requires ...

The law requires that you search records of the tax assessor and tax collector in the area where the person last resided.

The Reality

Start with the county of last-known residence and check the property tax records. Sometimes the subject still owns property in the county, even though he's not there. Sometimes the tax bill even goes to his new address.

Also, some states have their counties collect personal property taxes and intangible property taxes. (Intangible property always seemed like a contradiction in terms to me, but it's one of those things that if the government finds a way to tax it, they will.) Ask the tax collector what other taxes your subject might be liable for in the jurisdiction you're searching.

Search Professional PI Databases

I talk a lot about databases in Chapter 6. Isn't it interesting that even the government recognizes that private investigators have data resources that aren't affiliated with the government?

The Law Requires ...

Search of one internet databank locator service.

The Reality

You probably have searched your favorite database several dozen times by now. I always search the three that I have ready access to. In the affidavit, relate what your database told you: which address it showed as most recent and how you pursued all logical leads for that address.

LEGAL TRAP

Don't skimp on any of the steps I outline in this chapter. Sometimes it's tempting—don't do it. That would be dishonest and cheating, and in the end, you have to sign a notarized affidavit that you performed dutifully every required search in the process.

Filing Your Affidavit

Your affidavit is the culmination of all your effort. Win, lose, or draw, you've completed a thorough search for your subject—in other words, you've performed a diligent search. Upon conclusion, you will have successfully ended a complex investigation. You can be proud of your work, and if you've carefully documented each step, your affidavit will stand the test of any court, the probing of any attorney, and the hindsight of any person who might come along later.

Now that you've done the work, it's important that the finished product appear professional. Your client and the judge will not see all your notes in your file. They won't examine your telephone bill. So prepare an affidavit that lists each step I outline and the results you obtain. For a sample affidavit, check out Appendix D.

Make your affidavit look professional. The more professional your affidavit appears, the more satisfied your clients will be. And satisfied clients generate more business without any additional marketing.

How Much to Charge?

Don't bill diligent searches by the hour; instead, charge a flat rate by case. The minimum I charge for this type of case anywhere in the United States is $650. But in the case with the couple in Colorado, which involved searching for both parents, you might want to consider giving the client a discount.

How long will the case take? Figure on two weeks, mainly because of slow responses from the post office. Actual time spent on the phone, at the computer, and so on should be about three hours or a bit more. You do the math on the hourly rate.

The Least You Need to Know

- Many states require a diligent search in adoption and estate matters.
- Diligent searches are detailed investigations that command higher fees.
- Fourteen separate investigative steps make up a diligent search, including public, postal, governmental, utility, and hospital records.
- Upon conclusion of the search, if the subject is not located, a notarized affidavit detailing each step of the search is completed and presented to the court.

Evidence, Statements, Reports, and Bookkeeping

In This Chapter

- Using evidence to make a case
- Gathering recorded and signed statements
- Handling evidence properly
- Using the FBI FD-302 as a template for your reports
- Feeding the secretary

Reporting the results of your investigation to your client is just as important, if not more so, than the investigation itself. After all, no matter how well executed the investigation is, how valuable the information is to the client, and how sure the victory in court looks, it won't mean squat if you fail to submit a report detailing your findings, if your reporting skills are inadequate, or if the report is so faulty that it's unusable.

I've known investigative firms that have sent investigators into the field. The investigators shot good video on workmen's compensation claims and verbally reported the results to their clients. The firm sent the tape and a bill to the client but didn't include a detailed report—in other words, they provided no documentation of their investigation. Three years later, the case went to court. The attorney for the insurance company wanted to use the tape to prove that the claimant wasn't really hurt and needed the investigator to testify. Nobody in the firm could remember who shot the tape. Do you think they had a little problem?

In almost every investigation, there comes a juncture when you have to step back and analyze the direction of the case and how your efforts are directed. I deal with that analysis in this chapter. Then I show you how to wrap up the case and present it to the client in a professionally formatted report.

Sifting Through the Evidence

The general rule of evidence is, naturally, that somebody collected it and, logically, that same somebody needs to be present to introduce it into court. Later in this chapter, I discuss the importance of maintaining the chain of custody on the evidence. The same principles apply whether you're collecting evidence at the scene of a crime or gathering anything else of evidentiary value, including videos.

In surveillance matters, the video really isn't the primary piece of evidence. Actually, the investigator's testimony is what counts. Video just corroborates, albeit sometimes in a very dramatic way, what the investigator saw. The legal system relied on eyewitness testimony long before video was ever invented.

THE SCOOP

I can testify that I saw a workmen's compensation claimant with an alleged neck injury standing on his head on a surfboard while surfing. That's good testimony. But let me play the tape of that same scene, and the jury is totally convinced. You can tell when they laugh at the claimant that you've made your case.

Workmen's compensation evidence is fairly straightforward. Either you catch the claimant engaged in activities he says he can't perform, or you don't. In other types of cases, the evidence is often less clear cut, and you have to sift through it to see what you've got.

An 18-year-old boy, Darby, was employed at a restaurant as a server. The drinking age in the state is 21. One July evening after his shift was over, Darby left the restaurant in his pickup truck and prevailed upon his older buddy to buy some beer. They started club hopping, drinking the beers in his pickup truck on the drives between clubs. Darby claimed he had only two beers. Later, near closing time, Darby returned to the restaurant where he worked, entered through the back door to the kitchen, and proceeded to the bar area. According to Darby, the bartender gave him three free drinks made with an expensive brand of whiskey. Darby left the restaurant and, while driving home, drove off the road, hit a tree, and was paralyzed from the neck down for the rest of his life.

Darby and his parents sued the restaurant/bar for serving Darby because he was underage and for allowing him to leave the bar and drive while under the influence. It was a terrible tragedy. Now you be the judge and tell me who was at fault.

Two years later, the attorney representing Darby asked my agency to investigate the circumstances of that night in July. He wanted a blow-by-blow account of what had transpired in the restaurant and the bar. And, oh yeah, the restaurant/bar had gone out of business more than a year before he decided to take the case.

My agents and I had to track down the former employees and interview them, then sift through and evaluate what they could remember about that night. That night was momentous in Darby's life, but to everyone else, it was just another night. Can you remember where you were on July 23 two years ago? Neither can I.

We obtained the police reports and rescue reports detailing the accident investigation. No question about it, 18-year-old, underage Darby had been drunk. His blood alcohol level had been more than twice the legal limit.

We examined the bar records from that night. It included a log of the drinks served. About 11 P.M., when Darby says he was served, the log showed three double drinks of that same expensive liquor being rung up as complimentary drinks.

A pattern emerged from the interviews of the former employees: the young owners of the restaurant allowed their underage employees to drink alcohol on the premises. They were "cool." They sponsored several employee parties after work and provided the booze, allowing everyone there, regardless of age, to imbibe. They even had an employee meeting to discuss the subject of underage employees drinking, and the owners seemed to think that, even though 21 was the statutory drinking age, their employees could pretty well do whatever they wanted, as long as "it didn't get out of hand."

Not everybody we talked to was so forthcoming. Some, in an effort to protect the owners, said they never saw anybody underage drinking. Others maybe did. They came to work, did their job, and went home. Some seemed to hang around after hours until the lights were turned off.

As for the bartender who'd actually served Darby the drinks, all we had was a fairly common first name. No last name, no Social Security number, nothing we could use to help us locate him. Since we represented the plaintiff, we didn't have access to all of the employee records.

We also hadn't talked to any employee who could say definitively that Darby had been drinking at the bar. We had employees who saw Darby return to the restaurant. One of the cooks in the kitchen said when Darby came in, he was carrying a beer can, and the cook told him he couldn't bring outside beer into the restaurant.

Everyone in my office worked the case pretty hard for two weeks, locating and interviewing the former employees. Some of the former employees had worked at the restaurant for only a month; others had worked the entire two years it was open. Some of the former employees were never found. But let's sift through what we did get.

Positive for the plaintiff (Darby):

- Proof that Darby had worked at the restaurant

- Testimony of a clear pattern of underage employees being allowed to drink inside the restaurant

- Testimony that the owners knew underage employees were drinking and almost implicitly encouraged it

- Bar tab showing three doubles of the same liquor being served as complimentary beverages at about the time Darby says he was served that particular brand of liquor

- Proof that Darby was drunk when he hit the tree and that he'd just left the restaurant

- Beer cans in the bed of the pickup truck that could have been there for days or weeks before the incident and so be unrelated to the cause of the accident

Positive for the defendants (the restaurant):

- At the accident scene, numerous beer cans in the back of Darby's pickup truck

- Testimony that some employees had never seen underage drinking

- Testimony that Darby had left the restaurant sober after his shift was over

- Testimony that Darby had returned to the restaurant with a beer can in his hand

- No witnesses saw Darby drinking at the bar the night of the accident

Does Darby have a case? We don't want to get into a discussion here about personal responsibility, and a good PI must learn to compartmentalize such things from the hard-core legal issues of any case he's working. Legally, the bar has liability if Darby was served alcohol and had a traffic accident afterward. True, nobody poured the liquor down his throat, but it shouldn't have been offered to him. Even though the bar was now out of business, the bar owners and their insurance company would be on the hook if the case went to trial and Darby prevailed.

Our client, Darby's attorney, called and informed us that the next day they were to have a pretrial settlement hearing. What did we have? I gave him a synopsis of all the statements we'd taken and couriered them over to his office. The attorney wanted to know where the bartender was and why we hadn't found him. I told him that we were looking for him as hard as we could.

Periodically, while working a case, you have to take a step back and evaluate the evidence you've collected so far. Figure out what the attorney needs to make the case, and adjust your investigative efforts accordingly. Shift the focus or the direction you the investigator is going in order to meet those needs.

I'm not suggesting that you not report any facts that negatively affect your client's case. If you uncover any negative information, the attorney needs to know about it so that he isn't blindsided in a hearing. But you may need to redirect your efforts to get what he needs, which is exactly what we did with the bartender in this case.

Late that afternoon, I contacted another employee who used to room with the bartender. We got lucky. He gave me the bartender's complete name. He'd moved to another state, but we tracked him down on the West Coast, and the time there is three hours earlier. The bartender finally arrived home after midnight our time. I got a recorded statement from him saying that, yes, he did serve Darby three drinks, and his recollection was that the liquor was the particular brand which Darby said it was. His memory was pretty clear about it because, the next day at work, all the buzz was about Darby's wreck, and he knew he'd served him some drinks.

I called the attorney at home and woke him up. After I related what I'd just gotten, he was elated and said we'd just found the Holy Grail. The next morning, I faxed the attorney's office a synopsis of the bartender's statement. During the pretrial settlement hearing, he read the synopsis to a representative of the insurance company and the attorney representing the restaurant. After a few minutes of private consultation, the company agreed to settle for the policy limit, which was $1 million. Our client agreed to the settlement, and, right or wrong, it was done.

Taking Recorded and Signed Statements

Private investigators need to know how to take *recorded* and *signed statements*. A written statement, signed and sworn to by the person signing it, is a very good piece of testimonial evidence. Recorded interviews can be beneficial as well.

> **DEFINITION**
>
> A **recorded statement** is a voice recording made by a witness concerning facts and/or the witness's recollection of the pertinent incident. A recorded statement can be taken either over the telephone or in person. A **signed statement** is a written declaration made by a witness concerning facts and/or the witness's recollection of the pertinent incident that is signed by the declarant; it should be witnessed by the investigator and a third party, if possible. (If the statement is taken in a jail cell, have a guard witness the statement.)

You might recollect the law concerning recording of communications from Chapter 16. In that case, we talked about one-party and all-party states. Check out Appendix B for a list of which states are one-party states and which states require all parties to consent to being recorded. Those rules apply to the interception of telephone calls. Separate rules apply to the interception of oral communications not conducted over a wire.

> **LEGAL TRAP**
>
> When a telephone call crosses state boundaries, beware. The recording of the telephone conversation might be legal in one of those states but not in the other.

Many states make it illegal to record a conversation, other than telephonic, between two or more people unless all parties agree to the recording. Therefore, if you're going to take a recorded statement from a witness to an accident, be sure the witness affirms verbally on the recording that he is aware he is being recorded and states that you, the private investigator, have his permission to do so.

Why would you want to record a witness? Remember, a case might not go to trial for three or more years after an accident. Witnesses might forget what they saw, or at least what they told you they saw. There is nothing better to help refresh a witness's recollection of the incident than to let him listen to his own voice telling you what he witnessed.

As a PI, it's important to understand that the witness's sympathy might really be with the plaintiff. If your client is the defendant, that means you're asking for a statement from "the opposition." By getting the witness's statement on tape, you're protected so that when the witness's wife berates him for "helping" the wrong side, and suddenly he can't remember exactly what he saw, it won't matter. It's on the record. This happens all the time.

As I've noted over and over again, a good investigator merely gathers the facts and lets the evidence chips fall where they may, but witnesses often have their own agenda and flexible standards to suit it. A recording of the witness's statement, therefore, can be used to *impeach* her testimony in court if she has a sudden change of heart and testifies to something other than what she originally said.

> **DEFINITION**
>
> **Impeaching** a witness's testimony means to call into question the reliability or truthfulness of the testimony being given.

When a witness changes his testimony, the courtroom dialogue goes something like this:

> **Attorney:** Mr. Witness, didn't you tell our investigator that you witnessed the blue car run the red light and strike the white car?

> **Witness:** No, I don't believe so. The light was green when the blue car entered the intersection. I have a very good recollection of that.

> *The attorney plays the recording with the witness telling the PI that the light was definitely red and the blue car ran the red light.*

> **Witness (looking at his wife and shrugging):** I guess it must have been red. It's been so long, I got confused.

That's how impeachment works in a courtroom. You want the recording so the egg ends up on the witness's face and not yours.

Raymond was in a custody battle with his wife, my client, Sheila. Part of the court order was that Raymond, an alcoholic, would not drink. Raymond was about 28 years old, a tall, lanky, good-looking fellow who happened to own a very popular restaurant. Our client needed to prove that Raymond was still drinking and carousing.

I followed Raymond on numerous occasions. I photographed him using the drive-through window of a liquor store. There was an exchange of funds, and the clerk passed a brown paper bag with his purchases to him. I even photographed it.

Raymond also frequented topless bars. While in the bars, he drank a lot of beer. I documented how many beers he drank and what brand they were. When the case was ready to go to court, I interviewed the waitresses at these topless bars. (I know, you're thinking I probably interviewed more than I needed to, huh?) I found one good witness who remembered Raymond and what she served him. The waitress remembered the brand of beer he preferred, how he tipped, and how many beers he usually drank while he was there. He was a regular and would come in about three times a week.

We subpoenaed the witness the next day for the trial. In court, she testified that she never told me Raymond drank beer and said that, when he came in, he always ordered a soft drink. She didn't ever serve him beer or any other alcohol, always a cola drink. Do you think Raymond got to her? You can bet on it. I wished I'd had a recorded statement from her, but I didn't get one. What I did get was egg in my face in front of the jury. Took me a couple of hours to wash it all off.

People lie in court. It always amazes me that they will perjure themselves, but it happens every day. Oh, and what did Raymond say about the drive-thru liquor store? He claimed he bought a 2-liter bottle of cola. Right.

The Format for the Recorded Statement

A recorded statement should begin like this: "This is investigator [your name] and today's date is [today's date]. I am speaking with [the witness's name]. Mr. [witness], you are aware that I am recording this conversation, is that correct?"

Make sure the witness says "Yes." The recording device won't record head nods.

"And I have your permission to record this, is that also correct?" Again, make sure you get a verbal "yes."

"Now, Mr. [witness], for the record, please state your name and your address." Then make sure you get his telephone number, his date of birth, and his Social Security number.

Next, ask where he is employed and what hours he works. Why? You want all that detail because if it takes a couple of years for the case to go to court, that might be the only way you can track him down.

After the introduction, ask him to tell you what he witnessed. Let him talk. In addition to the recording, take good notes. I try not to interrupt the witness. When he has finished, I go back, using my notes, and ask appropriate questions for clarification purposes, or to elicit more details or facts that the witness didn't give the first time through.

If you want to ask the witness something, you need a potty break, or you need to talk about something that isn't relevant to the case, it is permissible to turn off the tape recorder and deal with whatever it is. Before turning off the recorder, state what time it is and that you are turning off the recorder. When you go back on the record, be sure to state the current time and get the witness's permission again to record the conversation.

You'll know you've exhausted the interview when you can't get another fact out of the witness. To officially conclude the recording, state the time, that the interview is finished, and that you're turning off the recorder.

It never fails. After I've recorded the interview, as I'm walking out the door, the witness remembers something very important and just blurts it out. If this happens to you, stop and discuss it in detail. Then sit back down, turn the recorder back on, reconfirm the person's identity and permission to record the conversation, and have the witness repeat that last tidbit of detail for the recording.

Do all recorded statements have to be done in person? No. Most of the recorded statements my firm takes are done over the telephone. We use the same Radio Shack device mentioned in Chapter 16. We follow the same rules as laid out here in the preceding paragraphs. The format is the same; you just don't have the eye contact with the witness. Remember the bartender from Darby's case? He was in California; I was in Florida. The settlement hearing was to begin in less than 12 hours. There wasn't even time to have a local investigator go to his house and take a statement. A telephonic recorded statement is just as valid as one done face-to-face.

To be successful at interviewing, you have to build a relationship with the interviewee. That's harder to do over the telephone, but it can be done. I prefer to perform all interviews face-to-face, but that's not always possible. Frequently, budget and time don't allow it, so you have to settle for a telephonic interview. If you utilize the techniques in Chapter 8, you can accomplish a successful telephonic interview and obtain a recorded statement that will hold up in court all the same.

Formatting the Signed Statement

Signed statements are a real pain for PIs. The reason is that you're usually the one who has to sit and handwrite the statement for the witness. And the statement might be several pages of handwritten material. I usually try to get a recorded statement. Then, if necessary, I type up what I need in the signed statement, go back to the witness, and have her sign it. If your client is an attorney, she'll want to have some input into what's included in a signed statement, and she may draft it herself. If the attorney has input or drafts the statement, I suggest you take a notary with you when you revisit the witness and she signs the statement. After she signs the statement, you should sign it as a witness and have the notary notarize it. If you think the witness may change her mind or be difficult to locate later, go ahead and have the witness write and sign the statement on the spot without worrying about a notary.

Why take a signed statement instead of, or in addition to, a recorded statement? An attorney can take the signed statement into court and present it as evidence. It's easily readable, it's concise and, if it's properly notarized, the person who signed it probably won't have to appear in court.

A signed statement should begin with this:

> I, [name of witness], reside at [insert residence address]. My date of birth is [insert DOB] and my Social Security number is [insert *SSAN*]. I am making the following voluntary signed statement: [Then proceed with the statement.]

At the end of the statement, the following sentence should appear:

> I swear that the above statement consisting of this and [insert the number of other pages in the statement] is true to the best of my recollection. (If the statement is a total of three pages long, that sentence would read, "consisting of this and two additional pages.")

Always have the witness sign the statement. If you are not a notary, take one with you and have her notarize the statement. You'll have to pay the notary for her time, but you can charge that to the client anyway and add a markup on it to increase your bottom line at the end of the month. PIs notarize lots of odd things at odd hours in odd places, so find yourself an adventurous one or become one yourself. In my firm, one of my investigators or secretaries always keeps her notary status current. When she goes with us into the field, we charge her time to the client at our investigative rate.

THE SCOOP

The requirements to become a notary vary from state to state. The National Notary Association's website (www.nationalnotary.org) lists the requirements for all 50 states and the District of Columbia.

Originals and Duplicates

As a private investigator, you keep evidence in your office. You've shot some video, recorded interviews, and taken signed statements. What do you do with all of that evidence? How do you store it?

An investigator needs to "maintain chain of custody on the evidence." This means that any evidence collected by you, video, beer cans from a crime scene, recorded statements, and anything else that might be introduced into court as evidence should be:

- Initialed and dated by the investigator
- Kept in a locked cabinet or room with limited access

When the case goes to trial, the investigator who gathered the evidence can testify that this evidence has been under his care, control, and custody (or in the custody of the agency) and has not been tampered with. If that investigator is no longer your employee, you can introduce it into court yourself as the supervisory investigator. Still, it's better if you can subpoena or otherwise have present the investigator who gathered the evidence.

Most importantly, when you send your report and your bill to your insurance client, you also want them to see the video you're so proud of. Send them only a duplicate of the video, and not the original. The last thing you want to do is mix up the original with a copy.

It took my firm a long time to educate the insurance companies not to ask for the original video. Insurance adjusters come and go. Companies merge, reorganize, and close offices. If the original tape is in their possession, it will most likely get lost or misplaced. In addition, the investigator who shot the video is going to have to testify in court and introduce the video into evidence, not the insurance adjuster.

HIDDEN HINT

Charge the dictation and the time spent writing the report at the same rate as your normal hourly rate. If you don't, you'll be losing money.

As to maintaining chain of custody on the evidence, here's the first thing one of the attorneys will ask you: "Is this video you're introducing an original?" The second question will be, "Has the video been in your care, custody, and control since it was made, and has it been tampered with in any way?" If the video has not been in your control the entire time, then you can't answer yes. And then you don't know whether it's been tampered with, do you?

I once had an insurance company client for which I worked a lot of liability cases, such as slip-and-falls in grocery stores. I took a lot of recorded statements. The insurance company representatives insisted that I provide them the original of the recorded statement. I refused, to a point, but they were paying the bills, so finally I agreed. I did make them sign a release saying that they had the original and would not hold my firm responsible in the future for the safety of the original. I can't tell you how many times they would call me a year or two down the road, asking me where the original was. I'd fax them a copy of the release and tell them happy hunting.

As far as recorded statements are concerned, now that we're in the digital age, I usually transcribe statements if the client wants it done, and I quote him my firm's secretarial rate for the service. If I'm paying a secretary $15 an hour, I charge the client at least $25 an hour for transcription. If they want a transcription, it's usually so that one attorney can send it to the other, hopefully encouraging him to settle the case. Be sure to separate out the transcription charge as a separate line item on the invoice.

What often satisfies the client is a synopsis of the witness's recorded statement that the investigator dictates into a handheld digital recorder. Our secretary types the synopsis, which is included in the full report to the client, and that way, the report of the interview is full and complete.

The Digital Age

Now that tapes are practically no longer available and many cameras use hard drives or compact flash cards to record video, how do you deal with "originals"? There is some debate in the PI community about this problem. Frankly, it's overblown and not really a problem at all.

Video

If you're working with video, the easiest thing to do is hook up the camera directly to a DVD burner and burn several copies. No judge or attorney will expect you to have a shelf full of cameras with the so-called "original" video on the camera's hard drive. When you testify, you testify that this is a copy of the original that you burned to DVD using a DVD burner, and that it has not been changed or altered in any way and accurately represents what you observed.

Some video cameras don't transfer the time and date stamp on the video if you use a computer to burn your DVD. They all transfer the time and date directly to a DVD burner, although it may be analog instead of HD. That's okay, though, because no judge is going to care if the video you play is HD or analog. Some investigators use various software programs that pull the time and date (which is actually on a different digital track than the video) and overlay it over the video. I don't recommend that because that alters the original video.

Have your investigator put his initials and the date of video on the DVD itself using a black or red marker so he can later testify that, yes, those are his initials that he put on that DVD at the time he made it. That will stand up in any court.

Recorded Statements

My firm uses Olympus digital recorders for all of our recorded statements. The more expensive Olympus recorders save the file as a Windows Media Audio (WMA) file. The less expensive units save them as an MP3. We like the software that comes with the WMA version. Take your pick. I have offsite secretaries that I email the WMA files to, and they type the statements from home and email them back to me as a Word file. Also, I recommend that you burn a copy of the recording to a CD on your computer, in case of a computer crash. I send a copy of the CD with our report to the client so he can hear it as well.

Superior Reports Are the Mark of the Professional PI

A competent private investigator should produce a clear and concise report, written in good, grammatical English. If the report has a lot of misspellings and grammatical errors in it, do you think the clients will be excited about you representing them on the witness stand? Or will they be embarrassed that they hired you?

This is often a problem when you use subcontractors to perform your work. You have to educate your subcontractors on what you expect in your reports. Sometimes they eventually learn the importance of a quality report. Sometimes they don't and you should move on to someone else.

If spelling is not your bag and you don't know the difference between *your* and *you're*, or *billed* and *build*, then hire somebody who has mastered proper English to do your paperwork. A talented secretary can make even a bozo look good.

Police departments are notorious for producing poorly written reports. They don't get much in the way of report-writing instruction in the police academies. Having had several years to cement some bad writing habits, an officer retires or leaves the force and starts his own private investigative agency. How is the quality of the reports he writes then? About the same as what he did on the force. They have the same mistakes and the same poor formatting because that's what he's done for 20 years.

FBI FD-302 Reports

A proper PI report should look very much like an FBI report. Why? What's the big deal? Because most law school graduates are familiar with *FD-302s*. An FD-302 is basically a blank sheet of paper. The format of the words on the FD-302 is important.

DEFINITION

An **FD-302** is a federal form number that the FBI uses for part of its report. Specifically, it reports the results of interviews conducted by FBI agents. All interviews are reported in a standard format and are typed or printed onto FD-302s. Law school students learn this early in their schooling, and the forms are referred to throughout judicial opinions.

One way or another, the whole purpose of most private investigations is to win a case in a court of law. Certainly, not every case you work will go to court, but you should prepare each and every one of your cases as if it will. FBI agents have been writing reports for a long time, and their reports are clear and unambiguous.

The following is a typical example of the wording at the beginning of an FD-302—or, in your case, a good investigative report:

> The following investigation was conducted by Steven K. Brown, of Millennial Investigative Agency, on April 15, 2012, at Jacksonville, Florida:

> On this date, Mary Jane Doe, date of birth 10/20/1947, SSAN 261-00-0000, was interviewed at her residence of 1234 Any Street, Jacksonville, Florida, and provided the following information:

> Doe advised that she witnessed an accident between ....

In the reporting of this type of interview, the investigator's name, agency, and date the interview took place are laid out at the beginning. Once that's done, the reader knows who did the interview, as well as when and where it was conducted. The investigator's name doesn't have to be repeated again anywhere else on the page, nor does the investigator refer to himself as "the writer," which is so often the case in police reports. By following this format, your reports will be plain, clear, easily read, straightforward, and done in a style that all attorneys are familiar with. If you tell your client up front that your reports are similar to FD-302s, they'll make you for a professional from the beginning.

Photographs

I cannot overemphasize the importance of including 35mm photographs (JPEGs) in your reports. It's a fairly simple and straightforward process if you're using Word. Just choose Insert > Picture > From File. When your client gets the report, the important photos are right there. I strongly recommend that you use a good color laser printer to print your reports with the photos. There is no need to include all the photos you took, unless you got only one or two. But include the good ones.

Burn all the photos that are applicable to the case on a CD and include a copy of the CD with the report. That way, your client can scroll through the photos on her computer and decide for herself which photos she wants to use in court or in a hearing. No rule says she has to introduce all of the photos. Chances are, she will call you and ask you to print copies of certain photos. Charge at least a dollar per photo to cover your costs. Also make sure each photo has the time and date stamp on it.

If you produce good reports, you will earn your client's respect and, most important, his repeat business. Remember, you can be the best investigator in the world, but your client sees only two things from you: the quality of your report and the quality of the evidence you collect, be it video or photographs. You can have a lousy car and a rotten pair of binoculars, and duct tape patches on your pants, but your client will never see those. If your reports and tapes are superior, he'll figure you for a superior investigator. This is the best way to produce a professional image. Talk is cheap. What's left on your client's desk when you leave his office is what counts.

Show Me the Money

In the business of running a private investigative firm, you must follow a couple of cardinal rules for the business to thrive:

1. You have to get paid.

2. You have to get paid soon.

Covering Administrative Costs

I'm about to share a company secret with you that I've never shared with any other PI, ever. It's something I came up with after a few years in business and several different attempts at weaving our secretary's time into our investigative invoice. She has to be paid. She told me so. That means I have to charge for it, and so do you. Just ask your secretary; I'll bet she says the same thing. The problem is, if you bump up your hourly rate to include her time, you might price yourself right out of the market. Your competition's rate will look much lower.

I came up with a solution that has worked for 30 years. In all that time, I've never had a complaint or even a question about it from a client.

On the invoice, under Expenses, we include a charge for Secretarial and Administrative Charges. We look at the total fees billed on a case and multiply that amount by 8.25 percent. That is our secretarial charge. This spreads our administrative costs over all of our cases and doesn't increase our quoted hourly rate. Other PIs have adopted this practice, but as far as I know, I originated it.

Collecting a Retainer

The best way to get paid is to collect a retainer before beginning a case. Always do this, without exception, in domestic cases or when your client is an individual instead of a corporation. View this as the acid test. If she can't scrape together the money to pay you the retainer, what makes you think she'll have any more money when you hand her the final bill?

Work the case up to the amount of the retainer you have, and then inform her that you'll need more money if she wants more work. Don't let her get into your pockets, and don't be shy about asking for money. If you don't ask, you won't get it.

If there is any advice I can give you that will help you succeed in the PI business, this is it: always present a bill with the report. We always put the bill on top so the client sees it first thing. And try to collect the money due right then. If you hide the bill on the bottom of the report, it'll get overlooked, and you'll be begging for your money six months after the case is completed.

It's best to keep the client apprised of the tab he's incurring as the case progresses. Nobody wants any surprises at the end of a case. He might be thinking he's spending only a few hundred dollars. Imagine his surprise when he receives a bill for a few thousand. Likewise, you're not going to be happy when he refuses to pay. It's best to keep a running tally and give him the current total periodically.

Being a professional investigator requires performing superior investigations, properly maintaining the evidence, and reporting the results of your investigative efforts in such a manner that you distinguish your firm from the competition.

In the more than 30 years I've been running a PI business, I can count on one hand the number of times I've been "stiffed" by a client. Two were attorneys, one of whom was out of state. One was a client whose retainer check bounced, but we didn't know it until the work was completed. She filed for bankruptcy. The other was a large out-of-state corporation that left me on the hook for more than $50,000. They filed for bankruptcy right after we completed the work. That's why a retainer is so important. I should have gotten one from that corporation, but they had several thousand employees and I figured they were good for it. I haven't made that mistake again.

The Least You Need to Know

- During the middle of a complex case, a good investigator steps back, looks at the direction of the case, and shifts the focus, if need be, to obtain what will be important in making the case in court.

- Recorded and signed statements are valuable items of evidence and can be used to impeach a witness's testimony if the witness changes the story during a trial.

- Original video and recordings should always be held in the investigator's control until needed for trial. Each CD or DVD should be labeled, initialed by the investigator who took the video, and dated as soon as the DVD comes out of the DVD burner.

- A superior method of report formatting is to follow the FBI's use of FD-302s. This is a clear, concise method of reporting and is a standard that all attorneys learn in law school. It will set your firm apart from the competition.

- Always submit a bill with each report. Getting paid is necessary when running a successful PI business. Always charge for report writing and secretarial time as well.

The Judges' Chambers

21

In This Chapter

- Ghostwriting from jail
- Swearing under oath
- Understanding privileged communication
- Testifying before a grand jury
- Putting your best foot forward
- Directing and redirecting in the courtroom

As private investigators, we deal with facts. I use the term *we* because if you've read this entire book, then you're pretty close to being an investigator, and *we* means "you and me."

All of an investigator's effort comes to fruition when the case goes to court. And the first step in going to court is receiving a subpoena. In this chapter, I walk you through the process of accepting a subpoena. After you've been subpoenaed, you need to be ready to testify. Your testimony may come in the form of a deposition, an appearance before a grand jury, or in a courtroom with a judge and jury.

I also touch on the topic of legal privileges, such as work product rules, and give you ideas for how to charge your client different rates for testifying and waiting to testify. Finally, I show you how to testify in court and maintain your professional "cool" while under cross-examination. Going to court is your final exam. You should be ready for it.

Just the Facts, Ma'am

Most of the cases that a PI works have something to do with the law. Divorces, traffic accidents, nursing home abuse, child custody, asset location, slip-and-falls, criminal defense, and witness locating all start out headed toward court. Few of those cases actually end up in court. Ninety out of a hundred will settle before reaching the trial date. Nonetheless, you must prepare your case as if it is going to a court of law. Your evidence and findings need to be prepared in such a manner that the judge, jury, and opposing attorney will recognize you as an impartial professional investigator.

If you learn nothing else by reading this book, learn that you must not only *appear* to be impartial in your investigation, but also that, in fact, you must *be* impartial. You should have this next statement memorized by now, since I've repeated it and similar statements throughout this book. It is the cardinal rule of private investigation. Say it out loud with me:

> *The professional private investigator searches for all the facts.*

There. You've got it. The best PI in the business seeks the truth and reports his findings to his client accurately and uncolored by the position his client has taken.

Unfortunately, many PIs don't follow this standard of impartiality. They report only the facts their clients want to hear. Some even deliberately misstate witnesses' statements to please their clients. Others even practice what is labeled in the industry as *ghostwriting*.

> **DEFINITION**
>
> **Ghostwriting,** in PI terms, refers to an investigator who makes up reports or details of reports. Instead of doing the work, dishonest investigators just write reports indicating that they performed the investigation, even though they didn't.

Thomas, an investigator I subcontracted with, worked in the Orlando, Florida, area. When Thomas began working for me, he shot some pretty decent video on my firm's insurance claimant cases. After a few months, I noticed that he no longer seemed to shoot any video whatsoever.

On one particular case, Thomas had been out on surveillance on a lady named Sarah. He submitted his report, but he didn't provide any accompanying video. The report showed absolutely no activity on Sarah's part on one particular day, June 22. I thought this highly unusual and, noting Thomas's lack of productivity, I reassigned the case to another investigator, Camille.

Camille went to check out Sarah's residence and discovered that Sarah no longer lived where we thought she had. I called Sarah on a pretext and chatted with her. In the conversation, I verified her new address and asked her when she'd moved. "Oh, it was June 22 I moved. I had my two nephews there, and the three of us spent all day moving my stuff down those stairs and into that pickup truck. We must have filled that pickup truck at least a dozen times, making runs back and forth to the new place, before we emptied everything out of that apartment. Why, I never knew I had so much stuff."

Amazed, I asked Camille to go to the apartment manager and verify the move-out date. She did. June 22. Do you think I ever subcontracted with Thomas again? Now think how embarrassed Thomas would have been if he'd gone to court to testify to the "facts" in his report. Sarah would have stood up and said, "That's not true. I was moving on June 22." And my firm's credibility would have suffered more than just embarrassment. It would have cost us some business and some bad word of mouth.

I know of another investigative firm that actually was criminally prosecuted for ghostwriting reports. The principals of the firm apparently just made up reports, like Thomas did, and went ahead and billed the insurance company for work that was totally fictional. Eventually, the Florida Department of Insurance found out about it and prosecuted the owners of the company for insurance fraud. They were fined and spent time in jail.

Do your job. Do it professionally. Gather all the facts, good or bad, for your client. Present them to your client in a professional manner. Then let the chips fall where they may.

Accepting the Subpoena

As an investigator, you will be receiving *subpoenas* for court appearances or depositions (I talk about depositions in the next section). Sometimes even your own client sends you a subpoena. Attorneys are strange that way. Even though they hire you, they still feel the need to subpoena you. I recommend telling your client there is no need to subpoena you—just let you know when and where they need you, and you'll be there. Save the client the $50 it will cost them to have you subpoenaed.

DEFINITION

A **subpoena** is a command from a judge, or an attorney acting as an officer of the court, requiring that the person or representative of an institution named in the subpoena appear in court or at another specified location on a specific day at a certain time.

Don't play hide-and-seek with the subpoena process server. Be professional about it. If your client doesn't want you to be served, then don't call up the opposing counsel and give him your schedule, but don't hide or try to evade the service, either. As much as you'd like to accommodate your client's desires, you are a professional, and you should conduct yourself as such. If you are served, the subpoena is an order from the court, or an attorney acting as an officer of the court, for you to appear. If you don't appear, then you're in contempt of that court. Better to have your client mad at you than to be held in contempt. Your client can always ask the court to quash the subpoena if he really doesn't want you deposed.

If you don't respond to the subpoena and you're held in contempt, you could be fined and will be required to testify anyway. The reality of the business is such that if you fail to respond to the subpoena and your client wanted you there, you'll lose a client. If the stakes are high and the opposing counsel issued the subpoena, you might find the sheriff on your doorstep with his handcuffs out.

If you are subpoenaed as a witness for trial, you're eligible for a witness fee. The witness fee, big deal that it is, usually amounts to about $20 or less. However, you can also bill your client for your time.

I always bill my own client, even if I am subpoenaed by the opposing counsel. I am there because of my client's needs, and I expect her to pay for my time and mileage. Make sure your contract with your client specifies a minimum amount that will be paid for courtroom appearances.

HIDDEN HINT

I include a sample contract in Appendix C. The sample contract is simple and straightforward; for a more complex contract, check out the one sold by the PI Store at www.pistore.com/retainer-agreement-p-961.html.

Usually, the subpoena you receive will be for you to appear at the trial at the courthouse. Other times, you'll get subpoenaed for depositions, which usually take place at an attorney's offices or at the office of the court reporter.

Most of your testimony will be given in your county, but not always. We routinely get subpoenaed for areas all around our state, and sometimes across the country. If your client is an insurance company, a large business, or an attorney, they know that the standard is to pay you for your time, including travel, and to reimburse your travel expenses.

If your client is an individual, get your travel expenses and anticipated hourly rate up front in the form of an additional retainer. It's always easier to get money from your client before you perform the service than it is afterward.

Some investigators bill their clients a lower rate for waiting time in the courthouse and at their usual rate for time spent testifying. I don't. I bill it all at our usual rate. Time spent waiting to testify at trial might go as long as several days. The attorney will usually have a good idea of what day she'll need you, but sometimes she guesses wrong. You've set aside everything in your schedule for this trial when you could be out working other cases. The attorney's office owes you for that time.

To speed the legal process along, I tell my secretaries that they have my authority to accept a subpoena on my behalf, as long as I am in town. If I am out of town on an extended trip, they ought not to accept the subpoena. Why? I might not be back in time to testify on the date desired, and I don't want to be held in contempt of court. Normally, you'll be given several weeks' notice, but I've been subpoenaed one day prior to my desired testimony.

Everything You Wanted to Know About Depositions

A *deposition* is the meat between the bread in the legal sandwich of our jurisprudence system.

> **DEFINITION**
>
> A **deposition** is a statement made under oath by a witness, usually written or recorded, that may be used in court at a later time. If the deponent (the witness being deposed) likely will not be available later—for instance, due to illness—it is not uncommon for the deposition to be videoed.

Private investigators are deposed by opposing counsel all the time. There's typically no need for your own client to depose you. Since you are working for him, he already has your reports.

Typically, a court reporter is present and makes an official record of the deposition. Your client, or your client's attorney, is there, as is the opposing attorney. The court reporter asks you to raise your right hand and swear under oath that what you are about to say is true.

LEGAL TRAP

Don't take the report you sent to your client with you to court or to a deposition, and don't refer to it in your deposition. If you need notes to refresh your memory, then take notes. There could be facts in your report that your client doesn't want the other side to know. If you refer to your report during your testimony, the other side has a right to a copy of it. And you certainly don't want anyone else seeing your bill. The last thing your client, the insurance company, wants is the claimant's attorney announcing to the jury that the company paid you $8,000 to sneak around and spy on that little old lady claimant instead of paying her doctor's bills with that money.

With all that high-priced talent in one place, you can just hear the cash register cha-chinging, can't you? There's the court reporter, both attorneys billing their clients for their time, and you, the PI, billing your client for your time. Conducting a deposition can be expensive. And that is the precise reason private investigators are in business.

By having the private investigator first go out and interview potential witnesses, attorneys can decide which witnesses to depose. There is no need to go to the expense of deposing someone if they have no recollection of the incident or matter at hand, or never even saw, for instance, the traffic accident you're investigating. It's a lot cheaper to pay the PI his hourly rate than to orchestrate a deposition that will be totally unproductive.

HIDDEN HINT

Give your client a progress report every few days. Your progress report can be as simple as a phone call or an email. This regular updating has two very beneficial purposes. First, your client will appreciate knowing how the case is moving along. Second, it's not unusual for your client to assign you additional work, either on the current case or on a new assignment. Just talking to your client makes him think about other cases he has for which your services could be useful. And more work means more billable hours and a better bottom line for your business.

Another reason for deposing someone is if there's a *reluctant witness*. A reluctant witness is an individual who might have considerable knowledge of the incident in question but won't discuss this incident unless she's forced to by a court.

Leslie was an emergency room nurse working in a local hospital. Our client, Hugh, had been a resident in a nursing home. The rules of common care in nursing homes require that patients be bathed daily. In addition, any sores or open wounds should be noted on their files, and a nurse specializing in wound care must tend to these sores.

The attendants, or certified nursing assistants, at these nursing homes are also supposed to make notes on whether the residents are eating their meals. If the residents don't eat, their health can quickly fail. Nursing homes have nutritionists on staff who can help residents with eating disorders.

Hugh was already in delicate health due to his age and some other exacerbating physical conditions. He apparently hadn't been eating any of his meals, but this had not been noted in his file.

Finally, one day, a nurse noticed that Hugh was having difficulty breathing. She called for an ambulance, and Hugh was transported to the emergency room, where Leslie was on duty.

In making a preliminary examination of Hugh, Leslie discovered many open sores and wounds on the lower portion of his body, including his legs, groin, and genitals.

Leslie made note that the wounds were infected. She saw maggots crawling throughout the open sores. She cleaned the wounds and admitted Hugh to the hospital because he was severely malnourished.

One of the witnesses that Hugh's attorney wanted me to interview was Leslie. I tracked down Leslie and one day dropped by her house unannounced. Leslie was cordial but insisted on calling the legal department of her hospital before talking to me. Note that the hospital was not being sued. In this case, the nursing home, a totally different institution altogether, was the defendant.

I had several discussions with the legal department at that hospital before they finally agreed to let Leslie talk to me—if she wanted to. The discussion had to be limited to Leslie's original observations when Hugh was admitted. We could not discuss his treatment while at the hospital. That was fine because all we wanted was her testimony as to the neglectful physical condition Hugh had been in when he arrived at the hospital.

Leslie still refused to be interviewed. She wouldn't tell me why she wouldn't talk to me. Consequently, my client, the attorney for Hugh, set her deposition. Once she was under oath and compelled to talk, she testified to what she'd seen that day when Hugh was admitted. Leslie was a reluctant witness. A witness will have her own reasons for not wanting to testify. It might be inconvenient. It might be company policy that employees don't testify unless compelled to, or she might harbor fears that her own actions—and, in this case, the quality of her care for this particular patient—might come into question.

HIDDEN HINT

Generally, it's better to talk to witnesses without first making an appointment to see them. If the witness knows you're coming and doesn't want to talk to you, he won't be there when you arrive at the appointed time. Also, the witness's sympathies might lie with the other party, and if he knows you're coming, he'll call the other party, who probably will tell him not to talk to you. Then when you arrive for your appointment, you will have wasted your driving time because the guy's not going to give you a statement. If you don't make an appointment, you might end up wasting a lot of time trying to catch up to your witness, so you need to weigh the time involved against the value of catching the witness by surprise.

Work Product from the Attorney's Office

A general rule of law states that work performed or originated by one attorney is not discoverable by the opposing attorney, unless the attorney shares that work with other parties. This is called the *work product* rule.

In a case headed for trial, each attorney is under the obligation to present to the opposing side a list of the witnesses he intends to use during the trial. The opposing counsel can then interview or depose these witnesses in an attempt to discover the nature of their testimony or the evidence the witness will introduce. This is called discovery.

DEFINITION

Work product is described as the attorney's notes and research materials and other documents or matters that the attorney makes, prepares, or uses as he works up the case. The reports of a private investigator, hired directly by the attorney or working out of the attorney's office, are also considered work product.

A **privilege,** under law, is a special right that someone enjoys that the public-at-large doesn't enjoy. For instance, the marital privilege asserts that a wife cannot be forced to testify against her husband, or vice versa. The clergy privilege declares that communications between a clergyman and his parishioner are considered privileged.

If the attorney voluntarily gives a particular piece of work product to the opposing counsel, then he has violated the work product privilege for that item, and that work product no longer enjoys the privilege. In this case, the opposing counsel can use it, even if the attorney who originated the material has changed his mind and doesn't want it to appear in the court record.

For instance, if your client, the attorney, shares a copy of your report with the opposing attorney, your report will no longer enjoy the work product *privilege*.

As most of us know, anything you discuss with your attorney is confidential and cannot be disclosed to another attorney, law enforcement officer, or the court without your permission. This is called the attorney–client privilege.

Why do private investigators care about work product and privileges? Whether you're an "in-house" private investigator who works directly for an attorney or you have a broad range of clients, including attorneys, your work for an attorney is usually considered work product from the attorney's office and isn't discoverable.

THE SCOOP

In some states, investigators who work solely for one law firm don't have to meet the licensing requirements of the state and don't need to have a private investigator's license. See Chapter 2 for details on licensing requirements for PIs.

If your client doesn't have an attorney, don't refuse the case. Just be aware that your reports will likely be discoverable by the opposing side, and the individual who called you will be your client, not his attorney.

HIDDEN HINT

If an individual who isn't an attorney calls you to discuss a new matter, ask if she is represented by an attorney. To protect the work product rule, the case needs to come from an attorney. I also encourage you to send your report and invoice directly to the attorney and have the attorney pay the invoice out of his own firm's funds. By routing everything through the attorney, you can answer truthfully that your client is the attorney, not the individual.

Mary Ellen was 69 years old. For her birthday, she took a weeklong cruise, departing from Fort Lauderdale and touring islands in the Caribbean. The cruise ship had an elevator to carry passengers between decks. Mary Ellen had the misfortune to be on the elevator when it broke down. She was trapped inside that small cubicle for about three hours.

Eventually, a mechanic managed to free the elevator but couldn't get it to stop exactly on the next floor. The elevator stopped about 2½ feet above the landing. To get out of the elevator, Mary Ellen was forced to jump down to the deck. In doing so, she fell and fractured her hip. She sued the cruise ship line and the manufacturer of the elevator.

Our assignment was to put Mary Ellen under surveillance to determine her lifestyle and range of motion. We followed Mary Ellen over several successive days as she drove to the grocery store and ran other normal errands.

She definitely walked with a limp and used her cane occasionally. The video evidence we collected basically was noncommittal. It pretty much showed a 69-year-old woman who'd undergone hip surgery. Our client, the attorney for the cruise line, did not want to use the video or any of our reports in the trial, not because there was anything damaging to his case, but because he was afraid that the jury would be incensed that the insurance company had hired private investigators to snoop on this nice little old lady.

The other attorney figured that there was probably a video of his client, and he wanted to play the "big bad insurance company" card at trial with the jury. He subpoenaed me for deposition. At the deposition, I refused to testify, on the grounds that my work was work product from an attorney's office.

This case went to trial, and the attorneys argued before the judge, out of the presence of the jury, about the admissibility of the videos. My client, who'd paid for the surveillance, didn't want them admitted. Mary Ellen's attorney did.

Finally, again, out of the presence of the jury, I was called in and I showed the video to the judge. He agreed that the video showed nothing significant that would help either case and declined to let the jury know that the video or the investigation even existed.

If the insurance company had hired me directly, there would have been no work product privilege, and the video and my testimony would have been admitted. Mary Ellen's attorney would have made a big deal about the insurance company stooping so low as to spy on this nice little old lady, and the jury's sympathy might have swayed toward Mary Ellen more than it otherwise had been.

In this case, Mary Ellen was awarded several hundred thousand dollars for her injury. At least her award was not prejudiced by the fact that the insurance company had hired a PI to check her out. Right or wrong? You be the judge.

LEGAL TRAP

States vary in what privileges they allow, so be sure you know the law in the states where you do business. The rules covering privileged communications are usually found in the state statutes concerning the rules of civil evidence or criminal evidence.

There's a general misconception that there is a privilege between a doctor and his patient in criminal matters. Most states recognize no privilege in that relationship with reference to a criminal matter.

However, in civil matters, a doctor–patient privilege applies to the doctor's treatment or diagnosis of any condition of the patient. But if the patient confides a matter to the doctor that isn't related to the patient's medical condition, there is no privilege.

The Grand Jury

It's not often that a private investigator is called to testify before a *grand jury*, but it does happen. If you ever are called to testify before a grand jury, present yourself as if you're in a regular trial before a judge and jury. In other words, be your usual professional self.

A grand jury is usually composed of 12 to 18 people who meet on a regular basis, usually once a week. These people are called to be members of the grand jury for the duration of the jury, which might run from 6 to 18 months, depending on the jurisdiction in which it is called.

DEFINITION

A **grand jury** is a group of people culled from the voter rolls that are called together for a specified period of time to listen to evidence concerning various crimes and return either a "true bill," which is an indictment, or a "no bill" which means that there isn't sufficient evidence to indict a person for a crime. In some states grand juries use the terms "information" or "no information" instead of "true bill" and "no bill."

A grand jury has no judge sitting with the jury while it is in session. The district attorney (or one of his assistants) or in federal matters, the U.S. Attorney (or one of his assistants) runs the grand jury. The assistant district attorney in charge of the grand jury presents evidence and calls witnesses pertaining to a crime under investigation. After the evidence has been presented and the witnesses have testified, the grand jury takes a vote to determine if there is probable cause that the crime occurred and that a particular individual committed the crime. The grand jury either returns a true bill, indicating probable cause, or a no bill, indicating insufficient evidence.

Unlike a regular jury trial, in a grand jury, the members of the jury can ask questions of the witnesses and of the assistant district attorney. Also unlike a regular jury trial, in a grand jury no attorneys are allowed to be present at the grand jury proceedings. Only the members of the jury, the assistant district attorney in charge, and the witness testifying are in the room.

The testimony given to a grand jury is usually considered secret. However, the names of the witnesses called to testify are not confidential. If a witness refuses to testify (unless he invokes his Fifth Amendment right to not incriminate himself), the assistant district attorney will ask a judge to order the witness to testify. If the witness continues to refuse to testify, the judge may hold the witness in contempt and put him jail until he does testify, or until the grand jury has disbanded.

The Cross-Examination

I've been asked by other investigators why I am in court all the time and they're not. I don't tell them this because I don't want to come across as an egomaniac, but the basic answer is that I know how to make cases that my clients can win. If your clients don't think they will win in court, they'll try to settle.

When you go to court, you stand before the judge, and the clerk swears you in. Then you take your seat on the witness stand, and you're asked for your complete name, address, and occupation. The attorney for your client asks you the questions she's prepared you for, and you give truthful answers.

Next, the opposing counsel asks you questions. Answer the questions straightforwardly and truthfully, even if you think the answers will hurt your client's case. The judge and/or the jury aren't stupid. You're only one part of the case. Be professional and answer assuredly. Don't hesitate while trying to phrase your answer in the best light possible. Just answer it.

There are a few exceptions to the "just answer it" rule. Sometimes your client doesn't want you to answer a question or to reveal certain information. I had a client who didn't want the ex to know how much he'd paid us. The ex's attorney asked me how much in fees we had been paid. I declined to answer. The judge ordered me to answer. I pulled out the Florida statutes and referred the judge to Florida Statute 493.6119. The judge had never heard of that statute, nor had the other attorney. It goes like this:

493.6119   Divulging investigative information; false reports prohibited.—

(1)   Except as otherwise provided by this chapter or other law, no licensee, or any employee of a licensee or licensed agency shall divulge or release to anyone other than her or his client or employer the contents of an investigative file acquired in the course of licensed investigative activity. However, the prohibition of this section shall not apply when the client for whom the information was acquired, or the client's lawful representative, has alleged a violation of this chapter by the licensee, licensed agency, or any employee, or when the prior written consent of the client to divulge or release such information has been obtained.

After conducting several rounds of discussions and searching through the law books, the judge agreed that I did not have to answer the question. I've used that statute on several occasions in court and in depositions. It's always fun to frustrate the other side. I have never found an attorney or judge who was previously aware of that particular statute. Check your own state laws. You might be surprised what you'll find.

After the opposing counsel asks you questions, your client's attorney has another chance to redirect questions to you. It's her job—not yours—to clear up any doubts that the questions from the other attorney may have raised.

Your job is the search for truth, the facts that surround every accident and every lawsuit. Let the attorneys present only the evidence that is beneficial to their cases.

The attorney's job is to sift through all the facts that you gather and present the evidence in an order that will substantiate the case. The attorney may omit facts. That's okay. No law or rule says they all have to be presented. There *is* a rule that says that, as a PI, you must present all of the evidence to your client or your client's attorney. After that, your job is done, and it's on to the next case.

The Least You Need to Know

- Some investigators are guilty of ghostwriting reports. This is illegal and is a prosecutable offense.
- Subpoenas command individuals to appear for trial or depositions. Not responding to a subpoena places you in jeopardy of being held in contempt of court.
- Privileged communications exist between attorneys and their clients. Also, if the circumstances are right, an investigator's work may be considered work product of an attorney's office, making it not discoverable by the opposing counsel.
- As a private investigator, your testimony in court should be straightforward and honest. It is the attorney's job to rectify any misleading impressions caused by the opposing counsel's questions.
- Your job is to search for truth. You must present your client with all of the evidence that you gather.
- The prosecuting attorney may present a case before a grand jury, which will either return a "true bill" or a "no bill."

Glossary

ANAC   Automatic Number Announcement Circuit is a telephone number that, when dialed, announces back to you the number you are calling from. These numbers vary within area codes and sometimes within switches in the same city.

arbitration   A process in which the plaintiff and the defendant in a civil lawsuit meet with a third party, known as a professional arbitrator. This arbitrator is skilled in negotiating and has the responsibility to help the two different sides come to an agreement. This process reduces the number of cases going to trial and helps clear the court calendar for cases that cannot be settled.

AutoComplete   A function in Internet Explorer that can be turned on or off. As a user enters a secure website, he or she is prompted for a user ID and a password. After the computer user has entered that ID and password the first time, AutoComplete remembers the combination as long as it's on. The next time you visit that website and begin to enter your user ID, AutoComplete recognizes where you are on the web and enters the ID and password for you, if you want. Utilizing AutoComplete means you don't have to type in your user ID and password at every visit. AutoComplete is handy but not very secure.

bandwidth   For our purposes, bandwidth means the amount of data that can be moved along a line of transmission at a certain time. The wider the bandwidth, the more data is moved.

being made   Being made means that a covert operation such as a surveillance has been exposed, and its presence has been made known to the subject of the operation. It's a clue that you've been made when the person you're following gives you the finger.

binding arbitration   Binding arbitration means that a settlement must be reached during arbitration. If the parties cannot decide upon a settlement considered fair by all, the arbitrator, after being fully informed of the facts, reaches what he considers a fair conclusion. His determination is binding on both parties.

blood spatter   The blood that is discarded during a violent crime. By the study of the blood spatter (not *splatter*), the size of the drops, and the velocity and direction of the spatter, one might be able to determine how the crime took place.

Brady violation   A Brady violation comes from a U.S. Supreme Court case, *Brady v. Maryland* (U.S. 1963), that ruled that a prosecutor has a duty under the Fifth and Fourteenth Amendments to disclose favorable evidence to defendants upon request if the evidence is "material" to either guilt or punishment.

breaking squelch   The squelch is the point at which a radio receiver is tuned to its most sensitive setting. If tuned beyond this point, the squelch is "broken" and the radio makes a loud, piercing sound similar to a screeching parrot.

burglary   The FBI's Uniform Crime Report defines burglary as the unlawful entry of a structure to commit a felony or a theft. The use of force to gain entry is not required to classify an offense as a burglary.

burned   Getting burned has the same meaning as *being made*. The subject has become aware of the surveillance.

butt set   A butt set is a handheld device that looks like a cordless phone, has a touchtone keypad, and is used by telephone and electronic service people to identify telephone lines. It has a set of wires with alligator clips at the end. You can buy butt sets for less than $100 over the internet or at Radio Shack.

center-weighted average   Many single-lens reflex cameras have a built-in light-metering capability that automatically adjusts the f-stop and the shutter speed. A good photographer will know whether a particular light meter averages the measurement of the light over the entire surface of the lens or center-weights the average, giving more importance to the amount of light coming through the center of the lens, where, presumably, the important image is located.

city directories   Sometimes called *reverse directories* or *criss-cross directories*, these books are privately published, frequently by Cole, Polk, Donnelly, and other publishers. These directories sort their listings by name, address, and telephone number. You can check a telephone number in the "reverse" listing and find the subscriber information. Likewise, for an address within the city, searching the directory by address gives you the person living there and the phone number. Most of these directories are now online, but public libraries may have older copies that you can use to find out who lived at a particular address in the last decade.

countermeasure sweep   A countermeasure sweep is an active measure by an individual with the goal of finding or countering an aggressive action taken against him or her. Typically, the term is used in the sense of actively searching for and eliminating any electronic transmitters (bugs) or wiretaps that are directed toward locations or facilities where the target of the measure would likely be heard. A variation of the term is also used with respect to surveillance.

countersurveillance   This is a surveillance initiated by an individual to determine whether he or she is under surveillance by an outside group. If properly conducted, a countersurveillance will identify the entity conducting the surveillance, so you'll know who at the diner counter is watching.

courtesy officer   A courtesy officer is usually a local police patrol person or sheriff's deputy who is given some sort of discount on his rent at an apartment complex in exchange for parking a marked patrol unit on the grounds and handling disturbance complaints at the complex when he is present. This is usually considered a good deal for the apartment management and the law enforcement department because it reduces crime and does not increase law enforcement costs.

credit scores   A credit score refers to one of several types of numerical rating systems devised by credit companies to give a credit grantor an instant evaluation of a person's risk as a credit applicant.

crime scene investigation   Conducting a crime scene investigation entails collecting evidence or possible evidence toward the goal of placing suspects at the scene of the crime. The evidence must be collected according to the rules of evidence, which have been established by law and judicial precedence.

criss-cross directories   *See* city directories.

data brokers   Also known as *information brokers*, these are individuals or companies that have access to specialized sources of information or use advanced techniques to gather information and then resell it to the private investigator. An example of this is asking an information broker to obtain a nonpublished telephone number.

defendant   Legal actions require a minimum of two parties. The plaintiff is the party who initiates the action or lawsuit. The defendant is the person on the receiving end of the action.

deponent   The deponent is the witness being deposed.

deposition   A deposition is a statement under oath, usually written or recorded, that may be used in court at a later time. If the deponent likely will not be available later—for instance, due to illness—it is not uncommon for the deposition to be videoed.

depth of field   The depth of field is the apparent range of focus in a photograph. In portrait photography, the background and the foreground may be intentionally blurred and out of focus while the subject, in the center of the photograph, is in focus.

diligent search   A diligent search refers to specific steps, often specified by state statutes, undertaken to locate an individual. Usually, diligent searches are required in locating parents of children who are about to be adopted or for heirs to estates that are needed to settle the estate.

drive-by   A drive-by is performed by private investigators to make a casual check of a subject's residence to see whether the subject is home or to observe what activities are taking place at a particular location during a specific time.

dropped   When a cell or telephone bill has dropped, it means that the billing cycle has ended and the charges are en route to the consumer. Usually, even the customer cannot access the list of phone charges until the bill has entered the billing system's computer. With enough pressure, in exigent circumstances like tracing a runaway, you might get the cellular company to give you the calls daily as they're made.

due diligence   A due diligence search is a check of an individual's ability or, more often, a company's reputed ability to perform under contract and verifies that there are no liens or judgments filed against the subject. A good due diligence search also encompasses any pending or potential lawsuits or other current or potential areas of liability, such as a pending bankruptcy. These are most often performed when one company is considering the purchase of another company or engaging in business with them.

ESN   An Electronic Serial Number is the unique number that identifies a single particular cell phone. This number is continuously broadcast to the cellular network from the phone, which lets the network know where you are when your cell phone is turned on and through which cell towers to transmit your calls.

f-stop   On an adjustable single-lens reflex camera, f-stops are numbers that indicate to what degree the iris of the lens is opened or closed. The f-stop setting is one factor in determining the amount of light that passes through the lens and exposes the film or light receptor. As the f-stop number increases, the iris is then "stopped down" to a smaller aperture, and less light is allowed through the lens. Larger numbers equal less light, with all other factors remaining the same. The f-stop settings also affect the depth of field; the higher the f-stop, the greater the depth of field.

FD-302   The FD-302 is a federal form used by the FBI that reports the results of interviews conducted by FBI agents. All interviews are reported in a standard format and are typed or printed onto FD-302s. Law school students learn this early in their schooling, and the forms are referred to throughout judicial opinions.

felonies   Criminal offenses are categorized according to the severity of the offense. Crimes that are punishable by one year of jail time or longer are called felonies.

Field Identification card   A Field Identification card is a card patrol officers fill out when questioning persons who might have been acting suspiciously. It contains the subject's identifying data, the date and location of the incident, and a short synopsis of why the subject was questioned.

GPS   GPS stands for Global Positioning System. It is a system of about 24 satellites that orbit Earth and send out very closely timed signals. The GPS receivers on Earth acquire the timed signals from multiple satellites and can calculate the receivers' latitude, longitude, and altitude.

grand jury   A grand jury is a group of men and women, usually culled from the voter's registration rolls, which hears evidence and determines whether there is probable cause to believe that a crime has been committed and that a particular person committed that crime.

gray areas   Gray areas are areas of investigative behavior that might be frowned upon by the state division of licensing but that aren't actually illegal or unethical.

HIPAA   HIPAA is an acronym for Health Insurance Portability and Accountability Act. It was passed in Congress in 1996. A minor part of the act, but the part most quoted by medical providers so they don't have to release any information to you, is a section that deals with the security and privacy of health data.

hot sheet   A hot sheet is a current list of recently stolen vehicles. Police departments sometimes have hundreds of patrol cars driving around their jurisdiction all day long. Patrolmen are on the lookout for any car that is on the hot sheet. Many police department patrol cars are now in communication with their headquarters by computer, and they access the hot sheet list on the computer rather than a physical printed list, as in smaller departments.

hyperlink   A hyperlink is an area, picture, word, or phrase on a web page that you can select with your cursor in order for your browser to take you to another page or website whose content is linked in some manner.

image stabilization   Image stabilization is a function available with almost all digital video cameras and incorporated into many newer SLR camera lenses. The camera or lens digitally stabilizes the image to reduce blurring from a not-so-firmly-held camera. An image-stabilized lens on an SLR camera means you can open the iris as much as four extra stops (good for low-light photography) when the image stabilization is turned on.

impeaching   Impeaching a witness's testimony means calling into question the reliability or truthfulness of the testimony being given.

informant   An informant is an individual that cooperates, usually without the knowledge of others involved in the case, by providing information during an investigation. She might or might not be a witness or a participant in the particular case under investigation. Frequently, an informant receives compensation or other benefit for information, whereas a witness never should.

information brokers   Also known as data brokers, information brokers are individuals or companies that have access to specialized sources of information or use advanced techniques to gather information and then resell it to the private investigator. An example is asking an information broker to obtain a nonpublished telephone number or a list of credit-card charges that the PI couldn't get himself.

judgment   Judgment refers to a final determination by a court of competent jurisdiction setting forth the rights and liabilities of the parties in a lawsuit. Usually, the term *judgment* refers to a money judgment in which the court may decide that a defendant owes a plaintiff money in a case. These judgments are recorded in the official records at the clerk of the courts office and are generally public records. Credit bureaus review these records on a regular basis and include them as part of their credit report.

junction box   A junction box is a piece of telephone company equipment that houses several customers' telephone lines and connects them to a phone company cable. Typically, these junction boxes house from two to two dozen connections. There is normally one on every block, or one for every 10 to 12 subscribers.

landline telephone line   This refers to a normal telephone line that has a physical demarcation point at a residence, business, or pay telephone. The phone call at least begins and ends its transmission along a pair of wires, regardless of whether transmission of the call includes microwave or satellite between both ends. This is in contrast to a cell phone or any type of radio communication, which is considered wireless communication—literally, not connected to the ground at some point with wires.

latent fingerprint   A latent fingerprint is a print that is not immediately apparent to the naked eye but can be made visible by dusting or fuming with chemicals. Latent prints can then be compared to inked prints of suspects. An inked print is a fingerprint taken in a controlled environment in which the pads of a suspect's fingers are covered with ink and rolled onto a fingerprint card.

light-meter averages   Many single-lens reflex cameras have a built-in light-metering capability that automatically adjusts the f-stop and the shutter speed. A good photographer knows whether a particular light meter averages the measurement of the light over the entire surfaces of the lens or center-weights the average, giving more importance to the amount of light coming through the center of the lens, where the important image presumably is located.

lines of resolution   This tells you how fine an image you'll get from the camera under optimal conditions. The higher the number, the better the resolution, and the better the picture.

lux   This refers to the camera video board's or video chip's sensitivity to light. Some cameras use charged coupled devices (CCD). For our purposes, consider them chips. Whatever they use, the lower the lux, the more sensitive the camera is to light, which is very helpful in indoor applications.

misdemeanors   Criminal offenses are categorized according to the severity of the offense. Less serious crimes, those typically involving a potential penalty of less than one year, are called "misdemeanors."

motor vehicle theft   For the purposes of the FBI's Uniform Crime Report, motor vehicle theft is defined as the theft of automobiles, trucks, buses, motorcycles, motor scooters, snowmobiles, and so on. This does not include taking a vehicle for temporary purposes by those having lawful access.

NCIC   This stands for the National Crime Information Center. Among other things, the NCIC maintains a huge database, run by the FBI, which lists subjects with outstanding arrest warrants. Also listed are stolen properties and missing persons.

no bill   The grand jury returns a "no bill" if it finds there is not sufficient evidence of probable cause that a crime has been committed or that a particular person committed that crime. Some jurisdictions use the term "no information."

optical zoom   On camera lenses, optical zoom refers to the focal length achieved by physically moving the lenses farther apart from each other, thereby achieving a greater focal length (hence the term "zooming out" with a zoom lens) and increasing the relative size of the image as it appears on the film or recording media.

PACER   An acronym for Public Access to Court Electronic Records.

parole   When an individual is on parole, he or she has been released from prison earlier than the original sentence called for. That person also must not violate any conditions of the parole, or the parole may be revoked and the person may be sent back to prison.

permissible purpose   Permissible purpose refers to 1 of 11 (depending on how you count) legal purposes for pulling a credit report, as defined by the Fair Credit Reporting Act, last updated by Congress in 2004.

pinhole lens   A pinhole lens is a lens for a camera that is about the size of the tip of a ballpoint pen. It's not literally "pin size," but it's close. It can be concealed quite easily, particularly in dropped ceilings, where the ceiling tiles have a rough texture. This size lens is also popular in Nanny Cams, with which the hole for the lens can be concealed behind a small piece of plastic, such as on radios or many other appliances. They are frequently used when installing a camera in an air-conditioning vent.

plaintiff   Legal actions require a minimum of two parties. The plaintiff is the party that initiates the action or lawsuit. The defendant is the person on the receiving end of the action.

plead down   To expedite the flow of cases and reduce the attorney's caseload and the burden on the court, the prosecuting attorney reduces charges from higher offenses to lesser offenses if the defendant agrees to plead guilty to the lesser offenses.

point man   The point man on a surveillance is the investigator who actually has "the eyeball" on, or physical sight of, the subject.

premise liability   A premise liability case involves the allegation that a property owner was negligent by not curing some default in the premise or real property owned or managed by the defendant, and this negligence led to the harm of the plaintiff. An example of this is the plaintiff alleging that the defendant failed to provide adequate exterior lighting, and the ensuing darkness was responsible for the rape or assault inflicted upon the plaintiff.

pretext   A pretext is a subterfuge or ploy used by private investigators to encourage an individual to reveal information about himself or herself or another party without being aware of the true reason for the conversation. In the course of responding to what appears to be a normal everyday query, the individual unsuspectingly releases the information the investigator actually is seeking.

private mailboxes   Commercial establishments, such as The UPS Store. Mail is delivered to the business and put into a box setup, much like post office boxes at the U.S. Post Office. In addition to the regular street address and box number, for a private mailbox, the address is supposed to contain the initials *PMB* (for "private mail box").

privilege   A privilege, under law, is a special right that someone enjoys that the public-at-large does not enjoy. For instance, the marital privilege states that a wife cannot be forced to testify against her husband, or vice versa. According to the clergy privilege, communications between a clergyman and his parishioner are considered privileged.

Pro Bono   *Pro Bono* derives from the Latin *Pro Bono Publico*, or "for the public good." Usually it's shortened to just *Pro Bono* and means legal work undertaken without expectation of payment.

probation   Probation indicates that a person was convicted of a crime, but instead of being sentenced to a jail term, the person is given probation to see if he or she can follow the law, stay employed, or complete any other terms of probation over a specified time period.

random access memory   RAM is an acronym for random access memory. It is the memory that the computer accesses when it processes information and runs computer programs. If a computer doesn't have enough RAM, the information being processed is swapped back and forth to the hard drive, which slows the processing speed and leads to more rapid hard-drive failure and computer program lockups and crashes.

real property   Real property is described as anything that is not personal property. Real property is anything that is a part of the earth or attached thereto that cannot be easily moved. Think dirt.

recorded statement   A recorded statement is a voice tape recording made by a witness concerning facts and/or the witness's recollection of the pertinent incident.

registered agent   An individual who agrees to be available to accept service, subpoenas, or other legal documents for a corporation is its registered agent. If you need to sue a corporation, your attorney must have it served with the lawsuit. The registered agent is the person who will accept notice of the suit on behalf of the corporation.

reluctant witness   An individual may have considerable knowledge of the pertinent incident relevant to the matter under suit but will not discuss that knowledge of this incident unless compelled to by a court.

repeater   A radio tower that receives the signal from a mobile radio, such as a walkie-talkie, and repeats the broadcast signal over a larger area than a 5-watt walkie-talkie can cover. The signal may bounce from one repeater to another, to another, possibly over an entire state. This is common with FBI radios. An agent in the field should be able to reach his division headquarters from almost anyplace within the geographical boundaries of his division's area. Most commercial repeaters, set up for business purposes, do not have such a broad area of coverage.

results billing   Results billing is the practice of charging more than a standard hourly rate if the results achieved justify a higher bill or a higher hourly rate.

retainer   Money paid by the client at the beginning of an investigation. Frequently a portion, or even all, of the retainer is nonrefundable if the case is canceled. Typically, the investigator bills his time against the retainer on hand. Once the retainer is used up, the investigator asks for additional funds before proceeding further with the case.

reverse directories   *See* city directories.

safe phone   A safe phone is a telephone that is not traceable back to the user. It does not reveal its number to the caller ID services on outgoing calls, but it has caller ID service for incoming calls. It is set up in such a way that it can be answered in any manner necessary and is used for only one case at a time. As a good PI, you should have one of these phone lines available in your office at all times.

search engines   Internet sites that allow a user to input a search criteria. The engine then searches its own database of researched internet sites and provides a list of sites that most closely meet your criteria.

service by publication or notification   This is a method whereby an individual is served with process without physically laying papers in his hand. If one party cannot be located, a notice may be published in a newspaper in the county where the court action is to take place over a period of several weeks. Once this is accomplished, the individual is considered to be served.

signed statement   A signed statement is a written declaration made by a witness concerning facts and/or the witness's recollection of the pertinent incident that is signed by the declarant and should be witnessed by the investigator and a third party, if possible. If the statement is taken in a jail cell, have a guard witness the statement.

single-lens reflex   A single-lens reflex (SLR) camera is a camera in which the light (the image) passes through the lens and is reflected by a mirror to the viewfinder, where it is viewed by the photographer. When the shutter button is depressed, the mirror flips out of the way and the image passes directly to the film or image receptor. The advantage of SLR cameras over other cameras is that the photographer sees the exact image that will appear on the final product. Also, with most SLR cameras, the photographer has a wide range of lenses from which he or she can choose.

skip tracing   Originally referring to collection agencies' attempts to locate a debtor who'd "skipped out" on his obligation, skip tracing generally now refers to anyone a private investigator is trying to find. Perhaps this person is intentionally eluding creditors or is merely a witness whose address is not currently known but is sought by attorneys for an interview or a deposition. Universally, however, a person who is eluding his creditors is referred to in the business as "a skip."

Social Security trace   A Social Security trace is the searching of a database by Social Security number. The search normally returns residence addresses connected to your subject for the last 10 years as well as phone numbers.

spoofing   Spoofing a caller ID is a technique in which numbers are substituted in the caller ID data stream so that the "real" originating number is not shown, but "fake" numbers appear, or seem to appear, on the caller ID screen.

SSAN   The standard abbreviation in most federal law enforcement circles for Social Security Account Number.

subpoena   In a subpoena, the judge of a court requires that a specific person or representative of an institution appear in court or at another specified location on a specific day at a certain time.

subpoena deuces tecum   A subpoena deuces tecum is a subpoena that requires the individual or institution to provide documents to the clerk of the court as outlined in the subpoena. A subpoena could require both an appearance and the retrieval of documents.

suspect   An individual who might have committed or aided the commission of a crime that is under investigation is a suspect or a subject.

telephone break   A telephone break is the process of obtaining, with no other identifying information, the subscriber information for a telephone number, including the subscriber's name and either the service address (if it's a landline) or the mailing address (if the number rings to a cell phone).

true bill   The grand jury returns a true bill if there is sufficient evidence to find probable cause that a crime has been committed and that a particular person committed that crime. Some jurisdictions use the term "information."

Voice Over Internet Protocol (VOIP)   VOIP is a popular and cost-effective method of making telephone calls. VOIP utilizes a broadband internet connection to transmit voice and make phone calls instead of using normal landline telephone wires.

web browser   A web browser is the software program you use to "surf" the internet. Most likely, it is Microsoft Internet Explorer, Google Chrome, or Firefox. Apple uses Safari as the default browser.

wild card   A wild card allows the use of only partial names in searches. This is accomplished by inserting an asterisk after the beginning of a name. For instance, if you're not sure whether a person's name is Rick or Richard, you can input "Ric*" (without the quotation marks), and the search will return "Rick," "Richard," "Ricky," and "Ricardo."

witness   A witness is an individual who might have testimony pertinent to an investigation.

work product   Work product is described as the attorney's notes and research materials and other documents or matters that the attorney makes or uses while working up the case. The reports of a private investigator hired directly by the attorney or working out of the attorney's office are also considered work product.

writ of execution   A writ of execution is an order from a judge of competent jurisdiction commanding that certain actions be taken or cease to occur. A custodial writ would command the person having custody to relinquish custody to the person named in the writ.

State Requirements for Telephonic Recording

Federal law allows any party of a telephonic conversation to record the conversation without notifying other parties participating in the conversation that the recording is taking place. Violators of the federal statute can be imprisoned up to five years and fined $10,000 (Title 18, Sec. 2511 (4)). The federal violation occurs if no parties to the conversation are aware that it is being intercepted or recorded.

Thirty-eight states and the District of Columbia follow the federal precedent. Twelve states insist that all parties to the conversation be made aware that the conversation is being recorded.

Also, different states have some peculiarities that don't apply to all states. Arizona, for example, may allow the subscriber to the telephone line (the person who pays the bill) to record conversations on that line with no party consent. Some states require that tones or beeps be placed on the line every 15 seconds during recording. If you have questions, check the statutes in your state. Don't rely solely upon this list, as state laws are subject to change. Keep in mind that the phrase "two-party state" is misleading; the correct term is *all-party state* because it applies to all parties (not just two individuals) in the conversation.

Search the list to determine what the law allows in your state.

All-Party States

California	
Connecticut	
Delaware	There is confusion between statutes in Delaware. Their wiretapping law specifically allows interception if one party gives his consent. Their privacy law forbids recording unless all parties are notified.
Florida	
Illinois	
Maryland	
Massachusetts	
Michigan	Michigan courts have ruled that just one-party consent is necessary, despite a statute requiring all-party consent.
Montana	
Nevada	
New Hampshire	
Pennsylvania	
Washington	

All others not on this list are one-party states.

Sample Client Retainer Contract

The following is a sample contract between a client and an investigative agency. It was provided by and is used with permission of Vicki Childs of Blazer Investigative and Security Consultants, LLC in Charleston, SC. It is also used by the author's agency. It is strongly suggested that, before using any contract, you have your company attorney review it. He or she will make some changes, to justify the fees. For a more complete retainer contract check out the one available for purchase at www.pistore.com. In the search field at the top of that page key in "retainer," and you'll find it.

INVESTIGATIVE AGREEMENT

This hourly rate investigator–client fee agreement is between ABC INVESTIGATIVE AGENCY, a licensed Florida investigative agency, and _____ client. The general nature of the case is _____
_____
_____

This case will begin on or about the date below and continue for 90 days or until Client withdraws.

Client employs and ABC INVESTIGATIVE AGENCY will accept employment to perform investigative services in connection with Client's case regardless of the disposition of this case. The Client agrees to fully cooperate with ABC INVESTIGATIVE AGENCY and provide accurate information as a basis for this investigation.

ABC INVESTIGATIVE AGENCY is not responsible for results of inaccurate information or leads provided by Client. Client understands that ABC INVESTIGATIVE AGENCY may withdraw from this contract if Client should fail to pay all fees and costs set forth below.

Reports, video, and photos will be provided within 10 days of a request by the Client but may be withheld until payment is received.

FEES AND RETAINER

ABC INVESTIGATIVE AGENCY shall be compensated for all services rendered Client at the rate of $ _____ per hour and $ _____ per mile. Client agrees to pay the sum of $ _____ as a nonrefundable retainer fee. ABC INVESTIGATIVE AGENCY will bill hourly against the retainer fee. Client further agrees to pay for any other expenses incurred during the investigation, including but not limited to hotel bills, videotapes, photos, etc. If travel is anticipated, a fee of $ _____ will be applied toward costs and expenses incurred in the pursuit of this matter.

COURT APPEARANCES

If any agent of ABC INVESTIGATIVE AGENCY is called as a witness for deposition or Court, the cost will be a minimum of $350.00. If the Court appearance or deposition requires more than 4 hour's time, the Client will be charged the hourly and mileage rate set forth above.

CLIENT AGREES THAT NO AGENT OF ABC INVESTIGATIVE AGENCY HAS MADE ANY PROMISE OR GUARANTEE REGARDING THE OUTCOME OF THEIR CASE OR FACTS GATHERED DURING THE INVESTIGATION PERFORMED BY ABC INVESTIGATIVE AGENCY.

Client does hereby bind his/her heirs, executors, and legal representatives to the terms of this contract as set forth herein.

I HAVE READ THIS CONTRACT AND AGREE TO ITS TERMS AND CONDITIONS.

_____   _____

CLIENT   ABC INVESTIGATIVE AGENCY

Date: _____

Affidavit of Diligent Search

Steven Kerry Brown, licensed private investigator in the State of Florida, has performed a diligent search for Jane Doe as required by Florida Statute Chapter 63.088 in an adoption matter with the following results:

Jane Doe's personal identifying information was discovered through investigation in this matter and determined to be the following:

Name: Jane Doe

Date of Birth: 06/13/1985

SSN: xxx-xx-xxxx

Last known address: An aunt, Martha Smith, provided a last known address of 6001 River Rd., Apt 240, Elyria, OH 44000, indicating Doe lived there in 2006. Property records for this address show it is owned by Richard and Carol Brown. Efforts were made to locate the Browns, and they were successfully located. Carol Brown advised on 7/6/06 that Jane Doe had occupied apartment 107 but had vacated the apartment near the first of the year. She had left owing the Browns rent money and had left no forwarding address.

Last known employment: No employment has been established for Doe.

Regulatory Agencies: Patrick Jones (440-329-5207) of the Loraine County Ohio Auditor's office, which regulates occupational and business licenses, advised on 07/12/06 that their office had no record of any license in the name of Jane Doe.

Relatives: The following individuals have been identified as relatives of Jane Doe:

> **Grandmother:** Shirley Doe, DOB 08/08/1934, SSN#: xxx-xx-xxxx, last known address of 123 Robin Rd., North Ridgeville, OH 44039. A letter has been directed to that address for Shirley Doe, but no response has been received.

Cousins: Patricia and Ricky Holt, 123 Robin Rd., North Ridgeville, OH 44039. The Holts are tenants at this property. The telephone number at this address is nonpublished. The landlord is Steven L. Duke, 1234 George Washington Ave., Lakewood, OH 44107. Duke was contacted and advised that the Holts currently reside at the Robin Road address. He agreed to contact the Holts and ask them to contact the investigator in this matter. The Holts have not contacted the investigator and presumably either do not know where Jane Doe is currently or have passed the information to her and she refuses to be contacted. A letter was directed to the Holts, but no reply either in writing or by telephone has been received.

Death Records: A search of the Social Security Master Death Index revealed no listing for Jane Doe, and the Social Security number of xxx-xx-xxxx was negative.

Telephone Records: A current search of telephone listings in the state of Ohio showed one listing in area code 440, which includes Loraine County. That listing was for a Michael and Janet Doe. A telephonic contact was made with Michael Doe, and he denied having any knowledge of Jane Doe or being related to her in any way.

Law Enforcement Records: Records from the Court of Common Pleas for Loraine County, Ohio, were searched from 1989 to the present (both criminal and civil records), and there was no record for Jane Doe.

Highway Patrol Records: Records of the Ohio Highway Patrol were searched, with negative results.

Ohio Department of Corrections: A current search for Jane Doe was performed of the inmates of the correction department, with negative results.

Hospitals: The following hospitals in Loraine County were checked for current patients and former patient information:

EMH Regional Medical Center, 630 East River St., Elyria, OH 44035. She was not a current patient, and the medical record department refused to disclose whether she had ever been a patient.

Allen Medical Center, 200 West Loraine St., Oberlin, OH 44074. This institution indicated that she was not currently a patient there, and they had no record of her ever having been a patient there.

Proceed with each required step and the results of those searches. End with a statement like the following:

I understand that I am swearing or affirming under oath to the truthfulness of the claims made in this affidavit and that the punishment for knowingly making a false statement includes fines and/or imprisonment.

_____   _____

Signature   Date

_____

Printed Name

_____

Address

_____

Telephone

State of Florida

County of St. Johns

Sworn to or affirmed and signed before me on _____ by _____

_____

Notary Public–State of Florida

_____

Print, type, or stamp commissioned name of notary

Index